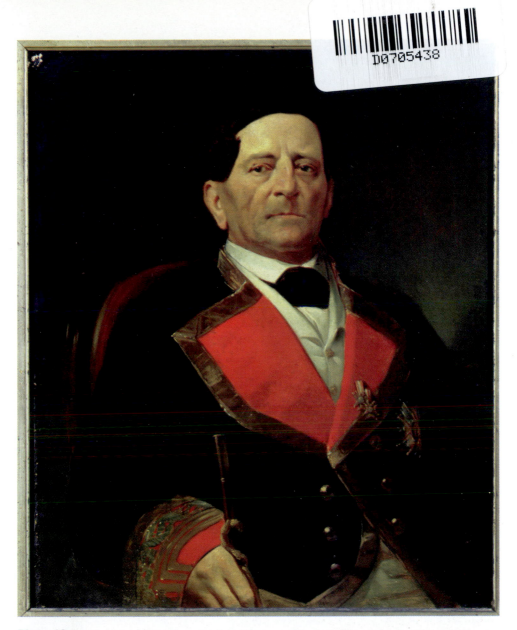

Plate 13 Antonio López de Santa Anna dominated Mexican politics and military during the first half of the nineteenth century.

Plate 14 C. Penuti and Alejandro Bernhein, *La Batalla de Monte Caseros*. The Battle of Monte Caseros in 1852 marked the defeat of longtime dictator Juan Manuel de Rosas.

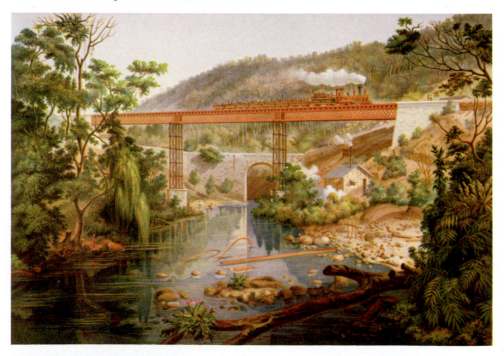

Plate 15 Railroads fueled Latin America's economic development in the late nineteenth century. Railway Bridge at Atoyac.

Plate 16 Édouard Manet, *Ejecución de Maximiliano* (*The Execution of Maximilian*), lithograph, 1868. Courtesy of the Museo de la Amada, Paris.

Plate 17 Frida Kahlo, *Las Dos Fridas* (*The Two Fridas*) (1939). Kahlo was one of the greatest Latin American painters of the twentieth century.

Plate 18 Juan Perón, the populist president of Argentina (1946–1955 and 1973–1974), and his wife, Eva Duarte ("Evita") de Perón.

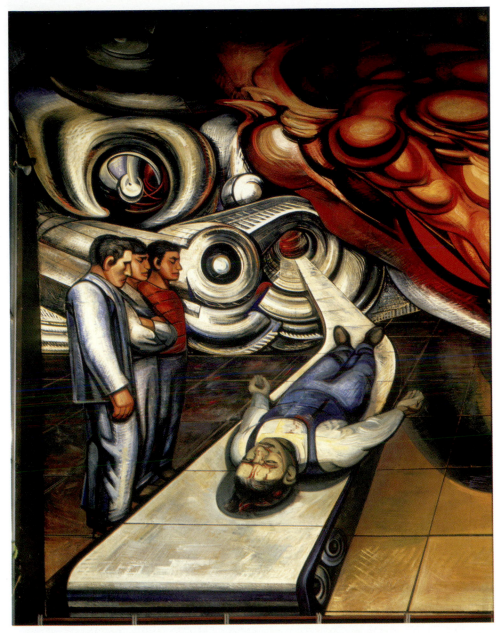

Plate 19 David Alfaro Siqueiros, *Por una Seguridad Completa para todos los Mexicanos (detalle), 1952–1954* (*For the Complete Safety of All Mexicans at Work, Detail of Injured Worker*). Siqueiros was one of three great Mexican muralists who focused their art on working people.

Plate 20 Globalization of commerce and media have brought U.S. brand names to even the smallest villages. Delicias, Chihuahua, Mexico.

Plate 21 Resourceful Brazilians built favela dwellings board by board and brick by brick.

Plate 22 Mexicans celebrate the Day of the Dead with colorful decorations of grave sites.

Plate 23 Juan O'Gorman, *La marcha de la lealtad* (*The March of Loyalty*). Francisco I. Madero, Mexico's first revolutionary president.

Plate 24 Latin American cities with more than one million inhabitants.

LATIN AMERICA AND ITS PEOPLE

VOLUME 2: 1800 TO PRESENT

Third Edition

Cheryl E. Martin
University of Texas at El Paso

Mark Wasserman
Rutgers University

Prentice Hall

Boston   Columbus   Indianapolis   New York   San Francisco   Upper Saddle River
Amsterdam   Cape Town   Dubai   London   Madrid   Milan   Munich   Paris   Montreal   Toronto
Delhi   Mexico City   Sao Paulo   Sydney   Hong Kong   Seoul   Singapore   Taipei   Tokyo

Executive Editor: Jeff Lasser
Editorial Project Manager: Rob DeGeorge
Editorial Assistant: Julia Feltus
Senior Marketing Manager: Maureen E. Prado Roberts
Marketing Assistant: Samantha Bennett
Production Manager: Kathleen Sleys
Cover Designer: Suzanne Behnke
Cover Photo: Robert Fried/robertfriedphotography.com
Full-Service Project Management/Composition: Hemalatha/Integra
Printer/Binder/Cover Printer: R.R. Donnelley & Sons, Inc.
Text Font: 10/13 New Baskerville

Credits and acknowledgments borrowed from other sources and reproduced, with permission, in this textbook appear on page C-1.

Library of Congress Cataloging-in-Publication Data
Martin, Cheryl English
  Latin America and its people / Cheryl E. Martin, Mark Wasserman. — 3rd ed.
    p. cm.
  ISBN-13: 978-0-205-05470-1 (alk. paper)
  ISBN-10: 0-205-05470-6 (alk. paper)
  1. Latin America—History. I. Wasserman, Mark II. Title.
F1410.M294 2012
980—dc22

2010046656

10 9 8 7 6 5 4 3

Prentice Hall
is an imprint of

PEARSON

www.pearsonhighered.com

ISBN 10:   0-205-05468-4
ISBN 13: 978-0-205-05468-8

To the students of Rutgers University
and the University of Texas at El Paso,
who have inspired us.

CONTENTS

8
THE NEW NATIONS OF LATIN AMERICA 216

9

REGIONALISM, WAR, AND RECONSTRUCTION: POLITICS AND ECONOMICS, 1821–1880 242

10

EVERYDAY LIFE IN AN UNCERTAIN AGE, 1821–1880 271

11

ECONOMIC MODERNIZATION, SOCIETY, AND POLITICS, 1880–1920 300

12

BETWEEN REVOLUTIONS: THE NEW POLITICS OF CLASS AND THE ECONOMIES OF IMPORT SUBSTITUTION INDUSTRIALIZATION, 1920–1959   327

13

PEOPLE AND PROGRESS, 1910–1959 352

14

REVOLUTION, REACTION, DEMOCRACY, AND THE NEW GLOBAL ECONOMY: 1959 TO THE PRESENT   375

15

EVERYDAY LIFE: 1959 TO THE PRESENT 401

LIST OF FEATURES

How Historians Understand

Latin American Lives

Slice of Life

List of Maps and Color Plates

National Capitals

PREFACE

Our aim in writing *Latin America and Its People* has been to provide a fresh interpretative survey of Latin American history from pre-Columbian times to the beginning of the twenty-first century. The millions of "ordinary" Latin Americans are the central characters in our story. We look at the many social and political institutions that Latin Americans have built and rebuilt—families, governments from the village level to the nation-state, churches, political parties, labor unions, schools, and armies—but we do so through the lives of the people who forged these institutions and tried to alter them to meet changing circumstances. The texture of everyday life, therefore, is our principal focus.

NEW TO THIS EDITION

Chapter 2
- REVISED: Map of "The Valley of Mexico" has been revised to indicate more accurate placement of *chinampas*

Chapter 3
- NEW: Latin American Lives: Domingos Fernandes Nobre

Chapter 6
- NEW: Illustration: Blacks in Trujillo, Peru

Chapter 7
- NEW: How Historians Understand: Latin America and the Atlantic World

Chapter 8
- NEW: Latin American Lives: Manuela Sáenz

Chapter 9

- NEW: Latin American Lives: Francisco Solano López

Chapter 11

- NEW: Latin American Lives: Evaristo Madero

Chapter 14

- UPDATED: Narrative updated throughout to reflect recent events and new scholarship
- UPDATED: Pink Tide
- NEW: Indigenous Political Movements

Chapter 15

- UPDATED: Narrative updated throughout to reflect recent events and new scholarship
- NEW: Environment: Natural Disasters
- EXPANDED: The Great Migrations
- NEW: Informal Economy: Narcotics Trade

The list of suggested readings at the end of each chapter, Learning More about Latin America, has been updated throughout, with some older titles having been replaced by recent publications.

THE TEXTURE OF EVERYDAY LIFE

Life has not been easy for most Latin Americans. Poverty, hard work, disease, natural calamities, the loss of loved ones, and violence have marked many people's lives. Many have lacked educational opportunities and the chance to speak their political opinions openly. In the chapters that follow, we will devote a lot of attention to the daily struggles of men, women, and children as they faced these difficult challenges and adapted to changing times. We are also interested in how people managed to find meaning and enjoyment in their lives. Even in the midst of hardship and tragedy, they came together as families and communities to celebrate, dance, eat and drink, flirt, marry, and pray. Our readers will meet the people of Latin American history "up close and personal," in their houses and on the streets, on the shop floors and in the fields, and at work and at play, for it is the texture of everyday life that makes the history of Latin America so fascinating and compelling.

THE DIVERSITY OF LATIN AMERICA

Latin Americans are a very diverse people. They have spoken Spanish, Portuguese, Nahuatl, Quechua, Maya, Aymara, Guaraní, and scores of other languages. Their ethnic and cultural roots can be traced to the indigenous civilizations of the Americas and to many generations of European, African, and Asian immigrants. A few have been very rich, but many more have been very poor. They have adapted to many climatic zones, some at altitudes as high as 11,000 feet above sea level. Many Latin Americans have lived in rural areas, but they have also built some of the world's most sophisticated cities, from the Aztec and Inca capitals of Tenochtitlan and Cuzco to such modern industrial giants as São Paulo, Brazil, and Monterrey, Mexico, to cosmopolitan urban centers like Mexico City and Buenos Aires. Following their independence from Spain and Portugal, they have experimented with a variety of political regimes—monarchy, liberal democracy, oligarchy, socialist revolution, and brutal military dictatorships, to name a few.

Despite this diversity, Latin Americans have faced certain common challenges. European conquest and subsequent shifts in world economic and political configurations have shaped the region's history over the past five centuries. Latin America's rich natural resources have attracted foreign investors who have profited handsomely, while the people who worked in the mines and oilfields have seldom garnered an equitable share of the bounty. The region's ability to produce a stunning variety of agricultural staples has shaped patterns of landholding and labor throughout the region, again to the detriment of the many and the benefit of the few. How to achieve political stability in nations divided by class, ethnic, and regional differences has been an enduring conundrum for Latin Americans, even if they have tried many different means of resolving that dilemma.

Our goal, then, is to explore Latin Americans' common history without losing sight of their diversity, and to compare how the many different peoples of the region have responded to similar situations. We have therefore organized our text thematically rather than proceeding country-by-country. There are too many countries and too much time to cover for us to thoroughly document the history of every Latin American nation. No doubt, some country specialists will feel their area slighted, but textbooks are as much about the choices of what to exclude as they are about what to include. Unlike many other texts on Latin American history, *Latin America and Its People* interweaves the history of Brazil with that of its Spanish-speaking neighbors, rather than segregating it in separate chapters, while also pointing out the special features that distinguish it from other Latin American countries. Volume I includes coverage of those portions of the present-day United States that were once part of the Spanish colonial empire.

Our underlying assumption is that, in order for our students to gain an introductory (and, we hope, lasting) understanding of Latin America, it is best not to clutter the narrative with too many dates and names. We believe that students will remember the major themes, such as the struggle to control local affairs, the impact of war, the transformation of women's roles, and the social changes wrought by economic development. And they will remember, perhaps even more clearly, that many Latin Americans lived and continue to live in overwhelming poverty.

VOLUME I

Volume I of *Latin America and Its People* looks at the ways in which people have continually reinvented the hemisphere that Europeans called the "new world." This world was first "new" for the nameless ancestors of today's Native Americans, who migrated across the Bering Strait and fanned out across North and South America over the course of many millennia. Generation after generation, they adapted to the many different climatic zones of the hemisphere and gradually accumulated the surpluses necessary to found the great civilizations of the Aztecs, the Inca, the Maya, and so many others. Chapter 1 is devoted entirely to the long trajectory of cultural development in the Americas down to the year 1400 C E, while Chapter 2 includes an extensive comparative discussion of the Aztec and Inca empires and the simultaneously emerging national monarchies of Spain and Portugal.

Spanish and Portuguese colonists not only found this world very different from what they had known but also remade it as they discovered its potential for yielding silver, gold, sugar, and other commodities of value to them. The changes introduced by European conquest and colonization profoundly altered the world of the indigenous peoples of the Americas. Over the course of three centuries, the hemisphere witnessed the rise of a new people, the biological and cultural offspring of native peoples, Europeans, and Africans, who yet again made this world something new. Chapters 3, 4, 5, and 6 explore the constantly changing worlds of Latin American peoples under Spanish and Portuguese rule. Chapters 7 and 8 look at the transformation of Latin American society in the eighteenth and early nineteenth centuries, the period known to historians as the "Age of Revolution."

The most important theme of Volume I is how ordinary people built these successive new worlds and continually renegotiated the complex and overlapping hierarchies of class, ethnicity, political status, and gender that supposedly governed their lives. Native peoples endured military and political conquest, catastrophic epidemics, highly oppressive labor regimens, and the imposition of a new religion. Yet, despite these enormous challenges, they survived and rebuilt their communities, selectively incorporating cultural elements introduced by the Europeans along with traditional practices and beliefs as they formed their new society.

Against what might seem like insurmountable odds, Africans brought to the Americas as slaves managed to retain something of the life they had known before, especially in places where their numbers were sufficiently great that they could form some kind of identifiable community. Some found ways to escape the bonds of slavery and passed that freedom to successive generations of descendants. Like the indigenous peoples, they too borrowed selectively from European cultures.

Throughout three centuries of Spanish and Portuguese colonial rule, Latin Americans of all races and social classes contested, sometimes successfully, sometimes not, the many "rules" that dictated how men and women should behave and how people in subordinate social positions should render deference to those who supposedly ranked above them. Volume I argues that it was not just kings and priests and other authority figures who built the world of colonial Latin America. Men, women, and children of all classes and all racial groups had at least some say in the outcome, even if the colonial state sometimes wielded enough power to silence the most vocal among them.

VOLUME II

The overarching theme of Volume II is how ordinary people struggled over the course of two centuries to maintain control over their daily lives. This meant that they sought to determine their own community leaders, set their local laws and regulations (especially taxes), establish and keep their own traditions, practice their religion, supervise the education of their children, live by their own values and standards, and earn a living. This endless struggle came to involve more than just the narrow view and experience of their village or urban neighborhood or their friends and neighbors. Rather, it brought ordinary people and their local lives into constant, not always pleasant and beneficial, contact with the wider worlds of regional (states, provinces, and territories), national, and international politics, economy, and culture. Although the local struggle forms the backbone of the narrative, we must include summaries and analyses of the contexts in which these struggles occurred, as well. Because all Latin Americans, regardless of country, participated in this struggle, the economic and political narratives proceed thematically and chronologically.

Volume II offers three chapters (Chapters 10, 13, and 15) that describe the everyday lives of Latin Americans at different points in time. We want students to know what people ate and drank, how they had good times, how they worshipped, where they lived, and what their work was like. The descriptions are individual and anecdotal and collective and quantitative. Thus, it is our hope that students will remember how a Brazilian small farmer raised cassava, or the tortuous efforts of Chilean copper miners. Perhaps, readers will remember the smells of the streets of nineteenth-century cities or the noises of late twentieth-century megalopolises. The struggle for control over everyday life and the descriptions of daily life are related, of course, for the struggle and its context and the reality were joined inseparably. Students should know what the lives were like for which so many bravely and often unsuccessfully fought.

There are other themes interwoven with that of the struggle for control over everyday life. Unlike many other texts in the field, our book gives full and nuanced coverage to the nineteenth century, incorporating the most exciting new scholarship on that period. In the nineteenth century, we assert, chronic war (external and internal) and the accompanying militarization of government and politics profoundly shaped the region's economy and society. We maintain, as well, that race, class, and gender were the crucial underlying elements in Latin American politics. Moreover, warfare, combined with the massive flow of people to the cities, most particularly transformed the place of women.

In the twentieth century, conflict between the upper, middle, and lower classes was the primary moving force behind politics. No ideology from either Left or Right, nor any type of government from democracy to authoritarianism, has brought other than temporary resolutions. We also follow the continued changes in the role of women in society and politics in the face of vast transformations caused by technology and globalization.

It is also our belief that the history of Latin Americans is primarily the story of Latin America and not of the great powers outside the region. To be sure, Europeans and North Americans invested considerable sums of money and sometimes intervened militarily in Latin America. Their wars and rivalries greatly affected Latin America's possibilities. We do note the importance of such key developments as Mexico's loss of half its national territory to the United States in 1848, the impact of the Cold War on Latin America, and the training that right-wing Latin American military establishments received at the hands of U.S. military forces in the late twentieth century. But we prefer to keep the spotlight on the people of Latin America themselves.

SPECIAL FEATURES

In addition to the main narrative of our book, we have included three separate features in each chapter. Each chapter offers a feature called "Latin American Lives," a biography of an individual whose life illustrates some of the key points of that chapter. Many of these figures are not well known. Chapter 2, for example, highlights Tanta Carhua, a young woman sacrificed to the Inca sun god in Peru, while Chapter 4 discusses a seventeenth-century Spaniard who made a fortune mining silver in Bolivia. We also give a "Slice of Life" for each chapter—a vignette that takes students to the scene of the action and that illustrates in detail some of the social processes under discussion. We include, for example, deliberations of the Spanish cabildo at Cuzco, Peru, in 1551, living conditions in Chilean copper mining camps in the late nineteenth century, and the circumstances that provoked Mexico City's so-called "Parián Riot" of 1828.

We hope, too, to convey a sense of the methods that historians have used in bringing that texture of everyday life to light and the many debates the intriguing history of Latin America has generated. Each chapter therefore includes a piece entitled "How

Historians Understand," designed to give readers better insights into the way that historians go about their work or the ways in which historical knowledge is used and transformed according to the concerns of a particular time and place. Chapter 5, for example, describes how historians have measured Indian acculturation under colonial rule by analyzing the incorporation of Spanish words into indigenous language sources. In Chapter 9, we show how changing political conditions in Mexico are reflected in the many myths and interpretations that have arisen concerning the life of President Benito Juárez.

AIDS TO LEARNING

Because students are at the heart of this enterprise, we have included a number of aids to learning. A glossary explains technical terms and Spanish and Portuguese words used in the text. Discussion questions at the end of the special features Latin American Lives, Slice of Life, and How Historians Understand are intended to stimulate classroom discussion and individual research projects. We have also included suggestions for further reading at the end of each chapter. In keeping with our emphasis on everyday life in Latin American history, we have chosen books that give readers especially clear views of "ordinary" men, women, and children as they went about their daily lives and made Latin America what it is today, at the beginning of the twenty-first century.

ACKNOWLEDGMENTS

Textbooks are inherently collective enterprises. In synthesizing the work of other scholars we have come to an extraordinary appreciation for the remarkable researches and analyses of our colleagues all over the world. We have tried to use the best old and new discoveries to illuminate Latin America's past. The list of those to whom we are beholden is endless. Because space constraints forced us to eschew scholarly apparatus, we have not presented formal recognition of these contributions. Many will recognize their work on our pages. They should regard this as our highest compliment. Some, but by no means all, we mention in our "Learning More about Latin Americans" at the end of each chapter. But the latter include only books in English that primarily pertain to everyday life, so it is incomplete.

We would like to thank the editors at Longman, especially Erika Gutierrez, whose patience and encouragement fostered the project. Thanks, too, to Danielle E. Wasserman, who read and commented on the chapters in Volume II, and to our colleagues Sandra McGee-Deutsch and Samuel Baily for their helpful suggestions. To Marlie Wasserman and Charles Martin, our gratitude for putting up with us, during the years that this book was in the making. Special thanks to the many students who have taken our courses at Rutgers University and the University of Texas at El Paso over the last three decades. Their questions and enthusiasm for learning about the people of Latin America helped inspire this book.

Finally, we would like to thank the following reviewers for their helpful comments and suggestions:

Ida Altman, *University of Florida*

Thomas Benjamin, *Central Michigan University*

Christina Bueno, *Northeastern Illinois University*

Nicola Foote, *Florida Gulf Coast University*

Orlando A. Hernandez, *New York University*

Michael K. Ward, *Ventura College*

Cheryl E. Martin
Mark Wasserman

ABOUT THE AUTHORS

Cheryl E. Martin has taught Latin American History at the University of Texas at El Paso since 1978. A native of Buffalo, New York, she received her bachelor's degree from the Georgetown University School of Foreign Service and her M.A. and Ph.D. from Tulane University. She studied at the Universidad de Cuenca, Ecuador, on a Fulbright Fellowship and was a visiting instructor at the Universidad Autónoma de Chihuahua, Mexico. Her publications include *Rural Society in Colonial Morelos* (1985) and *Governance and Society in Colonial Mexico: Chihuahua in the Eighteenth Century* (1996). She also co-edited, with William Beezley and William E. French, *Rituals of Rule, Rituals of Resistance: Public Celebrations and Popular Culture in Mexico* (1994).

Professor Martin has served on the council of the American Historical Association and on the editorial boards of the *Hispanic American Historical Review*, *The Americas*, the *Latin American Research Review*, and H-Borderlands. She has received two fellowships from the National Endowment for the Humanities and Awards for Distinguished Achievement in both teaching and research at the University of Texas at El Paso. She is the proud grandmother of Mackenzie and Zachary.

Mark Wasserman is a professor of history at Rutgers, The State University of New Jersey, where he has taught since 1978. Brought up in Marblehead, Massachusetts, he earned his B.A. at Duke University and his M.A. and Ph.D. at the University of Chicago. He is the author of three books on Mexico: *Capitalists, Caciques, and Revolution: The Native Elite and Foreign Enterprise in Chihuahua, Mexico, 1854–1911* (1984); *Persistent Oligarchs: Elites and Politics in Chihuahua, Mexico, 1910–1940* (1993); and *Everyday Life and Politics in Nineteenth Century Mexico: Men, Women, and War* (2000). He also coauthored the early editions of the best-selling *History of Latin America (1980–1988)* with Benjamin Keen. Professor Wasserman has twice won the Arthur P. Whitaker Prize for his books. Professor Wasserman has received research fellowships from the Tinker Foundation, the American Council of Learned Societies/Social Science Research Council, the American Philosophical Society, and the National Endowment of the Humanities. He has been Vice-Chair for Undergraduate Education of the Rutgers Department of History and Chair of the Department's Teaching Effectiveness Committee. Professor Wasserman was an elected member of the Highland Park, New Jersey, Board of Education for nearly a decade and served as its president for 2 years. He is an avid fan of Duke basketball and enjoys reading mystery novels, hiking, and travel.

LATIN AMERICA AND ITS PEOPLE

8

THE NEW NATIONS OF LATIN AMERICA

FOR 300 YEARS, Spain and Portugal ruled their enormous American empires with few serious challenges from people living in the colonies. But within less than two decades between 1808 and 1824, Brazil and most of Spanish America won independence, leaving Spain with just two islands, Cuba and Puerto Rico, and Portugal with nothing. From Mexico to Argentina, the new nations of Spanish America emerged from drawn-out, hard-fought wars, costly both in terms of lives lost and damage to the economic infrastructure (roads, buildings, mines, and agricultural estates). Brazil's independence came somewhat less violently, in 1822, when a son of Portugal's king agreed to become emperor of the new nation, but there too the years since 1808 had witnessed considerable political turmoil.

The movements for independence in Latin America resulted from the convergence of two sets of factors, one international and the other internal to the individual colonies. Although the most important cause of the rebellions for independence was the demand from Latin Americans to obtain more control over their daily lives, as manifested in local governance and practice of traditions, the timing of the independence movements depended to a considerable extent on events that occurred in the metropolises and in the rest of Europe.

The specific character of the struggles for independence and the kinds of nations that emerged varied greatly across Latin America, reflecting the tremendous geographical and historical diversity of the region. The independence movements were bitterly divided along class and racial lines. Wealthy creoles (people who claimed European descent, though born in the Americas) needed tactical support from the lower classes to win the battles against Spain and Portugal and in the political struggles of nation building that ensued. But they despised the masses of poor Indians, blacks, and *castas* (racially mixed people) that surrounded them. One of the principal reasons why the Spanish and Portuguese empires endured so long was that upper-class whites were terrified that any act of rebellion against the mother country might unleash popular unrest that could easily turn against them.

Creole fears were anything but groundless. The colonies were sharply split between the haves and the have-nots, and the gap had widened in many parts of Latin America during the last few decades of the eighteenth century. Popular discontent had mounted accordingly, usually meeting brutal repression by colonial governments and the creole upper class. When external events finally began unraveling the ties that bound the colonies to Spain and Portugal, lower classes joined the battles, but with their own agendas in mind. Their specific objectives varied from place to place, but included the abolition of slavery, an end to special taxes levied on Indians, and land reform.

The movements for Latin American independence divided on geographical lines as well. The racially and ethnically diverse people of the countryside thought mostly in terms of local autonomy at the village level and at least initially paid relatively little heed to the ideas of nationhood formulated by the creole upper classes in the larger cities and towns. The upper classes had their own local and regional loyalties as well. Peruvians and Venezuelans and Argentines all distrusted one another, and people who lived in towns across southern South America resented the domination of Buenos Aires. All of the divisions—racial, social, economic, and geographical—that became so evident during the wars for independence were to shape Latin American politics for much of the nineteenth century.

SPANISH AMERICA AND THE CRISIS OF 1808

During the last half of the eighteenth and beginning of the nineteenth centuries, upheavals in the Caribbean, Europe, and North America profoundly affected events in Latin America and contributed to the development and success of independence movements in the region. The French Revolution (1789) and subsequent conquest of Europe by the Emperor Napoleon, the slave rebellion in the French sugar colony Saint-Domingue (1791) that caused the birth of Haiti, and the uprising of British colonists in North America that created the United States deeply transformed how Latin Americans viewed contemporary society and the colonial governance of Spain and Portugal, causing them to question the underlying principles and structure of colonial rule that had lasted for 300 years. These revolutions disrupted the international balance of power and the uneasy equilibrium in domestic society. Most immediately, the Napoleonic invasion of Portugal and Spain in 1807 and 1808 provided the catalyst for the emergence of the Latin American independence.

Spain, the Napoleonic Invasion, and Representative Government, 1808–1814

From the 1788 death of energetic King Charles III, who had instituted widespread administrative changes in the empire, Spain experienced considerable political turmoil. No sooner had the dimwitted Charles IV ascended to the throne than revolutionaries overthrew the French monarchy, setting off a reign of terror, executing King Louis XVI, and going to war against the rest of Europe. From 1793 to 1795 Charles took up arms as an ally of traditional foe England in order to stem the French revolutionary tide. He quickly reverted to the old alliance with France once the revolutionary fervor there abated. The disruptions and war took a heavy toll on both Spain and its American colonies, for the burden of taxation was high and British naval blockades ruined commerce. The crisis came to a head in 1808, when faced with domestic opposition and an impending invasion by Napoleon, Charles IV abdicated. His son, Ferdinand VII, who had secretly plotted against his father, succeeded to the throne, only to have the French force him out to make way for Napoleon's brother Joseph Bonaparte to take over as king.

Spaniards resisted the imposition of a Frenchman as monarch, fighting a guerrilla war and claiming that sovereignty lay in the hands of the people. They experimented with various forms of representative government on both sides of the Atlantic. But with the defeat of Napoleon, the victorious European powers forcefully returned Ferdinand to the throne in 1814. Six years of self-rule, however, had convinced many Americans, particularly the creoles, that they were quite capable of governing themselves and that Spanish colonial rule was far too costly and the benefits too few.

At the same time that Spaniards rose to fight the invading French in 1808, municipalities throughout the country formed *juntas* to govern in place of the monarch. They also set up a central junta that claimed to represent the entire nation and its overseas territories. Spaniards soon called for the reestablishment of the Cortes, a parliamentary body that had existed during medieval times, but had not met in three centuries. Looking for support among Spanish subjects in the colonies, the organizers invited Americans to send representatives to the central junta and the Cortes. The Cortes first met in Cádiz in September 1810 and over the next few years enacted a series of sweeping political changes for both Spain and its American colonies. Most important was the writing of a constitution in 1812, which considerably limited the powers of any future restored monarchy. The absolute kingship was to be no longer.

Americans needed no prodding from Spain to take matters into their own hands in this time of political crisis. Juntas comprised mostly of creoles appeared in cities and towns throughout the empire as soon as news of Ferdinand's captivity reached them. All of these bodies proclaimed their loyalty to Ferdinand. Many, however, objected to any form of subservience to the ad hoc government in Spain, arguing that they were not colonies but separate kingdoms fully equal to Castile, León, Navarre, Catalonia, and the other peninsular territories that comprised the realm of the Spanish monarch. They were technically correct, for only in the time of Charles III had Spanish bureaucrats begun using the term "colonies" in reference to the overseas possessions.

This sentiment for self-rule gathered strength in early 1810, when Americans favoring local autonomy feared that the French armies might overwhelm all Spanish resistance and then Napoleon might impose his regime on the overseas kingdoms. In some places, politically active groups moved quickly to an outright break with Spain. Town councils in Venezuela, for example, convened a national congress that declared independence in July of 1811.

Other Americans preferred to cooperate with the ad hoc government in Spain and welcomed the opportunity to send spokesmen to the sessions of the central junta and the Cortes. Men in cities and towns all over Spanish America participated enthusiastically in elections. The Constitution of 1812 permitted the formation of elected municipal councils (cabildos) in all towns with 1000 or more residents. Hundreds of cities exercised that option. In Mexico, for example, only 20 communities had had cabildos prior to the enactment of the Constitution, while afterwards that number rose to nearly 900. Eighteen new cabildos were formed in Puerto Rico, and dozens more in the highlands of Ecuador. This process empowered men in Latin America as never before. Women, however, were excluded from participating in elections until well into the twentieth century.

The "American Question"

The disruptions to the rule of the monarchy between 1808 and 1814 provided the first practical demonstration of the principles of popular sovereignty and a taste of active political participation for the colonies. Autonomy without independence, however, proved impractical. Moreover, the inherent distrust that both creoles and Spaniards felt toward indigenous and casta peoples permeated the discussions.

The first objections to American autonomy arose in the heated debates over how many American delegates the Cortes would include. Authors of the Constitution of 1812 assumed they would allocate representation according to population. Americans easily outnumbered Spaniards, but they included large numbers of Indians and racially mixed people. Were all of these groups to be allowed to vote or even to be counted for purposes of representation? The Constitution of 1812 gave the franchise to Indian and mestizo men but not to castas, whom it defined as people with any trace of African ancestry (Latin Americans themselves used this term to describe many types of racially mixed people). It also excluded felons, debtors, and domestic servants—provisions that might eliminate many Indians and mestizos, and even some people of Spanish extraction, from the

How Historians Understand   WERE THE WARS OF INDEPENDENCE THE TURNING POINT?

Periodization—the dividing of history into segments and identifying crucial turning points—is a major device historians use to explain and simplify the past. Traditionally, historians have considered the Latin American wars of independence between 1808 and 1825 as the crucial watershed in the region's history, and many Latin American history courses are divided into terms focusing on the colonial and national periods. This interpretation inferred that Latin America abruptly ended its colonial era and entered into modern times with a sharp break from Spain and Portugal. We know, however, that while independence hastened many transformations already underway during the previous century, all vestiges of the colonial order did not disappear in the 1820s. Slavery and discrimination against indigenous peoples endured well past independence, and many laws and government procedures carried over from the colonial regimes to the new nation states. Puerto Rico and Cuba remained colonies of Spain until after 1898. The traditional

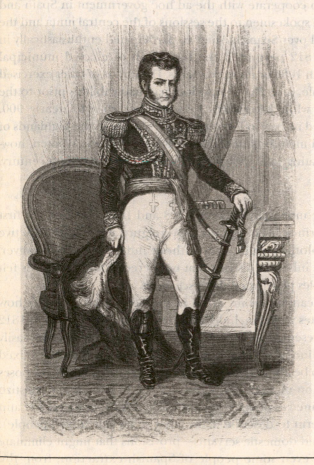

Bernardo O'Higgins, Chilean leader who symbolized the efforts of the colonial elite to maintain its power after Independence.

division of eras obscured critical continuities and made it difficult to assess the effects of change.

During the 1960s, an alternative approach arose, viewing the independence era as part of a broader period stretching from approximately 1720 or 1750 to 1850. This "Middle Period" incorporated the transition from traditional to modern society and from colonial to independent politics. The newly configured century allowed historians to trace the evolution of the trends and forces that caused the independence movements and to evaluate the impact of the end of colonial rule.

Investigating the half-centuries before and after independence has elucidated a number of new themes and hypotheses. First, traditional assumptions that the Spanish Empire was peaceful in the century before 1810 were incorrect. In the Mexican countryside, for example, there was constant unrest. Second, colonial rule was far from omnipotent. Historians had long ago documented corruption and inefficiency, but recent explorations have revealed the considerable extent of local autonomy. We have only scratched the surface of understanding to what degree the innovations introduced by the Spanish Bourbon kings and their counterparts in Portugal not only disrupted accommodations reached earlier but also began processes of change that independent governments built on after 1830. The Iberian monarchs of the eighteenth century, for example, took steps to reduce the power and political influence of the Catholic Church in Latin America. Many independent governments in the nineteenth and twentieth centuries continued to pursue this objective. Economic development, especially that of frontier regions, was a major concern of late colonial kings and independent governments alike.

While the inclusion of the wars of independence as part of a longer period and as part of longer historical processes has provided much new knowledge and many new insights, the more traditional periodization (adopted by the authors of this text) has considerable advantages. First, the break with Spain and Portugal had an enormous political impact. As we will see in Chapter 9, it set off decades of conflict over who was to rule and how. Independent governments tried for a century to establish their legitimacy and control. Moreover, there is little doubt that the wars of independence were economically cataclysmic. The damage to property and people over the course of nearly two decades of fighting was massive. It required nearly the entire century to recover to the level of production and prosperity in 1800. Independent Latin America had broken significantly from the past and begun a new era.

Questions for Discussion

What examples of significant historical turning points can you think of that have occurred during your own lifetime? What has changed? What continuities are there? Is periodization a useful tool for understanding history? Why or why not?

political process. Many American upper-class people feared the empowerment of castas and others they considered their social inferiors. Thus, the creoles were torn between their need to assure that their own concerns would receive ample hearing in the emerging political debate and their overwhelming fear of the lower classes. Full representation of all people regardless of ethnicity would have given the Western Hemisphere a three-to-two majority in the Cortes. Not surprisingly, Spaniards opposed this prospect.

The Spaniards prevailed on the question of representation, retaining control of the new parliament and using that advantage whenever their position differed from that of the Americans. One particularly divisive issue was the freedom to trade with all nations, a right that Spain's American colonies had never enjoyed. Spanish merchants preferred to maintain existing rules that allowed Americans to trade legally only with other Spanish subjects. Other American demands included the abolition of crown monopolies and, most crucially, equal access to jobs in the government, the military, and the church.

As they witnessed Spanish intransigence on issues such as representation and freedom of trade, even those Americans who initially favored some degree of cooperation with the new government moved toward a stance of greater self-determination for the overseas territories. Once they began to assert themselves politically, few Spanish Americans were willing to go back to old routines of subservience to the mother country. In the words of Simón Bolívar, a major leader of the independence movement in South America, by 1815 "the habit of obedience . . . [had] been severed."

SPANISH AMERICAN GRIEVANCES AND THE CRISIS OF 1808

The French invasion of Spain exacerbated decades of festering political and social tensions. Population growth, which had begun in the previous century, intensified during the 1700s, increasing the pressures on scarce land and water resources. There were an estimated 150 village riots in central Mexico from 1700 to 1820, as a result. In the early 1780s a dangerous rebellion, led by a man who claimed to be a descendant of the last Inca emperor, had shaken the viceroyalty of Peru.

The so-called Bourbon Reforms (named after the ruling dynasty of Spain installed after the Hapsburg line had expired in 1700) introduced by Kings Charles III and IV added to the undercurrents of dissatisfaction. The new monarchs sought to tighten Spain's control over its colonies to improve its defenses against threats from England and France, curb the influence and wealth of the Catholic Church, and increase the flow of revenues into the royal coffers. The reforms adversely affected Americans across all classes, with new taxes hitting everyone, conscription for the new standing armies striking fear into the vulnerable lower classes, and the arrival of swarms of Spanish bureaucrats thwarting the rising expectations of creoles. Riots protesting high prices erupted from Mexico to Ecuador. The Crown further agitated Americans by expelling the Jesuits, a powerful religious order, from the empire in 1767.

The disruption of Spanish sovereignty in 1808 brought all of these grievances to the forefront and sparked different kinds of revolts in the colonies. Three of the most important of these upheavals, each with its own special character but all with important implications for the future independence of Latin America, occurred in Mexico, Argentina, and Venezuela.

Mexico

The kinds of political, social, and economic changes that Latin Americans experienced at the beginning of the nineteenth century were especially apparent in the region of Mexico known as the Bajío, located between 100 and 200 miles northwest of Mexico City. As the colony's population grew in the late colonial period, wealthy individuals had invested in the commercial production of wheat, maize, and other crops, taking advantage of the area's rich soil and its proximity to the principal urban markets of New Spain. To expand their estates, these landowners forced many poor sharecroppers and other small farmers off the land.

At the same time, people who had worked in the region's many cloth factories and artisans who had made textiles in their own homes lost their livelihoods when the Spanish crown eased trade restrictions and opened the Mexican market to cheaper merchandise manufactured abroad. Production at the Bajío's silver mines also declined sharply as the new century began, leaving thousands of workers without jobs. Meanwhile, droughts and crop failures added to the misery. In the worst of these agricultural crises, from 1785 to 1786, almost 15 percent of the Bajío's population died of hunger. A new round of crop failures struck the region in 1809. The combined effects of economic change and natural disaster left thousands of people with little left to lose as the nineteenth century began.

Father Miguel Hidalgo y Costilla was a priest in the Bajío, in the town of Dolores, about 20 miles from the old silver mining town of Guanajuato. Born in 1753 to a middle-class creole family, Hidalgo had his own grudges against Spanish authority. He had received his early education at the hands of the Jesuits, and their expulsion from Mexico angered him and many others of his class. As an adult, he read the books of French Enlightenment thinkers who disputed the divine right of kings to exact unquestioning obedience from their subjects. His unorthodox ideas got him dismissed from his position as rector of a college in Valladolid (today, Morelia), one of the principal towns of the Bajío, and he narrowly escaped prosecution by the Inquisition. Policies of the Spanish king also hurt him in the pocketbook. He owned a small hacienda, but in 1804 royal officials seized his property when he could not pay special taxes levied to meet Spain's rising costs of defending itself against Napoleon. Meanwhile, Hidalgo took up his post as parish priest in Dolores. There he tried to promote new industries such as ceramics, tanning, and silk production to help his parishioners to weather the economic hard times they were facing. He also continued to meet with other intellectuals conversant with Enlightenment ideas and disgruntled with the Spanish monarchy.

Hidalgo's concerns and those of many other people in the surrounding region merged with the international crisis provoked by Napoleon's invasion of Spain. Since 1808, the government in Mexico City had been in the hands of conservative forces who favored maintaining ties with Spain at all costs. Father Hidalgo joined one of many conspiracies to overthrow them, and when authorities learned of his plans he decided to take the preemptive strike of declaring open revolt in his famous "Grito de Dolores" on September 16, 1810. Word of his rebellion quickly spread among the desperate and dispossessed classes in the Bajío. Within a few days, Hidalgo enlisted thousands of supporters who held a variety of grievances against the status quo. At its height, his army included 60,000 people, of whom about half were Indians and 20 percent were mestizos. In the words of historian Eric Van Young, many rural people joined Hidalgo's insurgency, and the many revolts that followed because they were "driven by hunger and unemployment, pulled into the maelstrom of violence by the prospect of daily wages in the rebel forces, the easy pickings of looting, or simply to escape from depressed conditions at home." The Indian rebels also wanted to retain control over their own communities, and for the most part, they did not stray far from their homes to fight. Their concern was less with independence from Spain than with local power and traditional values.

Hidalgo's forces sacked several towns and killed hundreds of Spanish men, women, and children who had taken refuge in the municipal grain warehouse in Guanajuato.

Creole elites, some of whom had once flirted with the cause of autonomy, recoiled in horror at the violent turn of events and joined forces with pro-Spanish authorities in Mexico City to crush the insurrection. Within a few months, they captured and executed Hidalgo, but another priest, José María Morelos, continued the fight, controlling virtually all of southern Mexico from 1811 until his defeat in 1815. Followers of Morelos, in particular the casta Vicente Guerrero, then continued guerrilla operations against Spanish authorities for several more years, but continued Spanish control seemed almost certain. It would take another round of events in Spain to propel Mexico toward the final step of independence.

Venezuela

The Bourbon Reforms included an emphasis on the economic development of formerly peripheral parts of the empire. Venezuela was one such region. Cacao production flourished as the popularity of chocolate grew in Europe during the eighteenth century. Its principal city, Caracas, became the seat of a new *audiencia*, or court of appeals, created in 1786.

Creole upper-class men in Caracas began efforts to create a self-governing junta in 1808 but succeeded only in the spring of 1810, when they overthrew the audiencia and the Spanish governor. A year later, they officially declared independence, created a three-man executive body, and drafted a constitution that excluded the lower classes from political participation. The new government lasted just a year. After a powerful earthquake hit Caracas in 1812, royalists regained control after convincing the popular classes that God was punishing Venezuela for its disregard for divinely constituted authority.

The young creole aristocrat Simón Bolívar took command of the forces favoring independence and began a campaign to retake Venezuela in the spring of 1813. Like so many others of his social standing, Bolívar detested the lower classes, and his enemies eagerly took advantage of this situation. In 1814, he suffered a humiliating defeat by royalist armies led by a black man José Tomás Boves and comprised largely of black and mulatto *llaneros* (plainsmen, cowboys by trade) angered at the harsh treatment they had received at the hands of those favoring an independent republic. Boves himself had suffered imprisonment by the insurgents in 1810. Now 4 years later, his "Legion of Hell" slaughtered wealthy creoles. Boves died on the battlefield, but his troops routed Bolívar and forced him into exile. In Venezuela as in Mexico, the outlook for independence looked grim as Ferdinand VII returned to power in Madrid in 1814.

Argentina

Like Venezuela, southern South America and the port town of Buenos Aires reaped significant benefits from the Bourbon kings' efforts to develop the empire's periphery. Formerly subject to the authority of the Spanish viceroy in Lima, Peru, in 1776, Buenos Aires became the seat of a newly created viceroyalty. The port now became the principal outlet through which silver from Bolivia and hides and tallow from the vast plains of Argentina and Uruguay reached markets abroad. The town's merchants also enjoyed abundant opportunities for contraband with British and Portuguese traders. The population of Buenos Aires quadrupled in the last half of the eighteenth century, reaching almost 40,000 by 1800.

Merchants and civic leaders took pride in the growing prosperity of their community. That sentiment deepened in 1806, when local citizens organized themselves and many of Buenos Aires's blacks and mulattos to drive out a British naval force that had taken control of the city. The following year, this combined militia thwarted yet another British invasion and forced the British to evacuate the city of Montevideo, across the Río de la Plata estuary from Buenos Aires, as well.

Creole militia officers thus positioned themselves to play key roles in the politics of Buenos Aires in the volatile years that followed the Napoleonic invasion of Spain. They figured prominently in a gathering of some 250 members of the town's upper class in May of 1810. That meeting produced a new governing junta that proclaimed nominal allegiance to Ferdinand VII, but in fact Spanish authority had ended in Buenos Aires, never to reappear. Those who dared to voice opposition to the patriot agenda were soon silenced.

SPANISH AMERICAN INDEPENDENCE

Buenos Aires was the exception, however. Only there, at the southernmost extreme of the empire, did prospects for the political independence of Spanish America seem good when Ferdinand resumed the throne. Everywhere else, the cause of independence appeared doomed. Hidalgo and Morelos were dead in Mexico, and within a few years thousands of those who had fought beneath their banners accepted amnesty from the crown. Bolívar had fled to Jamaica and King Ferdinand sent new armies to crush the Venezuelan rebellion once and for all. Once again, however, the determination of Latin Americans to assert control over their own affairs combined with events in Europe to bring about independence.

The Final Campaigns

When Ferdinand returned to power, he dissolved the Cortes and rejected the Constitution of 1812. These actions reinforced the determination of those Americans who had decided to break with the mother country and disillusioned those who had hoped he would be a just and fair monarch attentive to the concerns of all his subjects. Despite the many setbacks they had experienced, Americans persisted in their efforts to wear down the strength and morale of Spanish military forces.

By 1820, liberal politicians and army officers, fed up with Ferdinand's absolutist policies and the unpopular war in America forced the king to accept the 1812 Constitution and reconvene the Cortes. This led to the formation of provincial governments and elections to the Cortes in areas loyal to Spain. But the metropolis's new leaders proved unwilling to grant the overseas kingdoms an equal voice in government or the liberalization of trade.

The way now lay open for the Americas to break with Spain. In Mexico, the flurry of political activity among the lower classes, once again enfranchised by the resumption of constitutional government, alarmed Mexican conservatives who remembered the excesses of Hidalgo's forces in Guanajuato and elsewhere. Nonetheless the upper classes needed the support of the lower classes to obtain independence. In February 1821, the royalist general Agustín de Iturbide switched sides, forming an alliance with the rebel leader Vicente Guerrero, who had carried on guerrilla operations against royalist forces following the death of Morelos. Iturbide's proclamation of independence, known as the Plan de Iguala, was designed to calm conservatives. He proposed independence for Mexico and the creation of a constitutional monarchy. He also promised protection to the Catholic Church and to all Europeans in Mexico who agreed to support him. Over the next several months, Spanish authority simply collapsed in New Spain. In September of 1821, exactly 300 years after the Spanish conquest of Mexico, Iturbide entered Mexico City in triumph.

In South America, Simón Bolívar returned to Venezuela in 1816 and scored major victories against the Spanish, in part because he incorporated black troops, a tactical reversal of his prior refusal to allow them a role in the struggle for independence. Thousands of llaneros also joined with Bolívar at this critical juncture. By 1822, he had assured the independence of the Republic of Gran Colombia, consisting of present-day Colombia as well as Venezuela and Ecuador.

Meanwhile, the cause of independence won new victories in southern South America, led by José de San Martín, an Argentine-born officer in the Spanish army who

Independence or Death, the Shout of Ipiranga on September 7, 1822.

LATIN AMERICAN LIVES

MANUELA SÁENZ, 1797–1856, LIBERATOR OF SOUTH AMERICA

The life of Manuela Sáenz demonstrates how South Americans, and women in particular, experienced the transition from colony to independence. Manuela was born in Quito, the illegitimate daughter of a Spaniard who served on the city council and a woman from a prominent creole family. Her father provided for her upbringing in the largest and most affluent of Quito's convents, where she learned to read and write. In 1817, her father arranged for her to marry one of his business associates, the wealthy British merchant James Thorne, some 20 years her senior.

Manuela relocated to Lima with her husband and over the next few years helped manage his business affairs. Meanwhile, she became involved in Lima's political intrigues. She joined other women who supported Peruvian patriots' efforts to overthrow Spanish rule and actively helped recruit men to serve in José de San Martín's armies, even though both her husband and her father supported the royalist cause. In 1822, she paid a visit to her native Quito, in part because she wished to claim a portion of her mother's estate. She observed Simón Bolívar's triumphant arrival in the city on June 16, 1822, and shortly thereafter met him in person. The two soon began an intimate relationship that would last the remaining 8 years of Bolívar's life. She left Quito for Lima and from there accompanied Bolívar on his final campaigns against royalist forces in the Andes, serving as his personal archivist. After independence, she continued to support Bolívar against the many enemies who opposed his dominance of the newly emerging nations of northern South America. In 1828, when they were both living in Bogotá, she foiled an assassination attempt against her lover, winning for herself the title of the "Libertadora del Liberatador."

Bolívar resigned the presidency of Gran Colombia in 1830 and died of tuberculosis later that same year. Manuela's subsequent years were difficult. Bolívar's political adversaries in Ecuador refused to let her return to Quito, citing her unbridled ambition, outspoken nature, and past sexual improprieties. In 1835, she settled in Paita, a small port on the northern coast of Peru, not far from the Ecuadorian border. There she lived in poverty for the remainder of her life, depending on proceeds from the sale of handicrafts, occasional remittances from property in Ecuador, and the generosity of friends. A debilitating hip injury eventually confined her to a wheel chair. Her involvement in politics continued, however. She connived with other exiles and provided intelligence to her long-time friend, Ecuadorian President Juan José Flores, alerting him to Peruvian plots afoot to seize Ecuadorian territory and topple him from power. Even after Flores left office in 1845 she continued to maintain ties with other prominent conservative politicians in Quito. Gabriel García Moreno, a future president of Ecuador, was a frequent guest at her home during his period of political exile in Peru.

While in Paita Manuela began corresponding with her estranged husband, whom she had not seen since her departure for Quito in 1822. Thorne was murdered in 1847 at his hacienda in Chancay province, some 500 miles to the south of Paita.

Manuela was devastated when she heard the news, dressing in black and demanding that authorities identify and punish the perpetrators of the crime. She corresponded with her attorney in Lima, hoping to claim the dowry she had brought to their marriage and a share of Thorne's assets. Her husband's executor dismissed her pretensions, citing her notorious affair with Simón Bolívar. She died in 1856, as a diphtheria epidemic swept through northern Peru.

Sáenz has long been a controversial figure in Latin American history, denounced in her own time and subsequently for transgressing societal norms of proper feminine conduct. She smoked cigars, rode horseback, sometimes wore men's military uniforms, and was exceptionally outspoken, but many other literate and well-connected women, less flamboyant in their personal style than Manuela, participated in Latin American political life in the turbulent years surrounding national independence. Although Manuela and other women of her generation could neither vote nor hold office, their social networks proved vital for the emergence of new political ideas. They hosted political gatherings, and in the words of historian Sarah Chambers, "were active in social spaces between the public and private spheres, where philosophies were discussed, plots hatched, and alliances formed."

In recent years a novel by Colombian Nobel laureate Gabriel García Márquez, a film by Venezuelan director Diego Rísquez, and a carefully detailed biography by historian Pamela Murray have portrayed Manuela Sáenz as a strong, intelligent woman who made important contributions to the independence of Latin America. Feminists in her native Ecuador and elsewhere in Spanish America have seen her as a role model and a precursor of women's emancipation. She has also become a symbol of Ecuadorian patriotism. In 2007, she was posthumously promoted to the rank of general in the national army.

Questions for Discussion

Why do you think Manuela Sáenz is considered a national hero in Ecuador? Does her life story suggest that the independence era was a time of significant change for women? Why or why not? If Sáenz were alive today, how would her status as the mistress of a prominent male politician affect her involvement in political life?

had fought against Napoleon in Spain but returned home to join the independence struggle in 1812. After years of careful preparations, in January of 1817, San Martín led 5500 troops through treacherous mountain passes, some at altitudes approaching 15,000 feet above sea level, to Chile. Decisive victories over Spanish forces then paved the way for Chile's final independence in 1818.

San Martín's plan to liberate Peru stalled, because of distrust between the Peruvians and the invaders from Argentina and Chile. Although, Peruvian creoles declared independence and accepted San Martín as their military and civil ruler in 1821, royalist forces remained firmly in control of much of Peru. The following year San Martín and Bolívar met in Guayaquil, Ecuador, to determine how to complete the Peruvian campaign and realign the continent. As a consequence, San Martín withdrew and retired, leaving

A monument at the waterfront in Guayaquil, Ecuador, commemorating the meeting of South American independence leaders Simón Bolívar and José de San Martín there in 1822.

Bolívar to occupy Lima in 1823 and Bolívar's lieutenant Antonio José de Sucre to the secure victory at the Battle of Ayacucho in 1824.

Regional Conflicts in the Spanish American Struggle for Independence

The surrender of the royalist armies in Upper Peru in 1825 ended Spanish sovereignty in all of the Americas except for Cuba and Puerto Rico. The new republics that replaced the Spanish empire were taking shape, although their final boundaries underwent numerous alterations throughout the nineteenth century and beyond. The nation-states that emerged were the products of age-old local rivalries that drove Spanish Americans apart even as they fought for the common cause of independence. The movement for independence remained rooted in the desire of people from many different social classes to remain in control of their own communities.

Throughout the struggle for independence, the ad hoc governments created in major cities claimed to speak for entire provinces, but smaller towns resisted their domination. Declarations of "independence" proliferated, but the authors of these manifestos often meant independence from Lima or Buenos Aires or Mexico City, and not necessarily from Spain. Under royalist control in 1810, Quito formed a superior

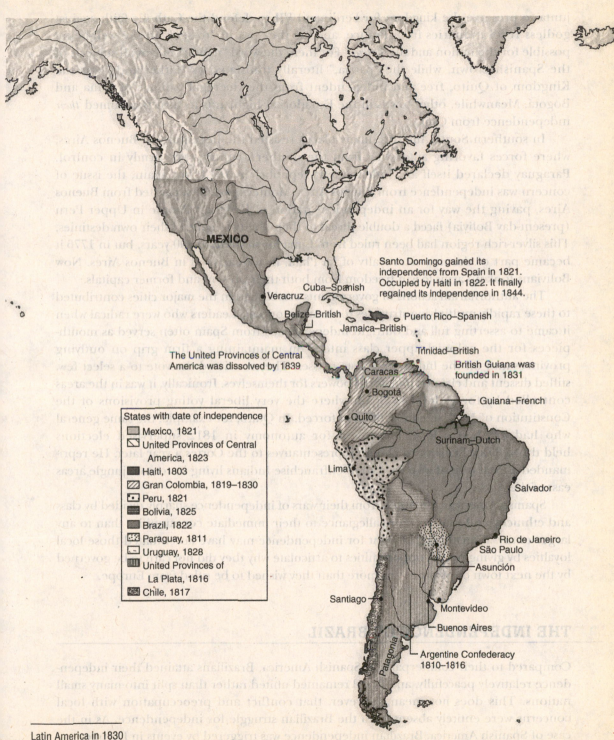

MEXICO

Santo Domingo gained its
independence from Spain in 1821.
Occupied by Haiti in 1822. It finally
regained its independence in 1844.

Cuba–Spanish
Veracruz

Belize–British

Puerto Rico–Spanish

Jamaica–British

Trinidad–British

The United Provinces of Central
America was dissolved by 1839

British Guiana was
founded in 1831

Caracas

Bogotá

Guiana–French

Quito

Surinam–Dutch

States with date of independence

Mexico, 1821
United Provinces of Central
America, 1823
Haiti, 1803
Gran Colombia, 1819–1830
Peru, 1821
Bolivia, 1825
Brazil, 1822
Paraguay, 1811
Uruguay, 1828
United Provinces of
La Plata, 1816
Chile, 1817

Lima

Salvador

Rio de Janeiro
São Paulo

Asunción

Santiago

Montevideo

Buenos Aires

Patagonia

Argentine Confederacy
1810–1816

Latin America in 1830

junta to preserve the kingdom for Ferdinand VII to defend the Catholic faith against godless revolutionaries from France, and, as they put it, "to seek all the well-being possible for the nation and the *patria*." For them the word "nation" meant all subjects of the Spanish crown, while the "patria," literally translated as "fatherland," was the Kingdom of Quito, free and independent from the viceregal capitals of Lima and Bogotá. Meanwhile, other towns in the Ecuadorian highlands in turn proclaimed *their* independence from Quito.

In southern South America, many places resisted the hegemony of Buenos Aires, where forces favoring autonomy from the mother country were firmly in control. Paraguay declared itself an "independent republic" in 1813, but again, the issue of concern was independence from Buenos Aires. Montevideo also separated from Buenos Aires, paving the way for an independent nation of Uruguay. People in Upper Peru (present-day Bolivia) faced a double threat to their ability to control their own destinies. This silver-rich region had been ruled from Lima for more than 200 years, but in 1776 it became part of the new viceroyalty of La Plata, headquartered in Buenos Aires. Now Bolivians took up arms to win freedom from both their present and former capitals.

The authoritarian actions of governments established in the major cities contributed to these rapidly multiplying struggles for local autonomy. Leaders who were radical when it came to asserting full and outright independence from Spain often served as mouthpieces for the colonial upper class intent on maintaining a firm grip on outlying provinces and on the Indian and casta masses. They restricted the vote to a select few, stifled dissent and claimed dictatorial powers for themselves. Ironically, it was in the areas controlled by forces loyal to Spain where the very liberal voting provisions of the Constitution of 1812 were most often enforced. In Quito, for example, the same general who had crushed a local movement for autonomy in 1812 supervised elections held throughout Ecuador to choose representatives to the Cortes a year later. He reprimanded a local official who tried to disenfranchise Indians living in remote jungle areas east of the Andes.

Spanish Americans emerged from their wars of independence sharply divided by class and ethnicity and with far more allegiance to their immediate communities than to any larger entity. If anything, the fight for independence may have accentuated those local loyalties by giving people opportunities to articulate why they did not care to be governed by the next town or province any more than they wished to be ruled from Europe.

THE INDEPENDENCE OF BRAZIL

Compared to their counterparts in Spanish America, Brazilians attained their independence relatively peacefully, and Brazil remained united rather than split into many small nations. This does not mean, however, that conflict and preoccupation with local concerns were entirely absent from the Brazilian struggle for independence. As in the case of Spanish America, Brazilian independence was triggered by events in Europe.

The Portuguese Monarchy in Brazil

Napoleon's invasion of the Iberian Peninsula was meant to sever Portugal's long-standing alliance with Great Britain. For decades, policymakers in Lisbon had toyed with the idea of removing themselves from the vicissitudes of European power politics by making Brazil, rather than Portugal, the center of the empire. The rapid approach of French troops in November of 1807 persuaded the government to consider this radical proposal as a temporary expedient in the face of a national emergency. The Crown decided to move the court and its entourage, numbering perhaps 10,000 people, sailing with a British naval escort. Queen Maria and her son, the de facto ruler Prince João, arrived in Rio de Janeiro in 1808. King João VI continued to reside in Brazil after his mother's death in 1816.

The presence of the royal court brought dramatic changes to Portuguese America. Intellectual activity flourished with the long-overdue introduction of printing presses at Rio de Janeiro and Salvador, the expansion of education at the primary level, and the establishment of two medical schools and a military academy to train officers for Brazil's new army. Rio de Janeiro thrived as never before, as local merchants found a market providing the court with its many needs. Most important, Brazilians took pride in their homeland, touting its greatness in new periodicals that circulated in major cities. As one young man from Bahia put it, "Brazil, proud now that it contains within it the Immortal Prince, . . . is no longer to be a maritime Colony . . . but rather a powerful Empire, which will come to be the Moderator of Europe, the arbiter of Asia, and the dominator of Africa." In 1815, Portuguese America was proclaimed the Kingdom of Brazil, fully equal with the mother country.

Other changes proved less welcome, however. Brazilians had to shoulder new tax burdens to pay for the expanded bureaucracy and the costs of waging war against the French in Portugal. Willingly at first but with increasing reluctance as time passed, prominent citizens of Rio de Janeiro vacated their homes to accommodate the courtiers and bureaucrats who accompanied the king to Brazil. People in Bahia in the northeastern part of the country chafed under Rio de Janeiro's growing dominance. Although the government in exile officially encouraged trade with all nations, it also bound Brazil more closely than ever before to an economic dependence on Great Britain that stifled the growth of local manufacturing.

Popular Unrest in Brazil

Some Brazilians dared to express their opposition to the adverse effects of the Portuguese occupation, and King João was no more sympathetic to their concerns than King Ferdinand was to the grievances of his American subjects. In March of 1817, a revolt began in Pernambuco in the northeast after royal authorities arrested a number of army officers and others suspected of harboring treasonous sentiments. The rebels destroyed images of the king and his coat of arms, proclaimed a republic, and trumpeted ideals voiced by their contemporaries in Spanish America, among them personal liberty, equality before the law, support for the Catholic religion, and devotion to their homeland, or patria. They also expressed their hatred toward the many Portuguese-born Europeans who had settled in Brazil in the years since 1808, but vigorously denied rumors that they advocated an immediate end to African slavery, a mainstay of the Brazilian economy. The revolt spread throughout the northeastern part of Brazil, the area that most resented the heavy hand of the royal government based in Rio de Janeiro.

King João was aghast at what he called "a horrible attempt upon My Royal Sovereignty and Supreme Authority." His forces suppressed the rebellion within just 2 months and about 20 of its leaders were executed, but the king could no longer take his Brazilian subjects for granted. He brought new armies over from Portugal and stationed them in Rio de Janeiro, Salvador, and Recife.

The Culmination of Brazilian Independence

Indeed, King João had cause for concern that the people of Portugal might attempt to throw off his authority. Discontent within the military sparked a revolt in August 1820 that strongly resembled the Spanish coup of that same year. The participants called for the convoking of a Cortes and the writing of a constitution modeled after the Spanish document of 1812. They also demanded that King João return to Lisbon, and he prudently acquiesced. Before embarking from Rio de Janeiro in April of 1821, he placed his 22-year-old son, Pedro, in charge as prince regent of the Kingdom of Brazil.

This was a period of important political change in Brazil. With the blessing of the Portuguese Cortes, many towns and cities formed juntas, asserting their local autonomy rather than accepting the continued domination of the government in Rio de Janeiro, much as Spanish Americans of their time tried to free themselves from the control of

Coronation of Emperor Pedro I, Rio de Janeiro, 1822.

capital cities. The Cortes also ordered the dismantling of superior tribunals created during King João's residency, and the local governing juntas refused to send tax revenues to Rio de Janeiro. The cumulative effect of these changes was to reduce Prince Pedro's authority, so that, in effect, he functioned as little more than the governor of the capital city and its immediate surrounding area. Affluent residents of Rio missed the good times their city had enjoyed between 1808 and 1821, and those imbued with a sense of Brazilian national pride fretted over the splintering of the great Kingdom of Brazil into a series of petty autonomous provinces, each under the jurisdiction of a separate local junta.

Meanwhile, delegates in the Cortes worried with considerable justification that those opposed to these constitutional changes might rally around Prince Pedro. The Cortes therefore commanded the prince regent to return to Portugal, as his father had done several months previously. In January of 1822, Pedro announced his decision to stay in Brazil,

Brazil States and Their Capitals

The final break came on September 7, 1822. Pedro I became the "constitutional emperor and perpetual defender" of Brazil, a position he held until 1831, when he abdicated in favor of his son, Pedro II, who in turn ruled until Brazil became a republic in 1889.

THE MEANING OF INDEPENDENCE

As they went about setting up governments, leaders of the new nations of Latin America borrowed very selectively from the egalitarian rhetoric of the North American and French Revolutions. They eagerly invoked ideas of representation and freedom of expression when it came to claiming a voice for themselves in governing their home-lands. Taking their cues from France and the United States, Latin America's leaders forged a new concept of citizenship, calling on all who lived within their borders to place loyalty to the nation above any ties to their church, family, or local community.

Slice of Life   THE 16TH OF SEPTEMBER: INDEPENDENCE DAY IN MEXICO

THE LEADERS OF LATIN America's new nations not only had to set up governments and rebuild economies disrupted by the independence wars; they also had to convince their people to pay allegiance to the nation. Historians sometimes speak of nation-states as "imagined communities" in which people who do not have face-to-face contact with one another and who may not have much in common all see themselves as citizens of the nation. In practical terms, forging these new communities in Latin America meant getting people as diverse as, for example, pampered creole aristocrats in Mexico City, Zapotec-speaking Indians in Oaxaca far to the south, and farmers who eked out a living on the far northern frontier of New Mexico, to set aside their racial, economic, linguistic, and cultural differences and swear loyalty to the new republic of Mexico.

Most Latin Americans of the early nineteenth century, whatever their back-grounds, did in fact see themselves as part of a universal community, that of the Catholic Church. Those who took command of the new national governments strove to persuade their citizens to transfer their loyalties from the church to the nation, and they borrowed some of the tools the church had used for centuries to instill a sense of community among the faithful. National holidays now competed with religious ones, and the heroes of the independence wars were invoked as examples of patriotism, much as saints had served as examples of Christian piety.

Leaders of Mexico lost little time in setting up a new ritual calendar intended to enkindle a sense of nationalism from Oaxaca to New Mexico. Foremost among the days they chose to commemorate was September 16, the anniversary of Father Hidalgo's "Grito de Dolores" of 1810, the proclamation that had ignited the first phase of Mexico's wars for independence. The initial celebration of September 16

Mexico States and State Capitals

took place in Mexico City in 1823. The festivities included the ringing of church bells, a splendid parade with music supplied by a military band, and speeches extolling the virtues of the new nation. The remains of national hero José María Morelos were brought to Mexico City for burial. Just as saints' days had offered a variety of secular entertainments in addition to the religious observances, the independence celebrations of September 1823 featured music and theatrical presentations in the Alameda, the city's centrally located park. Fireworks shows at the *zócalo*, the main plaza facing the cathedral, lasted far into the night.

From 1825, a private, voluntary organization supervised the celebration in Mexico City. For 30 years, with only one exception, when U.S. troops occupied the city in 1847, the *Junta Patriótica* (patriotic committee) oversaw the events. Beginning on the night of September 15 and continuing throughout the next day, there were patriotic speeches, artillery salutes, music, theater, and fireworks. The junta, the president of the republic, and other dignitaries marched through the city's streets on the morning of the 16th. Schoolchildren sang patriotic hymns specially commissioned for the occasion. The people of Mexico City turned out in droves dressed in their best. The junta also marked the day with charitable works such as cash payments to disabled or impoverished veterans and to widows and orphans of rebels who died in the wars. In the 1820s, poor children received new clothes. Every prisoner in the Mexico City jails received a good meal, a packet of cigarettes, a bar of soap, and one *real* (a coin, worth one-eighth of a peso) on September 16. In the provinces, the holiday was marked with equal fervor, if not with equal splendor. In San Luis Potosí, for example, local dignitaries marched and tossed coins to the assembled crowds, who also enjoyed music and fireworks.

From the 1820s to the present, the timing, scale, and specific content of Mexico's independence festivities varied according to the political climate of the time. Sometimes, members of the nineteenth-century upper class muted the celebrations because they feared a rekindling of the same kind of popular unrest that Hidalgo's proclamation had unleashed. On some occasions, they suspended all observances except for a few speeches in Congress. In times when national governments felt more securely in control, they praised the revolutionary aspirations of Hidalgo and Morelos, hoping to win the allegiance of the lower classes. The first celebrations of Mexican independence had commemorated Agustín de Iturbide's triumphal entry into Mexico City in September of 1821 along with Hidalgo's Grito de Dolores, but later leaders chose to focus exclusively on the first phase of the movement, when Hidalgo and Morelos had so forcefully articulated the grievances of the masses, even though it had been Iturbide's actions that had secured Mexico's final independence from Spain. Iturbide's victory represented the consummation of upper-class negotiations with insurgents—a backroom deal. Subsequent leaders of Mexico had more to gain politically if they claimed to be the heirs of Hidalgo and Morelos, even if their outlook and their means of governance far more closely resembled those of the conservative Iturbide. Ironically, the symbol of the people's movement, Father Hidalgo, triumphed just as governments grew strong enough to encroach upon the very local autonomy for which the people had fought.

Questions for Discussion

Are patriotic holidays effective in promoting a sense of national loyalty? Why or why not? What are some other means that governments use to win people's allegiance? Are there means that are available to governments today that were not available to the leaders of the new Latin American governments in the early nineteenth century?

The kind of equality proclaimed by the more radical factions of the French Revolution, and the specter of the bloody slave revolt that had brought independence to the former French colony of Haiti, terrified Latin American political elites. At the same time, fighters both for and against independence sought to enlist the lower classes on their side. Various insurgent leaders in Spanish America promised to abolish the tribute, a special tax on Indians and blacks levied by on the colonial state. In Peru, the insurgents also ordered an end to the mita, a highly oppressive system of forced labor that had sent thousands of Indians to work in silver mines and other enterprises. The tribute and the mita both symbolized the power of the colonial state that the insurgents were anxious to destroy. Indians often had few reasons to trust privileged creole patriots and sided with the Spanish. In Peru and Bolivia, for example, Indians comprised the bulk of the royalist armies. After independence, many leaders declared that the people formerly known as "Indians" were now citizens of the new national states. In practice, however, many forms of discrimination lingered long beyond the end of colonial rule.

Royalist commanders throughout the hemisphere promised freedom to slaves who helped them fight the rebel forces. Similar offers went out from insurgent camps as well, but sometimes blacks were advised that they would have to wait patiently for these promises to be fulfilled. In 1812, for example, the revolutionary junta at Buenos Aires told the city's slaves, "Your longed-for liberty cannot be decreed right away, as humanity and reason would wish, because unfortunately it stands in opposition to the sacred right of individual liberty." By "individual liberty," the Argentine patriots meant the property rights of slaveowners. Even when the offers of freedom were genuine, creole leaders of the independence movement often showed extreme prejudice toward blacks even as they tried to recruit them, and many people of color cast their lot with the royalists. After independence, victorious creoles devised means to deny blacks access to the political process in their new nations. Only in places where slavery was no longer economically viable did they carry through with their wartime promises to abolish slavery.

Both sides in the independence struggle also sought the support of women. Women often accompanied soldiers into battle, preparing meals, nursing the wounded, and sometimes taking up arms themselves. In South America, Bolívar's companion Manuela Sáenz played a prominent role in the final battles for independence. Throughout the Americas, women served as spies for royalist and patriot armies alike. María Josefa Ortiz de Domínguez, wife of a royal official in the Bajío and nicknamed "La Corregidora," alerted Father Hidalgo and his coconspirators that the authorities had learned of their plot. Women smuggled weapons, and—in one instance in Mexico—a printing press, to insurgents and persuaded soldiers in the royalist armies to desert. In Mexico City, however, a women's organization called the *Patriotas Marianas* drummed up support for the royalist cause. Despite the active involvement of many women in the independence movement, the new leaders of Latin America, like those who commanded the United States and all the nation-states of nineteenth-century Europe, included only males in their definition of who was entitled to play an active role in civic affairs.

CONCLUSION

In most of Latin America, the wars of independence were long-drawn-out, brutal contests. The Spaniards had defeated the insurgencies in the first phase by 1815. Popular and creole movements (in New Spain and northern South America, respectively) failed because of the deep-seated mutual distrust between the upper classes on one hand and Indians and castas on the other. Upper-class fear of the indigenous and mixed population cut short Hidalgo's campaign, and the unwillingness of creoles to make concessions to the lower classes in New Granada ensured Bolívar's initial defeats. Undercurrents of class and race war added a vicious, murderous aspect to the fighting.

Beginning about 1817, the tide turned in favor of independence, in part because the creoles learned from past mistakes and reached temporary arrangements with the lower classes, such as the llaneros of Venezuela and Vicente Guerrero's guerrilla forces of southern Mexico. Politics in Europe also played a role in pushing the colonies toward the final break with the mother countries. Following his restoration to the Spanish throne, King Ferdinand VII had paid little attention to colonial concerns, and the representative assemblies that reemerged in Spain and Portugal in 1820 proved intransigent on issues of vital concern to Latin Americans. Colonial upper classes finally felt confident they could declare independence and contain popular discontent without help from overseas. From 1817 to 1824, Spanish and Portuguese authority yielded to independent governments from Mexico to southern South America.

Soon after taking power, leaders of the new Latin American governments began declaring national holidays that honored the heroes of independence and their victories on the battlefield, but more than a decade of war left most Latin Americans with little to celebrate. Parts of the region were in ruins, and hundreds of thousands had died. Many survivors, armed and mobile, had nothing to which they could return. Facing an uncertain future, those who did have resources hesitated to invest in new enterprises. It would take much of Latin America a century to recover economically from the wars of independence. Poverty in turn undermined the political stability of the new republics.

And while it was easy enough to create new symbols of nationhood such as flags, monuments, and coinage, much more difficult was the task of forging new national identities, "imagined communities" in which racially and culturally disunited peoples who thought mostly in terms of their own towns and villages could live together and come to see themselves as Mexicans or Peruvians or Brazilians. The resulting tensions would undermine the stability of Latin American politics for a half century.

LEARNING MORE ABOUT LATIN AMERICANS

Bethel, Leslie, ed. *The Independence of Latin America* (New York: Cambridge University Press, 1987).

Chambers, Sarah C. *From Subjects to Citizens: Honor, Gender and Politics in Arequipa, Peru, 1780–1854* (University Park, PA: Pennsylvania State University Press, 1999). A look at how ordinary people in one Peruvian community experienced the transition from colonialism to independence.

Graham, Richard. *Independence in Spanish America: A Comparative Approach*, 2nd ed. (New York: McGraw-Hill, 1994). Comprehensive coverage of the wars for independence.

Henderson, Timothy J. *The Mexican Wars for Independence* (New York: Hill and Wang, 2009). Succinct survey.

Kinsbruner, Jay. *Independence in Spanish America: Civil Wars, Revolutions, and Underdevelopment* (Albuquerque, NM: University of New Mexico Press, 2000). Good overview of the process of independence.

Kraay, Hendrik. *Race, State, and Armed Forces in Independence-Era Brazil: Bahia, 1790s–1840s* (Stanford, CA: Stanford University Press, 2001). An examination of independence and early state-building in one of Brazil's historic sugar-producing regions.

Méndez, Cecilia. *The Plebeian Republic: The Huanta Rebellion and the Making of the Peruvian State, 1820–1850* (Durham, NC: Duke University Press, 2005). This study of a rebellion by peasants, muleteers, landowners, and military officers shows the kinds of challenges facing the new governments of Latin America in the era of Independence.

Murray, Pamela. *For Glory and Bolívar: The Remarkable Life of Manuela Sáenz* (Austin, TX: University of Texas Press, 2008). A definitive biography of Manuela Sáenz that dispels the many myths surrounding Simón Bolívar's mistress.

Rodriíguez, O., Jaime E. *The Independence of Spanish America* (New York: Cambridge University Press, 1998).

Schultz, Kirsten. *Tropical Versailles: Empire, Monarchy, and the Portuguese Royal Court in Rio de Janeiro, 1808–1821* (New York: Routledge, 2001). How the temporary presence of the Portuguese monarchy transformed life in the capital of Brazil.

Van Young, Eric. *The Other Rebellion: Popular Violence, Ideology, and the Mexican Struggle for Independence, 1810–1821* (Stanford, CA: Stanford University Press, 2001). A learned exploration of the reasons why Mexicans rebelled against Spanish authority.

Walker, Charles F. *Smoldering Ashes: Cuzco and the Creation of Republican Peru, 1780–1840* (Durham, NC: Duke University Press, 1999). Gives key insights into the roles played by the indigenous people of Cuzco in forging independence and a new national state.

9

REGIONALISM, WAR, AND RECONSTRUCTION:
POLITICS AND ECONOMICS, 1821–1880

THE NEWLY INDEPENDENT COUNTRIES of Latin America confronted two enormous challenges. The first was the need to persuade people who lived within their boundaries to render allegiance to the nation-state. Second, they had to rebuild their economies following the widespread destruction of the prolonged wars of independence. But before they could undertake these efforts, they had to resolve endless, seemingly intractable, disputes over who was to rule and what type of government was most appropriate. Most important, the new nations had to overcome the fact that the majority of people thought about politics in terms of their village, town, or province. Their concerns centered on how best to earn their livelihoods and maintain their local traditions, and for centuries, they had stubbornly resisted outsiders' attempts to meddle in their affairs. As we saw in Chapter 8, this regionalism shaped the independence struggle in many parts of Latin America, and it would continue to frustrate the efforts of nineteenth-century politicians bent on forging national communities.

Class and ethnic divisions further stymied nation-building, as people of different social classes fought for control of the new national governments. Underlying all politics was the deep fear the white upper classes had for the lower classes—comprised of African Latin Americans, native peoples, and mixed bloods—in part the result of a series of Indian and slave rebellions during the half century before the end of colonial rule.

Nor was there any kind of consensus about the form that governments should take. Some called for monarchy as the only way to guarantee stability, while others favored representative government. Among the advocates of democracy, some wanted a broad franchise, while others preferred to limit political participation to a select few. Often, charismatic strongmen, called *caudillos,* who were able to impose order by either mediating or coercing the various competing groups, took the reins for long periods. Finally, for many Latin Americans the struggle for independence was just the beginning of a cycle of intermittent and devastating warfare that would last for much of the nineteenth century. Civil conflicts, wars with neighboring Latin American nations, and invasions launched by nations outside the region all took an enormous toll in human lives, wreaked economic havoc, and undermined all efforts at achieving some kind of national political cohesion.

Building strong economies proved equally daunting. The damage caused by the wars of independence was extensive. The lack of continuity caused by changes in the form of government and turnover in personnel made economic development difficult.

DILEMMAS OF NATIONHOOD

The new leaders of Latin America embarked upon nationhood with many ideas about political life, but no clear blueprint of the forms their national governments should take. They all had recent experience with kings, much of it unfavorable. The principal model of self-government at the national level was that of the young United States, but some political leaders found it unsuitable for Latin America. Like their neighbors to the north, the larger nations grappled with the question of whether to create a strong central government or to leave substantial power in the hands of state, provincial, or local governments. Given the profound attachment that many Latin Americans had to their own regions and towns, this dilemma of centralism versus a loose confederation proved especially vexing. Then, too, Latin Americans disagreed about how much change their societies needed. What institutions and practices left over from the colonial period should they retain, and what colonial legacies should they discard? In particular, they quarreled over the proper role of the Catholic Church in their societies and how best to make their economies more productive. But before they could address any of these questions, they had to settle the argument over who was to control the new national governments.

Who Governs and What Form of Government?

From Independence through the 1870s, four broad groups vied in the political arena. At the top were wealthy, influential whites, such as prosperous merchants, large landowners, mine owners, and church officials, who expected to rule their nations for their own benefit. Military, comprised of national armies, provincial militias, and locally based private forces, formed the second contender. Mostly, the latter allied with the interests of the upper class, but on occasion had their own goals. The nineteenth century's many wars reinforced the role of the military. A small middle sector made up of professional bureaucrats, who allied with the upper classes and ran the everyday operations of government, lower-level clergy, and merchants, also competed. Lastly, the lower classes, which included sharecroppers, tenant farmers, small-scale merchants,

TIMELINE

1814–1840
Dr. Francia rules Paraguay

1822–1831
Pedro I rules in Brazil

1828
Gran Colombia breaks up

1828–1852
Juan Manuel de Rosas dominates the Río de la Plata

1836–1838
Peru–Bolivia Confederation

1846–1848
Mexican War with the United States

1857–1860
War of the Reform in Mexico

1862
Argentine unification
French Intervention in Mexico

1865–1870
Paraguayan War or War of the Triple Alliance

1879–1883
War of the Pacific (Chile vs. Peru and Bolivia)

unskilled and skilled workers, artisans, street venders, and domestics, demanded a say in the political debates. Although the upper class dominated politics and commanded most of the economic resources, the lower class wielded some influence at the local level. The upper class feared the lower classes but also needed their support, especially in times of internal conflicts or external war. The lower classes could negotiate, trading their assistance in return for local autonomy or other concessions.

The type of government was also under discussion. Mexico and Brazil first adopted monarchies. In Mexico, Emperor Agustín I (Iturbide) lasted little more than a year (1821–1822). The Brazilian monarchy, however, endured for 67 years (1822–1889) and two emperors, Pedro I (1821–1829) and Pedro II (1839–1889). For the most part, Latin Americans chose the republican model of government with three branches, the executive, the legislature, and the judiciary, with political participation limited to literate male property owners. For much of the nineteenth century, dictators who did the bidding of the upper classes ruled.

Federalism/Centralism and Liberalism/Conservatism

Regionalism was at the core of the political discourse with the political ideologies of the times focused on the roles of government at the various levels. On one side were the federalists who advocated weak national governments and strong provincial (state) governments. On the other were the centralists who favored strong national governments and weak provincial governments. Each counted landowners among their ranks, but the centralists also included urban merchants, top-echelon government bureaucrats, military officers, and high clergy. Neither factions trusted the lower classes, but nonetheless relied on their support, particularly at the local level.

During the middle decades of the nineteenth century, the political discourse expanded to include the role of the Roman Catholic Church in the economy and politics, the place of collective landholdings as practiced by Indian and mestizo villages, and the relative merits of free trade and protectionism. Federalism became subsumed in Liberalism (except in the Río de la Plata) and centralism in Conservatism. Each of these new factions for the most part incorporated the followers of their predecessors. The Liberals vehemently opposed the position of the Church as a large landowner, insisted on individual rather than collective property holding, and advocated free trade. They sought to create a nation of small farmers, practitioners of capitalism, who would form the backbone of the republic. Regional elites tended toward Liberalism, because it would maintain their traditional autonomy. Large-scale merchants were Liberals because they favored deregulation of commerce. Ironically, the Liberals discovered by century's end that their goals for economic development were incompatible with federalism, so they became centralists. They found too that free trade did not further modern industrial development. Conservatives fought most fiercely for the rights and privileges of the Church, which they believed served as the protector of social stability.

Whether Liberal or Conservatives, privileged groups distrusted, even despised, the lower classes, while at the same time they eagerly solicited their support. For most people in the countryside the struggles of everyday life remained paramount; access to good land and avoidance of oppressive taxation were at the center of their agenda. Keeping local community and religious traditions free of outside interference were also of utmost importance. Most country people had joined independence movements in order to reassert the local autonomy lost to the administrative reforms of the late colonial era. To them ideology meant far less than did control over local affairs. They often changed their allegiances, establishing links to whatever regional and national forces that seemed least likely to intrude on local prerogatives.

THE CHALLENGE OF REGIONALISM

The histories of almost every nation in Latin America recount decades of struggle to forge regions into larger entities and build national identities. The centuries-old desire for local autonomy on the part of many lower-class people lay at the heart of Latin American regionalism, but many other factors also worked against any quick achievement of national unity. Geography played a decisive role. Mountains, deserts, and jungles often impeded easy overland transportation and communication and made it difficult to determine clear national and provincial boundaries. In Mexico, the lack of navigable rivers further hindered contact among people across its vast territory that extended from present-day California to Central America. Linguistic differences and racial antagonisms divided many countries as well. Although a small group of upper-class whites in each country by the 1810s had imagined nationhood, the vast majority of the people owed loyalty to their home villages or cities. Mexico, Central America, northern South America, and Argentina all required a series of civil wars to create nations from regional conglomerations. Bolivia, Paraguay, and Uruguay owed their status as separate nations to their efforts to escape from the control of Argentina. Brazil avoided the ravages of civil war but still experienced serious conflicts among its many regions. Only Chile did not struggle to unify. It maintained orderly politics for 60 years, and Chilean presidents succeeded one another at 10-year (two 5-year terms) intervals until 1890.

Argentina, Mexico, Colombia, and Central America

Four areas, Argentina, Mexico, Colombia, and Central America, required a series of civil wars to amalgamate nations from their disparate regions. The rivalries between federalists and centralists and Liberals and Conservatives were often bitter and brutal. Independent Argentina (originally the Viceroyalty of Río de la Plata) consisted of four regions: the city and environs of Buenos Aires, the area along the coast north of Buenos Aires, the territory across the river (present-day Uruguay), and the interior (west of Buenos Aires to the Andes mountains). From the outset of independence, the people of the Río de la Plata struggled among themselves based on regional loyalties. Centralists, primarily export-oriented landowners and merchants in Buenos Aires, favored a unified, secular nation with an economy based on free trade. They earned their fortunes by exporting animal products, such as salted meat, to Europe. They also sought to limit the influence of the church and advocated religious freedom. Against them stood the regional bosses, usually landowners with armed cowboy (*gaucho*) followers, who objected to a strong central government and supported the church and fiercely fought to maintain their provincial autonomy.

The old Viceroyalty of Río de la Plata disintegrated as a political entity immediately after independence. It would take more than four decades to unite what is today Argentina. The northeast (Corrientes, Entre Ríos, and Santa Fe provinces) sought to throw off the domination of Buenos Aires as early as 1810. Upper Peru (now Bolivia) broke away in 1810, followed by Paraguay in 1811. Montevideo (across the river in present-day Uruguay) simultaneously rejected the rule of Buenos Aires. In 1819, several coastal and interior provinces declared themselves independent republics, each ruled by a local warlord.

The city of Buenos Aires, which was the strongest political and military entity in the Río de la Plata, led the struggle for centralization. Bernardino Rivadavia (1821–1827) and Juan Manuel de Rosas (1829–1852) established Buenos Aires's dominance until the provinces reasserted their autonomy, overthrowing Rosas in 1852. After nearly a decade of warfare, Buenos Aires finally defeated provincial forces in 1861 and imposed unification. Delegates from the provinces elected Bartolomé Mitre (1862–1868), the victorious general, Argentina's first president in 1862. He then used war with Paraguay (1865–1870) to further strengthen the power of the national government at the expense of provincial autonomy. By the mid-1870s, the government had eliminated the last of the regional bosses. The achievement of a centralized nation-state had been costly, however, requiring two civil wars and an external war.

Regionalism was also at the core of nineteenth-century Mexican politics. In Mexico, centralists and federalists alternated in power through the 1850s. The experiment with monarchy immediately after independence was short lived. Emperor Agustín I, who as Agustín de Iturbide had forged the negotiations between the upper classes and rebel guerrilla leaders that obtained independence from Spain in 1821, failed to unite the country and fell to a federalist insurgency. Mexico's first elected president, Guadalupe

Victoria (1824–1829), a hero of the guerrilla wars of independence, managed to balance the two factions. From 1829 until 1855, as the battle between federalism and centralism teetered back and forth, Antonio López de Santa Anna dominated the political landscape. Santa Anna began as a federalist, but quickly changed views when confronted with the fragmentation of his country. The centralists ruled for a decade from 1836 to 1846, lost out to the federalists from 1846 to 1853, and reasserted themselves in 1853. The loss of Texas in 1836 and defeat in the war with the United States (1846–1848) badly discredited the centralists led by Santa Anna. The federalist–centralist struggle was then subsumed in the new conflict between Liberals (who were federalists) and Conservatives (who were centralists). A terrible civil war erupted, which ended only in 1867 with the defeat of the centralists-Conservatives. Mexico began to come together under the presidency of Benito Juárez (1858–1872), a Liberal, who unified the nation through his heroic struggle against the French Intervention from 1862 to 1867. The Conservatives allied with the French and, as a result, suffered devastating defeat. Like Argentina, the emergence of Mexican nationhood had required a series of brutal civil wars and an external war in which there were hundreds of thousands of casualties.

Central America

How Historians Understand   BENITO JUÁREZ: THE MAKING OF A MYTH

Benito Juárez was president of Mexico from 1858 to 1872. Mexico's first Indian head of state led the nation through its bloodiest civil war, the War of the Reform (1858–1860), and its longest foreign war, the French Intervention (1861–1867). During his distinguished career, Juárez served at every level of government in both elected offices and the courts: from city councilor, to state legislator, national congressman, state governor, cabinet minister, and president, and from district judge to chief justice of the Supreme Court of the nation. Almost single-handedly, by force of his own determination, Juárez assured the triumph of Liberalism as the dominant political ideology and began the process of creating Mexico as a nation from the conglomeration of regions that had emerged from independence. Despite his obvious importance in nineteenth-century Mexican history, the myth of Benito Juárez has changed over time to reflect its creators' needs at the time. In the words of historian Charles Weeks: "…what Mexicans say about Juárez represents what they want to believe about themselves, as individuals and as a nation."

Because his career bridged and overlapped the careers of the two most vilified figures of nineteenth-century Mexican history, Antonio López de Santa Anna, who

Benito Juárez, symbol of the republic against French intervention in Mexico. Juárez, the first Indian president of Mexico, was a controversial figure.

dominated politics from 1828 to 1855, and Porfirio Díaz, the dictator from 1876 to 1911, Juárez should have attained the status of the nation's greatest hero. But mythical status came hard. In the fragmented politics of the era, his leadership was never uncontested. Two rivals vied for the presidency against him in 1861. He faced opposition to his continuation as president, during a time when the nation was at war, after his term ended in 1865. Two opponents confronted him in the elections of 1868 and 1872. (In the latter year he died shortly after his reelection.) Despite having defeated the French and their figurehead, the emperor Maximilian, Juárez found himself demonized by his enemies as a dictator.

For the first 15 years after his death, Juárez was almost forgotten. His successor, Porfirio Díaz, had tried twice to overthrow him by force, and the two men had ended as enemies. Díaz initially sought to get out from under Juárez's shadow. A radical change in attitude toward Juárez took place in 1887, when Díaz sought reelection for the first time. Díaz had served as president from 1877–1880, sat out for a term, and had run for election again in 1884 and also in 1888. Díaz needed to place himself as the heir to Juárez of the mantle of Liberal leadership, and it legitimized him for Juárez also to have run for reelection in a time of national crisis. The opposition to Porfirio Díaz supported the myth of Juárez, as well. They saw him as the champion of anticlericalism (anti–Roman Catholic Church), a strong legislative branch of government, and individualism. The celebration of Juárez the hero peaked in 1906 with the centennial of his birth.

Juárez then became a symbol of the radical opponents of Díaz, who sought to revive his program—democracy, and anticlericalism—that Díaz had betrayed. The major opposition to Díaz, which arose in 1910 led by Francisco I. Madero, named its political clubs after Juárez. Ironically, they called themselves anti-reelectionists. Madero deeply admired Benito Juárez as the epitome of legality. Madero's followers called him the modern-day Juárez. During the Revolution (1910–1920), Juárez emerged in yet another reincarnation as the model of a strong president. Amid the chaos and episodic tyranny of civil strife, Juárez stood for strength and law. The revolutionary leaders eventually constructed a centralized state led by a president with vast powers. They raised Juárez to hero status in order to legitimize strong presidential rule.

Questions for Discussion

Was Juárez a popular figure among common folk or just an icon created by the ruling class to suit its own purposes at various times? In the contest for control over their everyday lives, where did Juárez and his politics fit in? How do you think it is possible for historians to separate themselves from their times and to evaluate historical figures evenhandedly?

Regionalism destroyed independence hero Simón Bolívar's grand dream of a unified northern South America. From 1821 to 1830, Bolívar, as president, built Gran Colombia out of Ecuador, New Granada (present-day Colombia), and Venezuela. But by 1830, despite his enormous efforts, the three nations had separated and were individually beset by centrifugal forces. In Ecuador, the height of its regional divisions occurred in 1859, when no fewer than four governments with capitals in four different cities claimed to rule. Colombia was more divided than Ecuador. There were six major regions, five with an important city at its center: Cauca (Popayán), Antioqueña (Medellín), the coast (Cartagena), the Central Highlands (Bogotá), the northeast (Vélez), and the llanos (coastal plains). Francisco de Paula Santander, one of Bolívar's important lieutenants who was president from 1832 to 1837, maintained an unsteady peace. But after he left office, federalists and centralists fought a series of bitter civil wars from 1839 until 1885. Venezuela, through the skills of José Antonio Páez, another important lieutenant of Bolívar, resisted regional fragmentation into the 1850s. However, the nation erupted into the so-called Federal Wars from 1859 to 1863, which resulted in a federalist victory. The triumph was short lived, however, because in 1870 Antonio Guzmán Blanco (1870–1877, 1879–1884, and 1886–1888) reestablished centralized rule. In neither Colombia nor Venezuela did civil wars settle the conflicts between federalism and centralism.

Central Americans struggled against each other for much of the nineteenth century. In 1821, they put their fates in the hands of Mexico, joining the newly independent empire of Agustín de Iturbide. With the fall of Iturbide, a Central American congress met to declare the independence of the United Provinces of Central America in 1823, but the government of the United Provinces never gained control as the region plunged into civil war. Although the central government continued, the individual states increasingly expanded their influence. By 1865, Guatemala, under the rule of José Rafael Carrera (1844–1848, 1851–1865), defeated unification once and for all. In Central America, as in Argentina and Mexico, it took civil war to establish nation-states. Nothing, however, could unite the region.

Brazil and Chile

Although Brazil experienced no widespread civil wars, it, too, suffered deep regional divisions. Regional leaders never ceased their opposition to the nation's first ruler, Pedro I, and finally forced him to abdicate in 1831. Regional rebellions erupted during the 1830s, when a regent ruled during the minority of the heir to the throne. (Pedro I abdicated when his son was only 4 years old.) With Brazil seemingly on the verge of dissolution in 1840, Pedro II became emperor at age 14. War with Paraguay (1864–1870) to some extent served to push some Brazilians to think in national terms. Pedro II kept Brazil together until he abdicated, when regional tensions again overwhelmed the monarchy in 1889. Thus, to a large extent, regionalism determined Brazil's political fate, though the nation did not have to pay as great a price in bloodshed as had Mexico and Colombia.

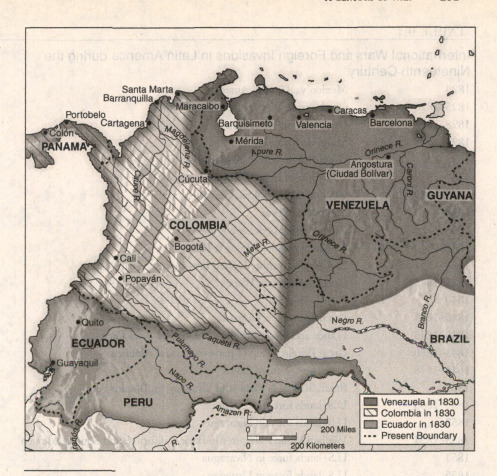

Gran Colombia: The failed experiment

A CENTURY OF WAR

War was the second major factor in the political instability in Latin America, as well as the primary reason for the lack of economic development. Hardly a year went by when there was not a war or some kind of military action somewhere in Latin America (see Table 9.1). Warfare inflicted enormous physical and economic damage; disrupted commerce, communications, and transportation; and drained governments of scarce financial resources. Political scientist Brian Loveman has identified four categories of wars in Latin America: transnational wars of political consolidation; international wars between Latin American nations; wars against foreign military intervention; and civil wars.

Wars of Political Consolidation

The best examples of wars of political consolidation were actually unsuccessful in unifying the contesting countries, leading instead to the dissolution of large confederations.

TABLE 9.1

International Wars and Foreign Invasions in Latin America during the Nineteenth Century

1823	Mexico vs. Central America
1825–1828	Cisplatine War: Brazil vs. Buenos Aires
1828–1830	Gran Colombia vs. Peru
1829	Spain vs. Mexico
1833	Great Britain takes Falkland Islands
1833	U.S. force in Buenos Aires
1836–1839	Chile vs. Peru–Bolivia Confederation
1836	Mexico vs. Texas
1838	Pastry War: Mexico vs. France
1838–1840	France blockades Río de la Plata
1838–1851	La Guerra Grande: United Provinces vs. Uruguay
1838–1865	Central American Wars
1840	Peru vs. Bolivia
1840–1841	Panama vs. New Granada
1840–1845	France and Great Britain blockade Río de la Plata
1843–1850	Great Britain occupies parts of Central America
1846–1848	Mexico vs. United States
1851	Brazil, Río de la Plata, and Uruguay vs. Buenos Aires
1852–1853	U.S. lands force in Argentina
1853	U.S. lands force in Nicaragua
1853–1854	William Walker filibuster in Baja, California, and Sonora, Mexico
1854	U.S. lands force in Nicaragua
1855	U.S. lands force in Uruguay
1855–1856	William Walker conquers Nicaragua
1856	U.S. lands force in Panama
1857	U.S. lands force in Nicaragua
1858	U.S. lands force in Uruguay
1859	U.S. displays force in Paraguay
1859	U.S. force in Panama
1860	William Walker filibuster in Honduras
1861	Tripartite (Great Britain, France, Spain) intervention in Mexico
1861–1865	Reoccupation of Santo Domingo by Spain
1862	Great Britain in Central America
1862–1867	French intervention in Mexico
1863	Guatemala vs. El Salvador
1864–1866	Peru, Chile, Bolivia, and Ecuador vs. Spain
1864–1870	War of the Triple Alliance: Paraguayan War

(Continued)

TABLE 9.1 (*Continued*)

International Wars and Foreign Invasions in Latin America during the Nineteenth Century

1864–1871	Guatemala and Honduras vs. El Salvador
1865	U.S. force in Panama
1868	U.S. lands force in Uruguay
1868	U.S. lands force in Colombia
1876–1885	Central America
1879–84	War of the Pacific: Chile vs. Peru and Bolivia
1885	U.S. force in Panama
1888	U.S. force in Haiti
1890	U.S. force lands in Argentina
1891	U.S. force in Haiti
1891	U.S. force in Chile
1894	U.S. force in Brazil
1895	U.S. force in Colombia
1896	U.S. force lands in Nicaragua
1898	U.S. force in Nicaragua
1894–1895	Great Britain in Central America
1898–1899	United States vs. Spain (Cuba)

Sources: C. Neale Ronning, ed. *Intervention in Latin America* (New York: Knopf, 1970); David Bushnell and Neill Macaulay, *Latin America in the Nineteenth Century*, 2nd ed. (New York: Oxford, 1994), pp. 305–309; and Brian Loveman, *For La Patria: Politics and the Armed Forces in Latin America* (Newark, NJ: SR Books, 1999), pp. 45–47.

Uruguay emerged as a separate nation as a result of the war between the Argentine Confederation and Brazil from 1825 to 1828. One of the longer wars of political consolidation took place in Central America, where the struggle for unification dragged on from 1824 to 1838, ending in failure. Peru and Bolivia, once together as part of the Viceroyalty of Peru, also failed to unify, engaging in a fruitless war from 1836 to 1841.

Intra-Regional Wars

The most important wars between Latin American nations were the War of the Triple Alliance (1864–1870) and the War of the Pacific (1879–1883). The War of the Triple Alliance, or Paraguayan War, in which Paraguay fought against the alliance of Argentina, Brazil, and Uruguay, was the most prolonged and destructive. The war began when Brazil invaded Uruguay (which Brazil claimed was part of its territory) and Paraguay responded by crossing a sliver of Argentine territory to attack the Brazilian province of Rio Grande do Sul. Argentina, Brazil, and Uruguay (with a government that was a puppet of Brazil) then allied and turned on Paraguay in May 1865. The war devastated Paraguay. It lost between 8 and 18 percent of its population and over one-third its territory. After the peace, alliance troops occupied parts of Paraguay for 8 years. All of the progress of the previous half-century toward a self-sufficient, relatively economically egalitarian society ended. Political instability followed for the next six decades.

Another extremely destructive conflict between Latin American nations was the War of the Pacific. Chile fought Peru and Bolivia over access to nitrate fields. Chile and Bolivia had a long-standing disagreement over the territory—located in a disputed area in northern Chile, southern Peru, and western Bolivia—while Peru and Chile disputed control over the taxes on nitrate deposits. Chile won a drawn-out struggle and occupied Peru from 1881 to 1883. Peace brought a substantial victory for Chile, for it acquired the nitrate fields and thus a monopoly on the world's supply of this fertilizer. Bolivia lost its access to the Pacific Ocean, which was a serious detriment to its future economic development.

Foreign Wars

The most devastating war with a nation outside the region was the Mexican War with the United States (1846–1848). Mexico had lost its northern province of Texas in 1836 to

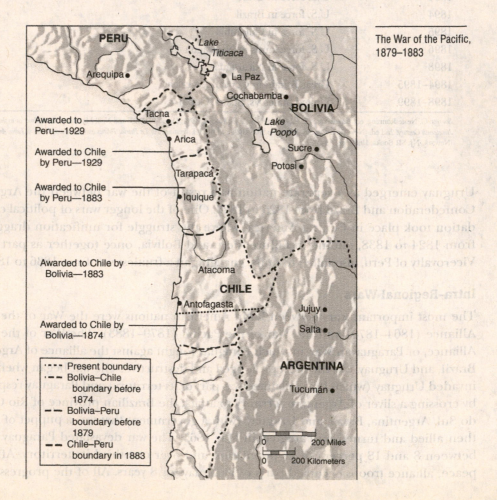

The War of the Pacific, 1879–1883

North American settlers, who had revolted against Santa Anna's imposition of centralist rule. Mexico never recognized the independence of the Republic of Texas and warned the United States that any attempt to annex Texas would be considered an act of war. In late 1845, the United States, ignoring Mexico's protests, annexed Texas. A few months later, a clash between Mexican and U.S. forces in south Texas led to war. In a relatively short but costly conflict, the United States eventually captured the major cities of Monterrey, Veracruz, and ultimately Mexico City. Mexico lost half its national territory, including present-day Texas, Arizona, New Mexico, and California.

In addition to the actual wars themselves, the potential for war with neighbors over boundaries and other issues was continuously present. Argentina and Chile disputed each other's rights to Tierra del Fuego. Peru and Ecuador were at odds over their Amazonian territories. The threat of foreign intervention was constant. For a decade after independence, Mexico feared Spain would attempt to reconquer it. It also anticipated invasion by the United States for almost a century after the two ended their war in 1848. Central America and the Caribbean lived in the shadow of U.S. intervention from the 1850s.

Civil Wars

The small civil wars that plagued Latin America in the nineteenth century were innumerable. There were 11 "national level rebellions" in nineteenth-century Colombia alone. From 1831 to 1837, Brazil endured continuous rebellions in Maranhão, Bahia,

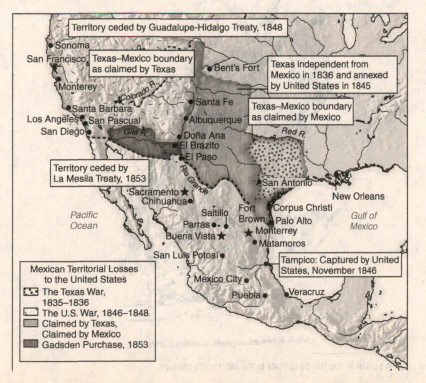

The Wars for Northern Mexico, 1836–1853

Territory ceded by Guadalupe-Hidalgo Treaty, 1848

Texas–Mexico boundary as claimed by Texas

Texas independent from Mexico in 1836 and annexed by United States in 1845

Texas–Mexico boundary as claimed by Mexico

Territory ceded by La Mesila Treaty, 1853

Tampico: Captured by United States, November 1846

Mexican Territorial Losses to the United States
- The Texas War, 1835–1836
- The U.S. War, 1846–1848
- Claimed by Texas, Claimed by Mexico
- Gadsden Purchase, 1853

Minas Gerais, Mato Grosso, and Río Grande do Sul. Thirteen military uprisings occurred in Peru in the months between June and October 1840. From 1852 to 1862, there were 117 uprisings of one type or another in the Río de la Plata.

The struggles between Liberals and Conservatives in some countries, Mexico and Colombia for instance, erupted in brutal warfare during the middle decades of the century, as the conflicts over the place of the church in society, politics, the economy and over collective landholding intensified. These were emotional issues, for at stake were the very essence of day-to-day life—control over one's religion and livelihood. In Mexico, neither Liberals nor Conservatives were willing to compromise. From 1854 to 1867, they fought a series of vicious civil wars, including the Plan of Ayutla Revolt (1854–1855), which ousted Santa Anna for the last time, the War of the Reform (1858–1860), and the French Intervention (1862–1867). The Liberals ultimately won the struggle because they won over the people of the countryside. Communal villages sided with the Liberals despite the fact the Liberals advocated destruction of communal landholding because the Liberals, as federalists, also advocated local autonomy in governance. Villagers calculated that it did not matter what laws the Liberals enacted nationally, as long as the villagers controlled their own local governments, they could evade them. The crucial factor was local autonomy.

Soldado de línea con su dotación de campaña y combate

A soldier in the Río de la Plata in the nineteenth century.

The Impact of War

The effects of warfare were profound both politically and economically. Wars militarized society, gave political prominence to military leaders, and undermined democracy; widened ethnic divisions; diminished daily life; killed tens of thousands of people; destroyed property, transportation, and communications; and squandered scarce resources. They made economic development nearly impossible and thus prevented any substantial improvement in living conditions for most Latin Americans (see Chapter 10).

Constant warfare militarized society as formal national and informal regional armed forces proliferated. The regular army functioned at the national level to defend the nation against external threats, but often its units attempted and succeeded in overthrowing the national government. In addition, there were local militias that formed the power bases of regional bosses who challenged national unity and authority. It seemed at times that everyone was armed.

Warfare spawned countless military leaders who dominated high government office in many countries. Six civilians and 16 generals served as president of Mexico between 1821 and 1851. Three of the civilian presidents lasted just a few days. Two generals, Antonio López de Santa Anna and Anastasio Bustamante (1830–1832, 1837–1841), dominated Mexican politics for the first half of the nineteenth century. The men who overshadowed all others in the politics of the Río de la Plata were in the military. Juan Manuel de Rosas was a noted military commander. Bartolomé Mitre (1862–1868) won fame for winning the decisive battle for Argentine unification in 1861. Despite its reputation as perhaps the most stable of the continent's republics, Chile was ruled by military officers through its initial three decades.

The presence of so many military figures gave politics an authoritarian air. Moreover, in times of war, governments often suspended civil liberties, such as freedom of the press and freedom of speech. National legislatures, when confronted with war emergencies, regularly chose to temporarily suspend the rule of law in order to bestow extraordinary powers on the president.

In addition, wars rubbed raw old ethnic and class divisions. The civil wars at mid-century in Mexico exacerbated local rivalries in the countryside to the extent that vengeance became an integral part of everyday life in the villages. There had been too many atrocities to be forgotten. In Mexico in the 1840s, the Caste War of Yucatán nearly resulted in the overthrow of white rule on that peninsula. In Peru, the War of the Pacific ripped open ethnic scars as Chinese coolies and rural blacks in the south sought vengeance for mistreatment. These conflicts only accentuated the fears of the upper classes.

Economically, wars were devastating. Lack of reliable sources makes it impossible to accurately assess the damage wreaked by a century of wars, but there is sufficient anecdotal evidence to suggest that in some areas it was debilitating. The mining sector was initially hardest hit. It took decades for production in the mines of Bolivia, Peru, and Mexico to regain their colonial levels. The destruction of mine shafts by flooding, scavenging of equipment, and deteriorating roads impeded redevelopment. No better example exists than Bolivia. It emerged from the wars of independence with its mining industry in ruins. The human cost of war in terms of casualties was sometimes catastrophic, as in the case of Paraguay in the War of the Triple Alliance. In Yucatán, in Mexico's southeast, more than 100,000 people lost their lives in the vicious rebellion during the late 1840s. Perhaps 300,000 people lost their lives in Mexico's War of the Reform a decade later. The tremendous losses among young males profoundly altered family structures and gender relations (see Chapter 10).

Wars and military preparedness bankrupted national governments. Armies drained scarce, precious financial resources that would have been better spent on roads and schools. The cost of the military was nowhere more evident than in Mexico. In 1836, the Mexican military expended 600,000 pesos a month, while government revenues totaled only 430,000 pesos. These figures did not include the cost of the Texas War (1836), which added another 200,000 pesos a month! Needless to say, this left no money for other functions of government. Dictator Rosas of Buenos Aires maintained a standing army of 20,000 and a militia of 15,000, the cost of which accounted for one-half to three-quarters of his annual budgets. In both these examples, the threat of foreign invasion was constant. Mexico feared Spain and the United States, while Buenos Aires worried about the Brazilians, the British, and the French.

Because armies regularly expanded and shrank in size, there were always a substantial number of out-of-work soldiers who were unwilling to return to their former homes to toil as tenants or peons on a hacienda or the communal holdings of their villages. Many became bandits, and lawlessness followed. From the 1820s to the 1860s, it was virtually impossible to travel between Veracruz, Mexico's major port, located on the Gulf of Mexico, and Mexico City without being held up. Some stagecoaches were robbed several times over the course of a single trip. It was not uncommon for passengers to arrive at their destination wrapped in newspapers, having been relieved of all their worldly possessions en route. This disorder greatly discouraged commerce and thus impeded economic development.

Not all of the effects of war were adverse, however. The military provided unparalleled upward social mobility. Indians, mulattos, and mestizos obtained unprecedented opportunities for economic and social advancement through war. Many of the national leaders who emerged from the wars of independence and subsequent conflicts had lower-class origins. Notable among them was Porfirio Díaz, who was dictator of Mexico in the last quarter of the century. Mobilization in Brazil during the Paraguayan War had conscripted mostly black and mulatto troops. The war probably assured the end of slavery as an institution, for slaves earned their freedom through military service. Returning soldiers were not the docile workforce they had been when they went to war. Some veterans received money bonuses and land grants. Others who had received nothing for their service refused to return to the status quo before the war.

Constant warfare undoubtedly eroded the fabric of everyday life and politics. Ironically, however, a few international wars may have actually contributed to the creation of nationalist sentiment and helped forge a sense of nationhood. Its two wars against Peru and Bolivia unquestionably helped consolidate sparsely populated Chile. These clear victories boosted popular association with the nation. The War of the Triple Alliance, which came only 3 years after unification, promoted a sense of Argentine national identity. The valiant fight of Benito Juárez against the French Intervention in Mexico also produced the first extensive sense of nation and Mexicanness.

POPULAR PARTICIPATION

Regional fragmentation, divisions among the upper classes, and war provided unusual opportunities for lower-class participation in political affairs during the first five decades after independence. Although Latin American civil conflicts rarely involved more than a few thousand troops, local and regional bosses required regular retainers recruited from their areas. Workforce requirements necessitated concessions and inducements. While personal loyalties were sometimes sufficient to secure followers, lower-class supporters demanded not only personal gain, such as wages, war booty, and promotions, but more importantly, maintenance of local autonomy for villages and protection from laws against collective landownership and taxes.

Popular participation in the politics of nation building resulted from the need of the lower classes at the very least to exert some influence over their everyday lives. As we have discussed, the policies of neither upper-class factions were acceptable. Country people increasingly opposed both Liberal and Conservative policies to develop the economy. The struggle to maintain control over their daily existence in the countryside manifested itself in the vast conflict over local autonomy, which translated into the national conflict between federalism and centralism. This in turn led the lower classes into broader political participation. In search of supporters, national leaders courted the concerns of everyday people, who comprised the armies of various competing factions.

In the cities, local issues revolved around food prices and employment. Riots were important expressions of political involvement in urban settings. Protests erupted in Latin American cities as a result of the high cost of corn and beans. For example, in 1831, the populace of Recife, Brazil, attacked Portuguese merchants believed to have been price gouging.

There were also a number of instances where the urban lower classes played crucial roles in national politics. Mexico City's lower classes formed the backbone of Iturbide's support during his last days. However, he was unwilling to use their support to maintain power, so strong was his sense of solidarity with the upper class and his fear of the lower classes. Mexico City dwellers erupted again in 1828 in the Parián Riot (see Slice of Life: The Parián Riot) in support of Vicente Guerrero, the hero of the war of independence, in his campaign for president. Mobs in the streets of Rio de Janeiro helped to force Pedro I to abdicate in 1831.

Slice of Life   THE PARIÁN RIOT: MEXICO CITY, 1828

IN NINETEENTH-CENTURY Latin America, common folk struggled constantly both to sustain themselves—furnishing sufficient food, adequate shelter, and safety for their families—and to maintain some measure of control over their everyday lives. During the first five or six decades after independence, the lower classes exercised a degree of political influence because the upper classes were divided, and in some places, periodically at war among themselves. Urban and rural working-class folk participated in the politics of the time in several ways: as voters in local elections, soldiers in civil wars and revolts, allies of upper-class factions, and perpetrators of specific, directed incidents of urban violence. Upper-class Latin Americans needed the lower classes to fight their battles and as allies. Nonetheless, the wealthy and powerful were wary, often fearful, of the lower classes, knowing fully well that to arm the masses risked unleashing the dangerous forces of centuries of pent-up resentment. The Parián Riot, which occurred in Mexico City in 1828, was an instance in which the lower classes took part in political events, leading to a tumultuous episode that shook the Mexican upper classes to their very core.

As in most history, the upper classes wrote the narrative of the riot, and, consequently, the actual events of the day were slanted in a way unfavorable to the masses. On the early afternoon of Thursday, December 4, 1828, simultaneous to and probably in association with a popular revolt that broke out against President Guadalupe Victoria (1824–1829), a crowd of 5000 assaulted and looted the luxurious shops located in the Parián Building in Mexico City's Zócalo. It ended sometime the same evening. Upper-class chroniclers of the era depicted the riot in graphic terms, such as a "savage invasion," "murders in cold blood," and a "stain on the pages of our history." We know that the rioters were people of the lower classes and some soldiers, probably part of the troop sent to bring the tumult under control.

There were two murders, neither committed by the lower classes (but by the upper class), and there was considerable damage to stores and houses around the Zócalo. Most of the heavy destruction actually resulted from 3 days of street fighting that preceded the riot. Considerable disorder followed, with the wealthy of the city notably absent from the streets.

The revolt against President Victoria began on November 30. The lower classes rushed to support the upheaval led by Vicente Guerrero, a hero of the long guerrilla war that had led to independence. One observer estimated that 30,000 to 40,000 people, 20 to 25 percent of the population of the capital, fought on the side of the rebels. Most soldiers abandoned the government and joined the rebellion.

Upper-class Mexicans disdained Guerrero, an uneducated, dark-skinned casta. Guerrero advocated two policies that were especially popular among the capital's poor. He propounded protective tariffs for the native textile industry, where many lower-class and artisan city dwellers earned their living. He also proposed to expel the remaining Spaniards, many of whom were quite wealthy and, given the dire straits of the Mexican economy, were bitterly resented. It may have been that some rioters shouted "Death to the Spaniards" as they stormed into the Parián. Many of the merchants in the building were Spaniards.

The Parián riot was indicative of the politics of lower-class mobilization in the first decades after independence. Mexican upper classes both in the cities and in the countryside needed popular support. But this came at a price—sometimes mobilization got out of control. In the countryside lower classes demanded local autonomy for their villages and delay in the implementation of many of the modernizing policies so dear to upper-class hearts. By mid-century it was clear to the Mexican upper class that the price of lower-class cooperation was too high. The Parián riot remained an indelible memory for Mexico's rich and powerful. Their fear of the masses, to their mind, was justified.

Questions for Discussion

Both during the colonial and early independence eras, Mexico had a long history of urban riots as a means for the common people to express their dissatisfaction with their governments. What were the alternative strategies for the lower classes in negotiating with the upper classes?

The lower classes also influenced national politics in some instances when they were willing to fight foreign invaders long after the upper classes, who, while looking after their own self-interests, surrendered to or collaborated with the enemy. After the United States army had defeated Santa Anna's army in a series of battles on the outskirts of Mexico City in 1847, the general withdrew from the capital. The population of the city continued to fight, however, sniping and throwing debris from the rooftops at the North American troops. During the War of the Pacific (1879–1883), after the total defeat of the Peruvian army, the civilian country people of the central sierras and the south of Peru continued to fight under the leadership of General Andrés Cáceres against the invading Chileans. Upper-class Peruvians collaborated with the invaders. In both Mexico and Peru, the upper classes signed disadvantageous peace treaties at least in part because they feared the expansion of popular upheavals.

Throughout the nineteenth century, the upper classes faced a decided dilemma. They needed support from the lower classes, but they were not always pleased with their allies, for the masses were not easy to control once an uprising began. They lost control of the 1831 revolt in Recife, Brazil, when slaves joined in hoping to obtain their freedom. In 1835, outraged blacks and Indians in Belém, Brazil, joined and then overwhelmed an upper-class–led revolt seeking independence for their province, engaging in widespread destruction of property and attacking wealthy whites. It took the government 5 years to finally quash the rebels. The death toll for this bloody uprising reached 30,000, approximately one-fifth of the provincial population.

The new rulers of Latin America were more successful at reimposing traditional gender roles in politics. Females were crucial participants in the wars of independence on both sides. This, of course, upset long-held views that women's place was in the home in the private sphere. The male casualties endured during the decades of war in some areas, however, created demographic imbalances that threatened male domination (see Chapter 10). In Argentina, females were in the majority until mid-century. The upper classes realized full well that in times of war and disruption, families rather than governments would hold society together. They therefore insisted on the model of a male-dominated family. In order to maintain stability, the upper classes sought to maintain long-established gender roles.

CAUDILLOS

Strong leaders, known as caudillos, often emerged to bridge the gap between the upper and lower classes and temporarily bring order to disrupted politics. The term *caudillo* refers to a leader whose notoriety and authority arose from the local level, where he had attained a reputation for bravery. The caudillos of the nineteenth century, who first emerged from the wars of independence, often obtained their economic and popular bases from landowning. A caudillo's army comprised the workers on his hacienda, and a web of patron–client relations (informal and personal exchanges of resources between parties of unequal status) served as the base of his support. Typically, a landlord expected labor, deference, loyalty, and obedience, while the employee, in turn, received a basic level of protection and subsistence. Many caudillos solicited support among the lower classes and consequently earned their fierce loyalty.

Juan Manuel de Rosas, who dominated Buenos Aires and allied provinces from 1829 to 1852, embodied the qualities of the nineteenth-century Latin American leader. He was rough, brave, ruthless, tyrannical, and a sharp political strategist. Rosas was a military leader with a common touch. Growing up on a large cattle estate (*estancia*) he shared the austere life and learned the ways and language of the people who inhabited the vast plains of the Pampas. Although he became a large landowner, Rosas presented himself as one of the people. He adhered to their "code" of honesty and discipline. It is said that he once ordered his servant to give him 20 lashes for being a bad gaucho, and when, unsurprisingly, the servant balked, Rosas threatened him with 500 lashes if he did not comply with the order. Virtually unchallenged through the 1840s, Rosas succumbed to his provincial opponents in 1852.

Like many other caudillos, Juan Manuel de Rosas had a crucial base of support among Indians and blacks. He organized a personal retinue from the poor of Buenos Aires and had a wide following among the gauchos of the Pampas. The lower classes regarded Rosas as the protector of their way of life. Rosas negotiated fairly with the Indians of the plains, thereby gaining their respect.

Rosas turned Afro-Argentines into a pillar of his regime, relying on them for his war machine. Through his wife, Encarnación, he worked with African mutual aid societies. Rosas lifted the previous bans on African street dances that reached the pinnacle of their popularity during his rule. His daughter Manuela attended dances and danced with black men. Once when the provincial government was strapped for money, 42 black nations (mutual societies) made special contributions to it. Rosas named his urban home after the black saint Benito de Palermo. His propaganda was written in African Argentine dialects. By 1836, Buenos Aires ended the forced draft for freed slaves and in 1839 ended the slave trade. Rosas promoted blacks to high military rank and took others as personal retainers. His large military force provided jobs for the chronically underemployed lower classes. He distributed land to the poor who were willing to live on the frontier and rewarded loyal soldiers with land.

LATIN AMERICAN LIVES

FRANCISCO SOLANO LÓPEZ

Some historians of Latin America have labeled the nineteenth century the "Age of Caudillos," when these often charismatic leaders imposed order through either negotiations or violence. The most notable examples, such as Antonio López de Santa Anna in Mexico and Juan Manuel de Rosas in the Río de la Plata (Argentina), dominated the histories of their nations, especially during the first decades after independence. In every instance the caudillos were controversial. This was particularly true in the case of Paraguay, whose three successive leaders—Dr. José Gaspar Rodríguez de Francia (1811–1840), Carlos Antonio López (1844–1862), and Francisco Solano López (1862–1870)—determined their nation's fate for 60 years. Historians have gone so far as to call two of them, Dr. Francia and Francisco Solano López, madmen. But to others both were national heroes.

At independence, Paraguay had carved itself out of the Spanish Viceroyalty of Río de la Plata (which also included current day Argentina and Uruguay). Its first caudillo Dr. Francia isolated the nation. The scrupulously honest dictator established a highly efficient government and a relatively egalitarian society, carefully curtailing the wealthy landowning class. He operated unusually successful educational programs and profitable state enterprises. He also created a strong military, ever in fear of larger neighbors Argentina and Brazil. His successor Carlos Antonio López for the most part continued his policies. López, in addition, broadened the rights of the nation's indigenous people, the Guaraní, expanded export agriculture, and developed independent military industry. His son Francisco Solano López took over after Carlos Antonio's death in 1862.

Francisco Solano López (1826–1870) was the material from which writers make great novels. Brought up as the privileged eldest son of a powerful dictator, to whom no one ever said no, the young López was a brigadier general at 18 and his father's chief advisor while barely in his twenties. Carlos Antonio sent him to Europe to be his chief procurement agent in 1853 and 1854. The experience yielded a close-up view of balance of power diplomacy and an Irish mistress, Elisa Alicia Lynch, who eventually bore him five sons. Many observers thought the beautiful Lynch the dark power behind the dictator; she was well hated by the local elite. López's mercurial temperament added to the drama.

Shortly into his 10-year term as president, López became enmeshed in the complicated politics of civil wars in both Argentina and Uruguay. As a result, Paraguay

Francisco Solano López.

entered into a 5-year long, catastrophic war against the Triple Alliance of Argentina, Brazil, and Uruguay. Uruguay was the 1828 creation of diplomatic compromise between Argentina and Brazil, both of which claimed its territory. At stake was access to the Río de la Plata-Parana-Paraguay river system. After more than a quarter century during which each nation turned inward, civil wars in Argentina that eventually resulted in its unification under the leadership of Buenos Aires, and in Uruguay restarted the rivalry between Argentina and Brazil over influence in the region. López became quite concerned that one or the other of his larger neighbors would upset the balance of power in the Rio de la Plata, endangering Paraguay. He attacked Brazil in late 1864 to prevent it from interfering in Uruguayan politics. In April 1865, he invaded an Argentine province, setting off war with the second neighbor. Although they had overwhelming advantages in population and resources, neither Argentina nor Brazil succeeded in taking advantage. López held them off until he died in battle in 1870.

Although often vilified by the victors and proclaimed a national hero by Paraguayans, recent scholarship has discussed more judiciously López's strengths and weaknesses, concluding that his motives for war were not unsound—he should have indeed feared his neighbors; he clearly commanded the loyalty of his people, who stayed with him to near extinction; he could have ended the war in 1866, but refused because the terms of the peace included his resignation; and as the war continued and his desperation intensified, he resorted to ever more brutal methods to maintain discipline.

The end result for Paraguay was, however, indisputably a catastrophe from which the nation never recovered. Although recent demographic studies have debated how many Paraguayans died in the tragic war, there is ample evidence that perhaps half the total population was lost and a much higher percentage of the male population. The nation also ceded tens of thousands of miles of territory to Argentina and Brazil. Brazilian troops occupied the country until 1878. Perhaps the most prosperous, stable, and egalitarian nation on the continent in 1865, Paraguay never came back from the debacle. Whether a madman or sound strategist, Francisco Solano López had led his homeland to ruin.

Questions for Discussion

How does the War of the Triple Alliance compare with other major wars in Latin America during the nineteenth century, such as the War of the Pacific or the Mexican war with the United States? Given the case of Francisco Solano López, do you think that colorful personalities were the dominant factor in nineteenth-century Latin American history?

Heroism and charisma were no guarantees for a long or successful political career. Several of the foremost figures of the wars of independence suffered tragic fates. Bernardo O'Higgins won independence for Chile, but as ruler, he lasted only until 1822. Antonio José de Sucre, one of Bolívar's best generals, was the first president of Bolivia (1825–1828), but he failed in his efforts to end the oppression of the Indian population.

THE CHALLENGE OF ECONOMIC RECOVERY

Regionalism and war adversely affected Latin American economic development. Regionalism created an uncertain political environment, which frightened investors, while war unproductively consumed vast human, material, and financial resources.

In Mexico and Bolivia, the loss of territory deprived the nation of valuable resources. During the years from 1810 to 1870, Latin American economies, with a few exceptions, stagnated due to the inability or unwillingness of the upper classes to establish governments that could create stable environments for commerce and industry. Institutional obstacles left from the colonial period, the widespread damages and disruptions caused by the wars of independence and subsequent upheavals, and the lack of capital further stifled economic growth. After 1850, the situation slowly began to change, as booming markets for Latin American agricultural staples and minerals, along with European capital investment in mining and transportation, brought renewed economic growth. From 1850 until World War I (1914), most nations in the region attached their economic fortunes to the burgeoning export markets in Western Europe and the United States. Still, economic development of Latin America faced substantial obstacles.

Obstacles to Development

In many regions, geography was a major obstacle to development. Most of Latin America lacked inexpensive transportation and easy communications. The lack of transportation greatly limited the establishment of national and regional markets. The cost of moving products to market was prohibitive. The Spanish colonial government had never invested much in roads, and the wars of independence left existing roads in disrepair. With the exception of the Río de la Plata, few major waterways ran through population centers. Coastal trade was not important in the nineteenth century.

Laws, attitudes, and institutions inherited from the colonial period further hindered growth after independence. These included local and regional autonomy; overregulation and underenforcement of rules; indifference to long-term planning and preference for short-term benefits; concentration on the export of precious minerals; state monopolies of commodities such as liquor and tobacco; strict limitations on international trade (including with neighboring nations); widespread corruption; a tradition of smuggling; and failure to invest in roads and ports. Three-hundred-year-old colonial habits and tendencies were not easy to break.

There were considerable institutional constraints to economic enterprise. Laws were often arbitrary and capricious, changing from regime to regime, and easily subverted through corruption. Laws often differed from region to region within the same nation. Each region also imposed its own taxes. Perhaps most important was the lack of modern systems of banking. The lack of credit handicapped both industry and agriculture. The shortage of capital prevented the repair and maintenance of mines and haciendas. The church, which had acted as a major source of credit during the colonial era, lost its primary base of income when the new governments abolished the tithe (an annual tax of 10 percent on all income collected by the colonial government from individuals for the church). The church's funds were still considerable, but they were tied up in land and virtually unredeemable loans to landowners. Europeans, with the exception of a few brief (mad) years in the 1820s, were unable or unwilling to invest in Latin America. Governments also experienced chronic revenue shortages because the newly independent states did away with many royal taxes and, because of their incompetence, were unable to collect those taxes that remained. The flight of Spaniards with their capital in the aftermath of the independence wars drained Latin America of crucial investment funds.

The new nations sought to make up for the lack of capital during the 1820s by borrowing funds abroad in the form of government loans. Several of the founders, like Bolívar, obtained loans from British investors, which they used to buy arms. From 1822 to 1825, seven Latin American nations (Brazil, Buenos Aires, Central America, Chile, Colombia, Mexico, and Peru) contracted for more than 20 million (British) pounds debt. Not surprisingly, economic difficulties prevented repayment. All the Latin American nations except Brazil remained in default of these debts for a quarter century. This foreclosed the possibility of attracting external capital to the region. After 1850, Europeans were attracted once again with the upturn of Latin American agricultural and mineral exports.

Export Economies

Although the general trend for the region as a whole was bleak for much of the first half of the nineteenth century, as continuous war and periodic political disruptions impeded economic growth, several nations prospered because of increasing demand for agricultural commodities. Buenos Aires became one of the remarkable economic success stories of nineteenth-century Latin America. Even when fighting raged, its foreign trade expanded. Markets for hides and cattle by-products flourished. A new industry arose to process hides and salt meat. The Río de la Plata provided the slaves of Brazil and the working class of Europe with their food. Entrepreneurial landowners began to raise sheep to provide cheap wool for the carpet factories of New England and Great Britain. Buenos Aires evolved into a complex of stockyards, slaughterhouses, and warehouses. The vast plains around Buenos Aires, the Pampas, became an enormous, efficient producer of agricultural products. In a more modest example, Venezuela experienced a coffee boom that brought two decades of prosperity from the 1830s through the 1840s.

After mid-century, European markets expanded rapidly. The increasing affluence of a growing population in Europe, a crucial aspect of which was the transfer of people from agriculture to industry, created a demand for Latin American products. Because most European nations were self-sufficient in basic agricultural staples, at first demand centered on luxury and semi-luxury commodities such as sugar, tobacco, cacao, coffee, and (later) bananas. Salted and dried beef also became a preferred part of the European diet. As industrialization in Europe accelerated, so too did the demand for raw materials. Cotton production grew rapidly during this period to meet the demand for inexpensive clothing. As the population continued to grow in Europe, there was less land available for raising livestock, and Europeans looked abroad for their tallow, hides, and meat. As Europe required more and more efficient agricultural production, the demand for fertilizers rose. Latin America had the natural resources to fill these demands.

The Haitian revolution of 1791, which destroyed the island of Hispaniola as the major sugar-producing region, sharply altered the trends of sugar production. Cuba and Brazil were the main beneficiaries. Brazil, which once had been the world's largest producer of sugar but whose ability to compete on the world market had atrophied by the end of the colonial era, was presented with new potential markets. Production doubled in the 1820s and nearly doubled again the following decade. Perhaps the most spectacular case of the rise and fall of an export economy occurred in Peru. The demand for fertilizers in Europe created an enormous demand for the natural fertilizer guano (bird excrement) found on Peru's offshore islands. Beginning in 1841, shipments of guano for export rose sharply. The Peruvian government used the prospects of future revenues from guano to compile an enormous debt. It also used guano funds to build the country's major railroad lines. By the early 1880s, however, guano deposits were nearly exhausted, and nitrate came on to the market as an alternative fertilizer. Consequently, the guano boom ended. Peru was left with huge debt to foreign companies and no possibility of repaying it because the revenues from guano had ceased.

A pattern of boom and bust cycles emerged. Latin America's national economies reacted to market forces using their competitive advantages in the production of agricultural and mineral commodities. Before 1850, when the market demanded

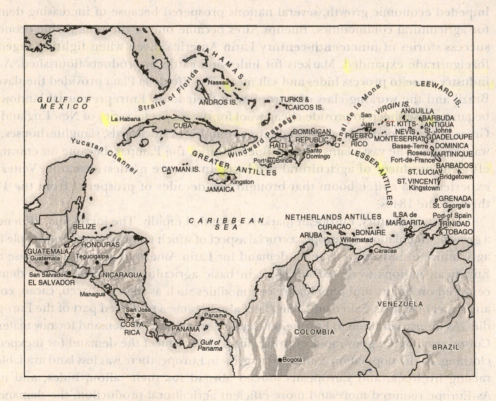

The Caribbean

mostly agricultural products, domestic entrepreneurs responded. Later in the century, however, when the demand was for minerals, foreign investors played an ever-increasing role. Latin American nations became increasingly dependent on foreign capital and vulnerable to fluctuations in world markets as the nineteenth century closed. Economic recovery from a century of war and political upheaval rested on an extremely precarious base.

CONCLUSION

The nineteenth century was a difficult time for governments and ordinary people in Latin America, but some progress occurred nonetheless. Once established, nations displayed remarkable continuity and cohesion in the face of strong regional forces. Despite the high turnover among high officeholders and the occurrence of civil wars, there were elements of stability in Latin American politics. Not infrequently, one or two figures dominated for a decade or more, though not continuously occupying the presidency. For example, Mexico had 49 national administrations between 1824 and 1857, and only one president, Guadalupe Victoria (1824–1829) finished his term. However, five chief executives held office on three or more separate occasions. Two, Anastasio Bustamante and Antonio López de Santa Anna, headed the nation for approximately half this period.

The high turnover was deceptive elsewhere as well. Though at times upheavals beset its politics, four men dominated Venezuela, José Antonio Páez (1831–1835, 1839–1843, 1861–1863), the Monagas brothers (José Tadeo and José Gregorio, 1847–1858), and José Guzmán Blanco (1870–1877, 1879–1884, 1886–1888). Pedro I (1822–1831) and Pedro II (1831–1889) ruled Brazil for more than six decades. Chilean presidents followed successively by election from 1831 to 1891. Rosas ruled the Río de la Plata from 1829 to 1852. Argentina's presidents followed one another by election from 1862 to 1930. Three dictators ruled Paraguay from 1815 to 1870.

Peru was perhaps the worst case of unstable politics. From its independence in 1821 to 1845, there were 24 major regime changes and more than 30 presidents. Strongman Agustín Gamarra (president 1829–1833 and 1839–1841) established some measure of order, interrupted only by Bolivian caudillo Andrés Santa Cruz's attempt to conquer Peru and establish the Peru–Bolivia Confederation from 1836 to 1838. During the early 1840s, Peru came apart. Finally, General Ramón Castilla reestablished order from 1845 to 1862 (as president 1845–1851 and 1855–1862), despite fighting a vicious civil war in 1854 and 1855.

Stability was more evident at the regional and local levels of politics. In Mexico, state (regional) politics were mostly in the hands of locally prominent merchant and landowning families who ruled for generations through control of municipalities and courts. In the Río de la Plata, provincial leaders like Estanislao López in Santa Fe ruled for decades. In Brazil, local bosses, known as colonels, and their families ran roughshod for generations.

Moreover, this era was in some ways the most democratic era in Latin America until nations introduced unlimited universal suffrage and mass voting after World War II. The lower classes not only participated in government, particularly on the local level but also took part indirectly in national politics and helped shape the political debates. It was also the period of the most extensive economic equity in Latin American history. In some areas, large landholdings suffered from disruptions and uncertainties. War and the expansion of the armed forces provided opportunities for upward mobility for the lower classes, including people of color.

Postindependence Latin America, as we will see in the succeeding chapter, was by no means the Garden of Eden, but common people had control over their everyday lives, a role in national politics, and often a chance to get ahead. The next 50 years were not to be as kind.

LEARNING MORE ABOUT LATIN AMERICANS

Barman, Roderick J. *Citizen Emperor: Pedro II and the Making of Brazil, 1825–91* (Stanford, CA: Stanford University Press, 1999). This is the best biography of the man who had the longest rule in Latin American history.

Fowler, Will. *Santa Anna of Mexico* (Lincoln, NE: University of Nebraska Press, 2007). Presents a balanced view of the most vilified Mexican ruler of the nineteenth century.

Graham, Richard. *Patronage and Politics in Nineteenth-Century Brazil* (Stanford, CA: Stanford University Press, 1990). Graham delves into the intricacies of politics in Brazil.

Guardino, Peter. *The Time of Liberty: Popular Political Culture in Oaxaca, 1750–1850* (Durham, NC: Duke University Press, 2005). A very good rendition of popular participation in Mexico.

Halperin-Donghi, Tulio. *The Aftermath of Revolution in Latin America.* Trans. Josephine de Bunsen (New York: Harper Torchbooks, 1973). Halperin has written a brilliant exposition of the impact of the wars of independence.

Jacobsen, Nils. *Mirages of Transition: The Peruvian Altiplano, 1780–1930* (Berkeley, CA: University of California Press, 1993). Traces change in the Peruvian altiplano.

Mallon, Florencia E. *Peasant and Nation: The Making of Postcolonial Mexico and Peru* (Berkeley, CA: University of California Press, 1995). Studies the ins and outs of rural local politics in communities in Mexico in Peru.

Thurner, Mark. *From Two Republics to One Divided: Contradictions of Post-Colonial Nationmaking in Andean Peru* (Durham, NC: Duke University Press, 1997). A study of the relationship between country people and the state in the early postindependence era.

10

EVERYDAY LIFE IN AN UNCERTAIN AGE, 1821–1880

IN LATIN AMERICA during the 60 years after independence, the uncertain political environment and frequent warfare adversely affected the material well-being of a large number of people of all social classes. The absence of consistent rules and regulations, the widespread lawlessness, and the loss of life and physical damage to property resulting from armed conflict often made day-to-day living quite difficult. It also substantially transformed important aspects of society, most importantly gender relations. Much changed profoundly over the course of the nineteenth century, but as much—good and bad—stayed the same. Despite these ofttimes troubled conditions, ordinary folk continued to earn their living and conduct their private lives much like their ancestors had for decades, even centuries. Ordinary people and to some extent their wealthier neighbors, particularly in the countryside, resisted the transformations sought by centralizers and modernizers.

The vast majority of Latin Americans during the nineteenth century lived in rural areas either as residents of large estates or villages with collective or small individual landholdings. Only a minority of country dwellers owned their own lands, though many were tenants or sharecroppers. In Brazil, most people in the countryside were slaves, forcibly brought in large numbers from Africa until 1850, when the trade in slaves from Africa ended as the result of enormous pressure put on the Brazilian government by Great Britain. A significant minority of Latin Americans lived in large cities, such as Mexico City, Buenos Aires, Lima, Rio de Janeiro, and São Paulo. Wherever they resided, most common folk lived in poverty, often barely surviving. Work was never easy, whether one was employed on a large estate, on one's own plot of land, in the mines, or as a domestic in a wealthier family's home in the city. Latin Americans toiled long and hard for their sustenance. However difficult their labor, they took pride in their jobs and did them well (no matter how much their bosses may have complained about them). Latin Americans, no matter how poor they were, mostly enjoyed their lives. There were *fiestas* (festivals) and other entertainments, the comfort of one's family, and the pageantry and solace of the Catholic Church.

The contrasts between rich and poor were enormous. Wealthy landowners often lived in palatial splendor in the cities, while only blocks away workers struggled in filth and squalor. Moreover, the well-to-do often had little sympathy for those less fortunate than they.

Let's turn, now, to the lives and work of Latin Americans, rich and poor.

THE PEOPLE

Who were the people who populated the newly independent nations? Latin America emerged from the colonial era with an ethnically diverse population, which had, during the eighteenth century, recovered from the horrific losses suffered in the sixteenth century, when the number of people had fallen by as much as 90 percent, mostly as a result of epidemic diseases brought by the Europeans. The vast majority of Latin Americans were Indians, Africans, or castas. Typical of Mexico at the turn of the nineteenth century, the population of the state of Puebla was 75 percent Indian, 10 percent white, and 15 percent castas. Less than one-third of Brazil's population was white, the rest black or mulatto. More than 30 percent were slaves. In the early 1820s, out of a total of 1.5 million Peruvians the white population counted only about 150,000. Mestizos numbered between 290,000 and 333,000. The African slave population was an estimated 50,000. The remaining million people were Indians. Approximately 65 percent of the people of Central America were Indian, 31 percent ladino (mestizo and mulatto), and 4 percent white.

The disruptions that followed independence slowed demographic growth (see Table 10.1), and, as a consequence, the region's economies stagnated. Mexico's population grew only at an average annual rate of 1 percent. Its population increased from 6 million in 1820 to 7.6 million inhabitants in 1850. Brazil's population rose from between 4 and 5 million inhabitants at independence (1822) to 7.5 million by the early 1850s. Unlike the other new nations, Argentina experienced rapid population growth, as its half-million people in the 1820s increased to 1.8 million by 1869. Latin America experienced growth after 1850, as Mexico's population rose to 15 million and Brazil's to 22 million by 1910.

In contrast, during the first half of the nineteenth century the population of the United States rose from less than that of Mexico in 1800—just over 5 million—to 92 million in 1910. The United Kingdom grew from 11 million to 45 million during the same period. These differences in population growth accounted for a large portion of comparable difference in economic progress between Latin America and these industrial leaders. While Latin America failed to grow economically, the United States and the

TABLE 10.1

The Population of Latin America in the Nineteenth Century

Nation	1820	1850	1880
Argentina	500,000+	1,800,000 (1869)	
Bolivia		1,378,896 (1846)	
Brazil	4–5,000,000	7,500,000	
Chile	1,000,000 (1835)		2,100,000 (1875)
Colombia			
Ecuador	496,846 (1825)		1,271,761 (1889)
Mexico	6,000,000	7,600,000	
Paraguay			
Peru	2,488,000	2,001,203	2,651,840
Uruguay			
Venezuela	760,000	1,660,000 (1860)	2,080,000
Costa Rica	63,000	101,000	137,000 (1870)
El Salvador	248,000	366,000	493,000 (1870)
Guatemala	595,000	847,000	1,080,000 (1870)
Honduras	135,000	203,000	265,000 (1870)
Nicaragua	186,000	274,000	337,000 (1870)

United Kingdom's economies expanded exponentially. Latin America has never been able to make up for these 50 or so years of economic and demographic stagnation.

The colonial heritage of large, dominant cities continued in postindependence Latin America. Mexico City's population fluctuated between 150,000 and 200,000. Rio de Janeiro experienced growth from 100,000 inhabitants in the 1820s to 275,000 in the 1850s. Buenos Aires blossomed from 50,000 inhabitants in 1810 to 189,000 by 1869. As we will see later in this chapter, the expansion of the cities outpaced governments' ability to provide a healthy and prosperous environment for their residents.

THE LARGE ESTATES: HACIENDAS, ESTANCIAS, PLANTATIONS, AND FAZENDAS

Most Latin Americans earned their living on the land, planting, maintaining, and harvesting crops and tending to the livestock of their wealthier neighbors. Other Latin Americans toiled on lands owned either collectively by the residents of their home villages or individually by themselves and their families. Some worked as both employees and owners. Whichever the circumstances, the land represented more than just a living: Farming or ranching was a way of life. As we will see, life in the countryside in the nineteenth century was difficult. Sometimes, as in the case of slaves, conditions were oppressive and cruel. But even those worst off, including slaves, made lives for themselves often with humor, love, and grace.

A large number of Latin Americans resided on large estates (known as *haciendas*, *estancias*, or *fazendas* in Mexico, Argentina, and Brazil, respectively), where they worked for the landowner or leased land as tenants or sharecroppers. In rural areas, the owners of these large properties (known as *hacendados*, *estancieros*, and *fazendeiros*) controlled much of the land. Conditions on these large estates varied widely according to era, region, property size, and crops under cultivation.

At the top of hacienda society in Mexico was the owner, the hacendado, and his family. Beneath him were the supervisors and administrators, headed by the chief administrator or *mayordomo*. Usually males headed haciendas, but occasionally a widow operated a large property. Mayordomos in the Río de la Plata managed the larger estancias, directing employees, keeping records, and communicating with the owner about all estate-related matters. The mayordomo controlled his workers through subordinate foremen (*capataces*). On smaller ranches the foreman took the role of the mayordomo. The living conditions of the capataces were hardly better than those of the workers. The mayordomo, however, was well paid.

Work Life

Estate employees worked long, hard hours. On the Mexican haciendas, there were two types of employees: permanent and temporary laborers. Permanent labor included resident peons (unskilled laborers), tenants, and sharecroppers. A hacienda's temporary labor came from neighboring villages, whose residents supplemented their incomes from communally held land or family plots by working seasonally at planting and harvest. Commonly, the hacienda's sharecroppers and tenants earned extra money by working for their landlord.

While some hacendados farmed their own land with their own employees, the most common arrangement was for owners to combine farming their lands with sharecropper- or tenant-cultivated lands. Tenants paid their rent to the hacendado in the form of cash or a portion of the harvest. Though most tenants leased small plots, there were a few who leased entire haciendas. Sharecroppers paid the landowners with a preset part of the harvest, usually 50 percent. A possibly typical such arrangement in the central region of Mexico included resident peons earning wages and rations of corn to feed their families and receiving the use of small plots of land for cultivation. Tenants received a hut, firewood, seeds, and some pasturage, along with their plots, in return for half their crop. Occasionally, tenants worked for the hacendado and earned additional cash. For peons, the crucial part of the arrangement was the corn ration. Custom obligated hacendados in some areas to provide peons with the ration, regardless of the market price of corn. Because corn comprised 75 percent of a peon family's diet, this arrangement ensured the peon's most important staple, even in periods of drought and crop failure, and partially insulated him and his family from the effects of inflation, which resulted from shortages of staples arising from crop failures. Tenants and sharecroppers had no such security, so their well-being depended on the vagaries of the weather. A good-size plot with oxen and plenty of rain might turn a profit, but there were no guarantees. We know little about the situations of such day laborers other than that agricultural wages varied according to the available supply of labor.

Conditions on the haciendas varied according to region, depending on the availability of labor. A relatively dense population, concentrated in mestizo or Indian villages, as in central Mexico, meant a large pool of potential workers and, therefore, low wages and less-favorable terms for tenants and sharecroppers. Labor shortages, as in the far north and the far south, produced one of two outcomes: heavy competition for workers, which raised wages and added benefits, such as advances on wages; or intensified coercion to retain employees.

Debt peonage was the most notorious aspect of hacienda labor relations. In this system, peons went into debt to the hacienda in order to pay church taxes and fees; expenses for rites of passage such as marriage, baptism, and burial; or for ordinary purchases at the hacienda store. Peons then were obligated to work until they repaid the debt—but, of course, they often could not repay it. In some regions, multiple generations were tied to the hacienda, because children were expected to repay their parents' debts. Debt peonage in a few areas was nearly indistinguishable from slavery. On one of the great estates of northern Mexico, the owner dispatched armed retainers to hunt peons who tried to escape their obligations. Some historians have observed, however, that debt was not always to the disadvantage of the debtor, for in some areas debt served as a kind of cash advance or bonus, attracting peons to work on a particular hacienda. In these instances, it was understood by both debtor and creditor that the debt was not to be repaid. Debt, in these situations, became a device to attract and keep workers.

The Hacienda del Maguey, a grain and livestock estate in central Mexico, provides us with an example of relatively benign living and working conditions. The normal workday on this hacienda lasted from 6 A.M. to 6 P.M. There were breaks for breakfast and a traditional midday dinner followed by a resting period, or *siesta*, which lasted for 2 to 3 hours. The complete workday was 8 to 9 hours long, which, compared to the contemporary industrial workforce in the United States and Western Europe, was not arduous. The workload was heaviest at planting, weeding, and harvest times.

Peons on the Hacienda del Maguey, according to the calculations of historian Harry Cross, were relatively well treated. The average peon laboring in the fields probably needed 2150 calories a day. His family, two adults and two children, required 9000 calories. The ration of corn provided by his employer contained 75 percent of this caloric need. The rest of the diet consisted of *frijoles* (beans), chile peppers, lard, salt, and meat. The peon added to these staples wheat flour, rice, and sugar, which he bought at the hacienda store. (Usually, there were no other stores in the area. Sometimes employers allowed employees to purchase goods only at the hacienda stores.) The typical family also gathered herbs, spices, and cacti from the countryside at no cost. Alcoholic beverages, particularly *pulque*—the fermented juice of the maguey plant—were consumed in large quantities, providing vitamins. The combination of beans and corn produced most of the diet's protein.

LATIN AMERICAN LIVES

THE GAUCHO

THE HISTORY OF the *gauchos* (cowboys) of the Argentine plains, known as the Pampas, reflects the evolution of the region's politics and economy in the postindependence era. Gauchos were the symbol of regionalism, fierce local independence, the crucial role of the lower classes in politics, and the importance of the export economy. Originally a product of the vast growth of wild herds of horses and cattle on the Pampas during colonial times, gauchos were skilled horsemen who roamed far and wide, taking the livestock that they needed to survive. Viceroy Arredondo, in 1790, considered them "vagabonds" who "live by stealing cattle from the estancias and selling the hides . . . to the shopkeepers . . . ." Like other members of Latin America's working classes, cowboys in the Río de la Plata and Venezuela were important participants in the wars of independence and the uncertain politics and warfare of the early nineteenth century. During the wars, gauchos were among the rebels' best troops. After the wars, they comprised the local private armies of the numerous regional chiefs who ruled in the Río de la Plata. As the Argentine economy grew by exporting hides, tallow, and dried salted beef, gauchos worked on the expanding estancias. During the first half of the nineteenth century their services were in such demand, both as soldiers and as ranch hands, that they escaped worker discipline.

To many upper-class Argentines, however, the mixed-blood gauchos were a symbol of backwardness. Domingo F. Sarmiento, in his famous polemic (*Life in the Argentine Republic in the Days of the Tyrants*) against Juan Manuel de Rosas, the notorious gaucho leader who ruled Buenos Aires from 1829 to 1852, defined the gauchos as representatives of "barbarism." He saw them as impediments to Argentine development.

Dressed in little more other than a poncho, mounted on horseback, armed with rope and knife, the gaucho was a formidable sight. He subsisted on meat, a bit of tobacco, and strong yerba mate (a strong, tea-like beverage) and lived in simple huts roofed with straw and possessing neither doors nor windows: "The walls were sticks driven vertically into the ground, and the chinks were filled with clay . . . ." Furniture in a gaucho's hut consisted of perhaps "a barrel for carrying water, a horn out of which to drink it, a wooden spit for the roast, and a pot in which to heat the water for mate." There were no chairs or tables or beds, and cutlery consisted of only a knife, for gauchos ate only meat. To cook and keep warm, gauchos burned dung, bones, and fat. Their clothing, shelter, and food made the gaucho no different from other Latin Americans who struggled to make their living in the nineteenth century.

Compared to most Latin American workers, however, gauchos retained a relatively high degree of freedom, because Argentina's growing economy increased demand for their services. For example, gauchos attained the right to enjoy leisure time on the numerous fiesta days. Often, cowboys worked for a few months, asked for their pay, and moved on. Offering them higher wages only delayed the inevitable. There was always another job somewhere for a gaucho to fill.

Time was against the gauchos, and their glory days did not last long. The export economy demanded their subordination, and the undisciplined gauchos, who were enthusiastic brawlers, and loved to sing, gamble, and drink, were not acceptable employees in the modern economy. In addition, modern technology, in the form of barbed wire, and a glut of immigrant agricultural labor in Buenos Aires province also worked to end their independence. The history of the Argentine gaucho parallels that of many other lower-class Latin Americans, who defended their local prerogatives, customs, and traditions in an ever more difficult struggle against government centralization and economic modernization.

Questions for Discussion

How did the life of an Argentine gaucho compare with that of a Mexican worker on a hacienda? Why were gauchos able to exert their independence and, thus, control over their daily lives so successfully during the first half of the nineteenth century?

Gauchos comprised the lower-class political support for local bosses of nineteenth-century Argentina.

But not all haciendas treated their peons so well. A passerby noted the conditions for resident peons on the Sánchez Navarro estate in northern Mexico in 1846: "The poor peon lives in a miserable mud hovel or reed hut (sometimes built of cornstalks, thatched with grass). He is allowed a peck of corn a week for his subsistence, and a small monthly pay for his clothes . . . ." Peons generally earned 2 or 3 pesos a month and 1 or 2 pecks (a peck equals a quarter bushel or 8 quarts) of corn a week. The Sánchez Navarro family paid their highly valued shepherds and cowboys (*vaqueros*) a bit more, 5 pesos a month and 2 pecks of corn a week salary, but these modest wages hardly covered an average family's necessities.

The Hacienda de Bocas, located 35 miles north of San Luis Potosí, also in central Mexico, for which we have extensive records for the 1850s, illuminates another example of hacienda life. Bocas had between 350 and 400 permanent workers. The better-off minority of these had free title to land they used for a house, corral, and farming. The best-treated permanent workers also received a corn ration. A resident earned 6 pesos a month, slightly less than $1.50 a week, with a corn ration of 15 liters a week. Because this was not enough to feed his family—1 liter a day per adult was necessary for sustenance—he purchased another 7 or 8 liters a week, on account, for 0.125 pesos each, leaving him with roughly 50 centavos a week to cover all the family's other expenses. The worker received a plot of 3000 square meters for which he paid no rent. He bought seed for planting from the hacienda. Other purchases during the year included food, sandals (*huaraches*), leather pants, and a burial. His expenditures totaled just over 72 pesos for the year, approximately the same amount as his annual salary. The circumstances for temporary workers on the Hacienda de Bocas were not quite as favorable as those for permanent workers. Despite earning 10 pesos a month (if they labored 30 days), versus permanent workers' 6 pesos, temporary employees were not guaranteed subsistence rations. Regardless of employee status, however, few of the 794 tenants and 200 sharecroppers at Bocas in 1852 made ends meet without supplementing their incomes with temporary work for the hacienda.

Work was equally hard in the Río de la Plata, where most of the employees on the estancias were wage labor called in for cattle branding and horse breaking. There were a few permanent workers who tended cattle or sheep and rode the perimeter looking for strays. Each of these workers maintained a hut and a corral in his area. Routine work consisted of tending to the herds and rounding them up every morning. Shepherds' chores were to wash and shear, brand, and slaughter, as well as to tend the herd. Cowboys earned wages, while shepherds shared in the profits. Some owners gave their shepherds one-third to one-half the increase in their flocks per year. Other sheepherders earned up to one-half of the sale of wool, grease, and sheepskins. Cowhands, in addition to their flat wage, received rations of salt, tobacco, *yerba mate* (a very strong tea-like beverage), and beef, and perhaps a small garden plot.

The estancias employed Europeans, mixed bloods, and both free and enslaved blacks. Part-time workers came from the interior of Argentina and Paraguay. Native-born mestizos and mulattos, migrants from the interior, tended cattle, while immigrants raised sheep, farmed, and traded. Labor for the cattle roundup and sheep shearing came from nearby rural communities. When labor was scarce, temporary workers earned more. Estancieros had to pay high wages to skilled workers, such as sheep shearers, who could demand as much as 40 to 50 pesos a day plus food. A native-born laborer, with his own string of horses, could hire himself out at 20 to 25 pesos a day in cattle-branding season. Some estancieros offered advances and credit at the ranch store to attract laborers. These workers, however, were often paid irregularly or in scrip to be used at assigned stores. Agricultural wages remained relatively high until the late 1880s, when immigration and improved stock-raising methods ended the labor shortage.

Domestic Life

The differences between the affluent and the poor were particularly evident in the conduct of their everyday lives. Daily routines for upper-class women and men focused on work and meals. Wealthy women on the hacienda began their day around nine and spent much of the morning doing needlework together in the drawing room in what was called "virtuous silence." After the midday meal, each female family member carried out chores before retiring for a nap (siesta). During the mid-afternoon, the women gathered again to continue their needlework. Males and females joined at eight in the evening to say prayers and eat the evening meal. Afterward, the women put in another hour of needlework, while one of the men read aloud to the family.

Women administered the domestic sphere and may have acted as heads of family when their husbands were away. Girls stayed at home while boys went to school. Young women learned needlework and enough reading skills to enable them to read the Bible and carry out religious observances. A curious relationship existed between wealthy families and their household servants, who simultaneously were part of and separate from the family. A hacienda's rich and poor children grew up together, even shared confidences, but real friendship was never possible, because the social barriers between classes were too great.

Slice of Life   URBAN SLAVES

MANY SLAVES WORKED in the plantation fields, but a few toiled in their master's home, and others had skilled occupations processing sugar and coffee. A surprising number of slaves worked in the cities, primarily as domestic servants, but also as artisans and in other jobs.

Slaves comprised 11 percent of the Brazilian industrial workforce in 1872. Approximately 13,000 slaves worked in textile factories. Slaves also made up 15 percent of construction workers, and slave women represented 8 percent of all seamstresses. Many of these slaves lived in the cities, numbering some 118,000 in total, or roughly 15 percent of the population.

Urban slaves usually found themselves in one of three working situations (or some combination thereof): the traditional relationship with a master; a largely traditional relationship with a master but which included being rented out to a third party; or self-employment (the latter arranged housing for themselves). Self-employed slaves generated considerable income and were a lucrative enterprise for their masters. Such slaves worked as bakers, barbers, carpenters, masons, porters, and prostitutes. It is likely that slaves in the cities had more control over their everyday lives than their counterparts on the plantations. Nonetheless, urban slaves were no less subject to abuse or the other hazards of survival. Thomas Ewbank, a traveler from the United States, observed at mid-century: "Slaves are the beasts of draught as well as of burden. The loads they drag . . . are enough to kill both mules and horses."

In Rio de Janeiro, the constant demand for domestic servants arose from the need for services later supplied by urban utilities and public works. As late as 1860, homes in the city had neither piped water nor a sewerage system. Residents also had no refrigeration, and perishable food could not be stored, because it spoiled easily in the tropical climate. Servants carried water, shopped, and did laundry. Most indoor chores were centered around the kitchen, where slaves were skilled cooks. Other household slaves saw to the considerable volume of cleaning required in the dusty, dirty city in houses chockful of furniture and other objects. Still other servants emptied chamber pots and wet-nursed babies. Trusted servants were so valued by wealthy families that parents sometimes passed such workers down to their children to ensure that the younger generation had a reliable staff when it established households of its own.

While a significant minority of slaves worked independently in the cities or held relatively privileged positions in their owners' households, they, nonetheless, remained in bondage. Their master still controlled their fate.

Questions for Discussion

How did the lives of urban slaves compare with those on the plantations? How and to what extent were slaves able to shape their own living and working conditions (and thus exert some control over their daily lives)?

Plantations and Slavery

Brazilian slaves lived perhaps the hardest lives of all the Latin American poor. About two-thirds of Brazilian slaves worked in agriculture. And of these, the largest group, one-third, worked on coffee plantations in the environs of Rio de Janeiro or São Paulo. Others toiled on sugar plantations in the northeast. On plantations, particularly in the south, masters practiced swift, brutal discipline. They regarded slaves as "by nature the enemy of all regular work." Planters lived in constant fear that their slaves would rebel.

At the beginning of the nineteenth century, Brazil had 1 million slaves and during the next 50 years imported another million. Perhaps surprisingly, slaves' life expectancy was not much different from that of the rest of the population: 23 to 27 years. The crucial difference, however, was the odds of a child born into slavery surviving infancy. One-third of all male slave babies died before the age of 1, and a little less than one-half died before the age of 5. If a male slave reached the age of 1, he was likely to live until he was 33.5. If the slave child survived until age 5, then he could expect to live more than 43 years. Twenty-seven percent of female slave children died before reaching the age of 1, and 43 percent died before age 5. If the female lasted until age 1, she could expect to live until 25.5, and if she endured to age 5, she would likely reach 39 years.

Slaves born in Africa had difficulty in adapting to the new climatic and biological environments of Brazil, and, as a result, their mortality rate was high. In the northeast, the climate was very humid and hot, but sudden drops in temperature were common.

Many Africans, unaccustomed to such swings in temperature, suffered chills, which, in turn, often resulted in pulmonary illness. Diseases such as tuberculosis, scurvy, malaria, dysentery, and typhus were endemic. Slaves lived in unhygienic conditions and medical care was crude or unavailable. The number of slave deaths in Brazil always exceeded that of births, and only the continual importation of newly enslaved people from Africa permitted the slave population to increase.

The flow of slaves to Brazil ended in 1850, a decision made as a result of pressure from the British. This brought about a massive transfer of slaves from the cities and towns to the countryside and from regions where markets for export crops were in decline to those areas where exports flourished. Regardless of a slave's age, the dynamics underlying every slave's relationship with his or her fazendeiro were coercion and violence. Owners required slaves to be loyal, obedient, and humble. In return, slaves might expect to be made part of the patron's family, with all the accompanying benefits and protections: Slaves who attained "family" status could become skilled artisans and attain positions as overseers.

Most slaves worked in the fields in regimented gangs closely supervised by overseers. Corporal punishment—being whipped or placed in stocks, for example—was common. The workday lasted 16 to 17 hours. Overnight work was rare, except when sugar had to be milled and coffee dried. Surprisingly, slaves did get breaks during the day. And while everyday work was always hard, it may have been truly unbearable only for short periods during harvest.

Many slaves had occupations other than being field hands. Men were given the skilled positions repairing equipment, constructing buildings, and sewing clothing. Planters even rented the services of slave artisans to other landowners. As a result, fewer male slaves and more women planted, weeded, and harvested. Slaves were also domestic servants. Slaves who worked in the masters' houses or as artisans experienced better living conditions than those in the fields.

In the nineteenth century most slaves worked in the São Paulo coffee region. The typical plantation had 70 to 100 slaves, though the largest coffee fazendas contained as many as 400. The average adult slave took care of well over 3000 coffee trees and produced approximately 1000 kilograms of coffee.

Slaves' daily routine began before dawn with breakfast, which consisted of coffee, molasses, and boiled corn. They then said prayers and divided into work teams, which were led by supervisors who were themselves slaves. At 10 A.M., slaves ate a meal of corn porridge, black beans, and pieces of lard covered with a thick layer of manioc flour. Sometimes they also ate highly seasoned sweet potatoes, cabbage, or turnips. At 1 P.M., there was another break for coffee and a corn muffin. Dinner was eaten at 4 P.M. Work then went on, often until well after dark, as late as 10 or 11 P.M. Finally, before retiring, slaves received a ration of corn, a piece of dried meat, and some manioc meal.

Slaves usually lived in a single unpleasant building. Some were given the use of a plot of land to raise coffee or vegetables and were even allowed to sell these crops and keep the proceeds. Coffee planters did not give slaves Sundays off because they feared that

How Historians Understand   THE CONSTRUCTION OF RACISM

The upper classes' fear of the lower classes that so impeded political developments in Latin America during the nineteenth century was founded in racism. Africans and Indians were people of color and, as such, were widely disdained, if not hated, by the white descendents of European colonials. Nineteenth-century historians, many of whom were prominent intellectuals and politicians, were the generators and pillars of this racism.

By mid-century, pervasive racism had overwhelmed Argentina. In their desire to modernize, Argentines firmly believed that European immigration was the only "civilizing" influence on their nation. Juan Alberdi, one of Argentina's leading intellectuals and author of the Constitution of 1853, disdained nonwhites, writing that to populate the Pampas with Chinese, Asian Indians, and Africans was "to brutalize" the region's culture. Domingo Sarmiento, another notable Argentine intellectual and later president of the nation from 1868 to 1874, also advocated the benefits of European immigration, because he believed that Africans and people of mixed blood were inferior. These men and others thought that Argentina in the 1850s was a mestizo country and that it would not progress unless it was Europeanized. Part of the consequent "whitening" campaign was having Argentine historians and government bureaucrats make Afro-Argentines disappear from the country's history and be excluded from its census. Similarly, Chileans saw to it that Africans disappeared from their history. They, too, firmly believed that development would come only with the Europeanization of local culture.

In Peru, intellectuals retained their hostility to Afro-Peruvians long after that country's abolition of slavery in 1861; one even insisted that "the Negro [is] a robber from the moment he is born . . . ." Another thinker decried that "in South America, civilization depends on the . . . triumph of the white man over the mulatto, the Negro, and the Indian."

The failure of Latin American governments to abolish African slavery at independence was not only an indication of the powerful political influence of planters, but also of the underlying fear and contempt the white upper classes felt for Africans.

Abolition of Slavery

Country	Year	Country	Year
Argentina	1861	El Salvador	1825
Bolivia	1831	Honduras	1825
Brazil	1888	Mexico	1829
Chile	1823	Nicaragua	1825
Colombia	1850	Paraguay	1870
Costa Rica	1825	Peru	1854
Cuba	1886	Uruguay	1846
Ecuador	1852	Venezuela	1854

Free and enslaved Africans were not the only victims of racism. In Argentina, Mexico, and Chile, governments conducted campaigns of extermination against nomadic indigenous peoples, who white officials believed also stood in the way of progress. Indians were perceived as barbarians and obstacles to the betterment of society by Latin Americans of European descent. These indigenous peoples fought back fiercely. In the north of Mexico, for example, the Apaches, Yaquis, Comanches, Mayos, and Tarahumara resisted incursions until the end of the century. In Yucatán the Maya Indians came close to eliminating whites from their peninsula in a bloody rebellion that began in 1847. (Historians did not confirm stories of this resistance until the late twentieth century, however.) Mexican historians of the era, such as Lucas Alamán and Carlos María Bustamante, had a predictably low regard for the nation's Indian peoples, even though by virtue of Mexico's first Constitution (1824) all Mexicans were equal before the law. Alamán once said that "it would be dangerous to enable the Indians to read the papers."

How could these historians legitimate such inaccurate and destructive beliefs? Historians, like everyone, are products of their times: Nineteenth-century historians such as Alamán, mostly from upper-class origins, shared the same prejudices and fears of the others of their status.

Questions for Discussion

Why do you think that historians in nineteenth-century Latin America, like Domingo Sarmiento and Lucas Alamán, were so biased against people of color? Why do you agree or disagree with the assertion that race underlay all of the region's politics during the century after independence?

Mistreating of a slave in Brazil in 1839.

religious or social gatherings of the entire slave population would lead to trouble. Instead, to prevent the possibility of any kind of unified revolt, rotating groups of slaves were given different afternoons off during the week.

Within the larger plantations, African slaves established their own communities, resembling small villages. There they established families and forged a new culture adapting African ways with those of the Americas. Almost all native-born slaves married. And though they were not usually married by the church, the fazendas commonly recognized the marriages. Maintaining a family was difficult, however, for there was always the possibility that one or more family members would be sold, thus permanently separating the family. And the reality of high mortality rates among slaves was a perpetual threat to family stability. On the plantations, enslaved women were subordinate in marriage to their husbands (like their free counterparts). As with every aspect of slaves' existence, their family and social lives were both separate from and intimately attached to the world of their masters.

Like marriage and family, religion played an important part in plantation slave communities. Slaves practiced godparenthood (*compadrazgo*), in which close friends of the parents of a child became godparents, which meant that they were obligated to care for the child if its parents died. Slaves also synthesized their African religions with Catholicism, producing a folk Catholicism and religious cults, such as *candomblé*, *voudoun,* and *santería.* In these hybrid spiritual practices, African deities often took on the guise of Catholic saints.

Ultimately, however, slaves confronted and resisted their conditions: They refused to surrender either their cultural heritage or their dignity. Slaves resisted passively, by slowing the work pace, working shoddily, or refusing to do work that did not fit their described assignment (i.e., work that was not in their "job descriptions"). Cooks would not do housework, for example. Occasionally, slaves struck back violently at their masters. More commonly, slaves tried to gain their freedom by running away. Those who fled sometimes found haven in isolated communities, known as *quilombos.* Whatever the approach—harsh or paternalistic—taken by the planters, few were entirely successful in controlling their slaves.

VILLAGES AND SMALL HOLDERS

The majority of the rural population in Mexico and Peru consisted of Indians, who continued to live in relatively autonomous villages, as they had during colonial times. The small, individual plot of land used for family subsistence farming was the basis of rural life. Villages had simultaneously symbiotic and conflicting relationships with haciendas: Villagers relied on the estates for work to supplement earnings garnered from farming their own lands. Haciendas, in turn, depended on village residents for temporary labor and tenants. Nonetheless, haciendas and pueblos frequently clashed over land and water rights. The relationship was, perhaps, most equal in the years from

1821 to the mid-1880s, a period when war and uncertain political conditions badly weakened the haciendas economically. Villages traded their political support for increased local autonomy and protection of their lands.

It is important not to idealize rural life, particularly in the villages. In Mexico, the *pueblos* (villages) had their own forms of social stratification, with local bosses (*caciques*), municipal officeholders, and lay leaders of religious organizations comprising the upper level. Small traders, muleteers, and some of the larger tenants (in terms of the amount of land they rented) at times entered the top group. At the bottom were poorer residents who worked permanently or temporarily as hacienda peons and tenants.

Generally, village leadership came from elder males, who nominated people for local offices, made decisions in times of crisis, and oversaw all dealings by local officeholders with the wider society. Elders attained their elevated status through hard work on the community's behalf or, perhaps, through economic achievement. As the century wore on, the ability of the elders to act justly and to reach community consensus lessened, as state and national governments intruded on their autonomy.

Politically, residents of all villages concerned themselves primarily with protecting their individual and collective landholdings, minimizing taxes (both of which required local autonomy), as well as maintaining the right to govern their everyday affairs without interference from state or national governments. Taxes oppressed country people, and throughout the nineteenth century taxes were a never-ending source of friction between pueblo residents and the various levels of government. Country people also bitterly opposed coerced military service. It was not uncommon for the armies of various factions to raid villages in order to drag off their young men, the loss of whom badly disrupted the local economy and society.

A considerable measure of competition, petty bickering, and serious disputes often existed among villagers. In many places, such as Oaxaca in southeastern Mexico, intervillage conflict was endemic, as rival pueblos fought perpetually over land and water.

For most rural dwellers in Mexico and elsewhere, life revolved around their land and their families. Country people lived in two worlds: the first was the traditional subsistence economy, which retained ancient practices, and the second was the modern money and wage economy, the incursion of which country people carefully limited. Indian people, such as the Maya of the Yucatán peninsula of Mexico, fiercely resisted the discipline and values of the plantation and the industrial workplace. North American John Lloyd Stephens, who traveled extensively in the peninsula in the 1840s, reported that "The Indians worked as if they had a lifetime for the job." Working slowly, though, was only one strategy for resisting the demands of overbearing employers. Unlike Brazil's slaves, however, passive resistance was not the only tactic available to rural folk: Attempts to alter existing custom or wages were met by strikes or mass migrations.

In many parts of rural Latin America, the family was an economic unit, both on small plots and on the large estates. Families worked together in the fields, especially during planting and harvest. The men worked their 8- to 9-hour days at the hacienda or, perhaps, even longer on their own land or in helping neighbors at planting and harvest times.

Families' small fields were watered only by erratic rainfall. If the rains did not come, crops failed, and people either starved or went deeper into debt to the hacendados in order to purchase their food. Often, the plots were cultivated by the slash-and-burn method, whereby a field was cleared of forest or scrub, the debris burned to create ash fertilizer, and the land tilled with a wooden digging stick. Crops quickly exhausted such lands' nutrients after only 2 or 3 years, whereupon the farmer abandoned it. Usually, it took 7 years for the land to restore itself for cultivation.

In Argentina, small, family landowners comprised the most common productive unit on the vast plains of the Río de la Plata. Most farmers lived in comparative modesty on land they worked with family members and a few hired hands. In one sector of Buenos Aires province, almost 70 percent of the landholdings were smaller than 5000 hectares in 1890. The typical rural residential unit was a farm or small ranch with six to eight persons: a man, his wife, their children, a peon, an orphan, and perhaps a slave or *liberto* (a slave born after 1813 who was to remain a slave until age 21). In the Brazilian northeast, small farmers eked out a living raising the region's staple crop, cassava. To plant cassava, farmers cleared the land with an iron axe and set fire to the brush, then the farmers' slaves used hoes to heap the earth into small mounds. These prevented the cassava roots from becoming waterlogged and rotting during the winter rainy season. Two or three pieces of stalk cut from growing plants went into each little mound. Corn or beans were planted in the rows between the mounds. In about 2 weeks, the cuttings took root and poked through the soil. For several months, slaves guarded the crops from weeds and other natural enemies, such as ants, caterpillars, and live-stock. After 9 to 18 months, the central stalks sprouted small branches. Below ground, each plant put down five to ten bulbous roots, which the farmer harvested.

The slaves then prepared the cassava for processing into coarse flour (*farinha*). Most important was to eliminate poisonous prussic acid from the roots, which involved scraping, washing, grating, pressing, sifting, and toasting. Workers first scraped the roots with blunt knives and washed them. Then they grated or shredded the roots with a grating wheel. The pulp fell through the wheel and dried overnight to remove the prussic acid. The fine white sediment that collected at the bottom of the trough, when dried, washed, and sifted, became tapioca. The grated pulp of the cassava root was sifted into a coarse grain with the texture of moist sand. Slaves placed the sifted cassava on a large griddle made of glazed clay or copper and then lightly toasted it over an open hearth, stirring often to prevent burning. Toasting made it taste better and removed the last of the prussic acid. Cassava was a crop that could be planted or harvested at any time. Harvesting, moreover, could be delayed for a year before the roots would spoil.

Regardless of where they lived, nonslave women's workdays and responsibilities went far beyond those of men. Women rose well before dawn to prepare the family's food. The backbreaking work of making tortillas took hours, and because men had to take both breakfast and lunch with them to the fields, women had to prepare enough food for both meals early in the day. Women drew the water, gathered wood for the fire, cared for the children, prepared three meals for their households, did the wash, spun thread and wove cloth, and made clothing. They also made pottery and then hauled it to the Sunday market. When men were hired on to a hacienda, it was common for the women in their families to function either as field hands or as domestics in the hacienda house—work for which they received no pay. All was not drudgery, however: The weekly market day provided a welcome respite from the dull daily routine, giving the women vendors the opportunity to meet, gossip, and laugh with friends. Despite the enormous amount of work done by pueblo women, employment opportunities for women in rural areas were very limited. Consequently, a large number of young women migrated to the cities, where, for the most part, they entered domestic service.

Religion

Religion occupied a central place in rural Latin American life, and permeated popular culture. The influence of Catholicism was everywhere. Almost every small town had at least one chapel, and many had several churches. Perhaps the most important religious institutions in the countryside were the *cofradías,* the village organizations that maintained the church and funded religious celebrations. Much of a village's social life revolved around these celebrations and rites of passage. Priests often lived only in the larger villages or towns, and so traveled periodically through the villages in their districts to perform masses (Catholic religious services) and sacraments (baptism, marriage, and burial). Though clergy were among the most important figures in Latin American society, most country people rarely encountered a priest. As a result, the folk Catholicism practiced in the countryside retained many indigenous customs from pre-Christian times. The characteristics of Christian saints were often indistinguishable from those of gods worshipped by pre-Columbian peoples. Religion was a daily presence in the lives of all villages, rich and poor. The literate wealthy, for example, read primarily devotional literature, and their houses were decorated with religious artwork. The huts of poor families were blessed by corner altar bearing candles, flowers, and the likenesses of saints.

URBAN LIFE AND SOCIETAL TRANSFORMATION

During the nineteenth century, most of Latin America may have been rural, but Latin American cities rivaled any in the world in size. These cosmopolitan centers were at once splendiferous and horrifying. Often situated in physically beautiful settings with impressive colonial architecture, they also were unsanitary and dangerous, filled to overflowing with poverty-stricken people. The cities were crucibles of change, for it was in the urban areas that modernization most directly confronted tradition—especially in the realm of gender roles and relations. It was in the cities that the transformation of the role of women was most dramatic.

The Cities

Mexico City was the largest city in the Western Hemisphere and the fifth largest city in the Western world during the early nineteenth century: Its population was 168,846 by 1811. Half its population was of Spanish descent, with the rest comprised of Indians, mixed bloods, and African Mexicans. During the next three decades, through the 1850s, the city's population fluctuated between 160,000 and 205,000 because of periodic epidemics, and migration from the countryside, rather than natural increase, accounted for the net population growth. At the beginning of the nineteenth century, Rio de Janeiro had between 50,000 and 60,000 residents. But its population rose to 423,000 in 1890. The city's residents included immigrants from Portugal, Spain, and Italy, free blacks and mulattos, and white Brazilians from the hinterlands. Buenos Aires was the fastest-growing large city in Latin America during the second half of the century, becoming the largest city in the region by 1890. By 1914, in all the Americas, only New York exceeded it in number of inhabitants. Half of Buenos Aires' population was foreign-born.

As mentioned previously, the physical spaces of the cities were impressive, but their beautiful buildings and picturesque settings hid the dismaying conditions of most of their inhabitants. Mexico City was laid out in a grid with an enormous central plaza, the Zócalo. The great cathedral stood at the north end, with the palace of government on the east, and the offices of the municipality on the south. Five causeways furnished access to the city over the lake beds that surrounded it. A legacy from Aztec times, the city was divided into distinct sections, known as barrios. The outer margins of the city were left to

View of Mexico City from northwest, taken from the terrace of the Mining School, ca. 1870.

the poor, while the affluent lived in the central area. Rio de Janeiro was located in a setting of overwhelming physical beauty but was just as shabby and disease ridden as Mexico City. With narrow, stinking streets and crowded tenements, it was jam-packed with poor people. In contrast, Buenos Aires at mid-century was little more than a large village, possessing none of Rio de Janeiro's topographical beauty or Mexico City's impressive architecture. One Scottish traveler remarked that there was a "filthy, dilapidated look" to the houses. Pastureland, adorned with grazing livestock, lay 20 blocks from the central plaza.

All these cities were unsanitary and unhealthy. The Spaniards had built Mexico City on the ruins of the great Aztec capital Tenochtitlan and surrounding dry lake beds. During rainy season, these beds flooded, frequently transforming the outlying districts into lakes, dumping mud, garbage, and human feces into the houses, and leaving the central plaza knee-deep in stagnant water. Buenos Aires also had poor drainage, making even paved streets difficult to pass when rains were heavy. Much of Rio de Janeiro was built on filled-in swampland, so its inhabitants suffered similar problems.

Mexico City never had enough water for any purpose or sufficient waste disposal (nor does it today). Walking its thoroughfares was dangerous to one's health. The air smelled horribly from the sewage and piles of garbage. The city dumped trash into Lake Texcoco, which, unfortunately, was one of the primary sources of municipal drinking water. These unsanitary conditions had an enormous cost. Diseases such as smallpox, scarlet fever, measles, typhoid, and cholera were endemic. In 1840, smallpox killed more than 2000 children, while cholera killed almost 6000 in 1833 and 9000 in 1850. Cholera killed 15,000 in Buenos Aires in 1870. These diseases and others, such as diarrhea and dysentery, were closely associated with the wretched living conditions. Rio de Janeiro also was chronically short of water. In the 1860s, the city built a new system of reservoirs to hold water from mountain streams. This did not solve the problem, however.

Governments, whose minimal resources were used up to finance their armies, were simply unable to provide the public works necessary to make the cities healthy and safe.

Life in the cities in early nineteenth-century Latin America differed in many respects from that in the countryside, but many of the societal dynamics were much the same in urban settings as in rural ones. The social structure was just as rigidly stratified in the cities as in the country, the work was equally hard and as badly paid, and the gap between rich and poor was comparably wide. And, the vast migration of the populace from the countryside to the city made these conditions worse, especially during the last half of the century, when the migration intensified. But this migration also made possible the transformation of certain aspects of Latin American society, particularly that of women's roles.

Society in Mexico City was divided into very small upper and middle classes separated by vast differences in wealth and status from the majority of people, who were tremendously poor. The upper classes were comprised of high civil government and ecclesiastical officials, merchants, and wealthy mine owners and landowners. The next layer of the strata, upper middle class, was inhabited by professionals, such as doctors, lawyers, prosperous merchants, civil servants, industrialists, and other business people.

This group was closely associated in circumstance and outlook with the uppermost class. The "true" middle sectors consisted of small shopkeepers, tradesmen, artisans, and the better-off skilled workers. At the bottom lived 80 percent of the city's population: the unskilled workers, peddlers, artisans of low-prestige trades, and others who lived at the margins of society, such as prostitutes and beggars (*léperos*). These urban dwellers tried desperately to live on wages barely sufficient for subsistence. There was never enough steady employment; only 30 percent of those employed had full-time jobs. Only 1.4 percent of city residents owned property.

A large number of tiny businesses supplied consumer goods; many of these merchants conducted their commerce on dirty blankets in the filthy main market. The most common occupations, much like on the haciendas and in the pueblos, were domestic service, manual labor, and artisanship. Shoemakers, carpenters, and tailors were the most common types of skilled workers, while bricklayers, domestics, and street peddlers made up the majority of unskilled laborers. The average daily salary was .5 to 1.0 peso per day for skilled workers and .25 to .50 for unskilled, while the minimum cost of subsistence was .75 to 1.0 peso per day. (Until late in the century, the peso was equal in value to the U.S. dollar.) The region's stagnant economy and a labor surplus ensured that wages did not rise much, if at all, through the 1830s.

Transformations

The nineteenth-century migration from rural to urban life transformed the situation of women. These brave, determined women, many of whom were single and aged 15 to 29, left their rural birthplaces in search of a better life. They often came to urban areas without a father or a husband and suddenly found themselves having to lead self-reliant lives of unprecedented, even undreamed of, independence. Now, they had to function in public spaces (such as factories and markets), make their own living, and even act as head of their own household.

Women made up between 57 and 59 percent of the inhabitants of Mexico City and the majority of the migrants from the countryside throughout the first half of the nineteenth century. As with the men, almost all were castas or Indians who came from the densely populated regions around the capital.

Work

A quarter of all women in Mexico City worked, accounting for one-third of the total work force in the capital. More than a third of casta women and almost half of Indian women worked. Sixty percent of women worked as domestic servants; 20 percent sold food from their homes, on the street, or in the markets. Other occupations ran the gamut from mid-wife to peddler to waitress. Women fared no better than men regarding the conditions and remuneration of employment. Work was hard to come by and wages were paltry. Even those who found employment were underemployed. Worse still, women were limited to the worst-paying occupations. The jobs most easily obtained, in domestic service, were regarded as humiliating. Some servants were well treated, but all owed their employers "submission, obedience, and respect." They were on call 24 hours a day and were often paid no more than their room and board. Because there were so many young women available for domestic service, the labor market precluded any improvement in these conditions. Factories paid no better. And, although work there was considered more honorable than domestic service, conditions in the textile and tobacco industries, large employers of women, deteriorated considerably over the course of the 1820s and 1830s. Women were not allowed into the clergy, the military, or government bureaucracy—which were, of course, the main paths to upward mobility in Mexico.

In Rio de Janeiro in 1870, 63 percent of free women and 88 percent of slave women were gainfully employed. Only a very few, however, were professionals, working as midwives, nuns, teachers, or artisans. Women were prohibited from holding jobs in the government bureaucracy and in law and medicine. Women found work in commerce only as street vendors or market sellers because employers preferred to hire men as clerks and cashiers. More often women found jobs in the textile and shoe industries. By far and away the most common occupation for women in Rio de Janeiro was, as in Mexico City, domestic service. More than 60 percent of free working women and almost 90 percent of urban slave women were servants.

Marriage and Children

As previously noted, urban women often were separated from their families and became necessarily independent, though desperately poor. Not surprisingly, then, many women did not conform to the traditions of their male-dominated society. In Mexico City, slightly less than half were married. Eighty percent of females married at some point, either in formal or informal unions, but most spent only a small portion of their lives married. If they migrated from the countryside, they delayed marrying. Because of the higher mortality rate among men, it was likely that they would be widowed. One-third of adult women were single or widowed at the time of the censuses (1811 and 1848). Seventy percent of married women between 45 and 54 had outlived their husbands. Rich or poor, women spent much of their lives on their own.

An average woman in the Mexican capital bore five children. With infant mortality (death before age 3) estimated at 27 percent, it was likely that she would outlive at least one of them. Although two-thirds of adult women bore children, less than half of these women had children at home.

For much of their lives, therefore, a substantial proportion of Mexico City's women headed their own households as widows. Widowhood afforded wealthy women a degree of independence. This, of course, should not be exaggerated, for in many wealthy families, an adult son or son-in-law controlled the finances and negotiated with the outside world for the woman. Half of white women headed their own households in 1811, while only a third of casta or Indian women did so. Wealthy widows benefited from inheritance laws, which forced the division of an estate among spouse and children. The wife would always have at least some control over the estate. Because affluent males commonly married late, the number of offspring was often limited, thus keeping the widow's share of the estate larger. These kinds of calculations, of course, were of no consequence to the poor. Poor women barely subsisted. They had few alternatives other than to turn to men for support. Even then survival was uncertain. Children were such women's only old-age insurance; it was hoped that children would care for and support their parents in their old age.

Marriage and motherhood did not end a woman's work outside the home. Poor women worked out of necessity, because families could not subsist on men's incomes without the addition of women's earnings. So, poor women, married or not, worked. Marriage may, however, have changed a woman's occupation. Domestic service, for instance, was not possible for a married woman because it required that she live apart from her husband, in the residence of her employer. Self-employment, on the other hand, allowed women to care for their children while generating income. They could prepare food for sale, sew, operate small retail establishments, or peddle various wares. The result was that women dominated the markets.

Marriage, an entirely patriarchal institution, was an unequal relationship for women. A wife was expected to submit to her husband and to "obey him in everything reasonable." Domestic violence was common. Sexuality was another arena defined by double standards: It was perfectly acceptable for men to engage in extramarital relations, but totally unacceptable for women to do so.

FOOD, CLOTHING, SHELTER, AND ENTERTAINMENT

For most Latin Americans the fabric of everyday life—the food they ate, the housing that sheltered them, and the clothes that covered them—remained much the same throughout the tumultuous decades of the nineteenth century. Nowhere were disparities between social classes as clear as in these three basic aspects of daily existence.

Food

The staples of the Brazilian diet were black beans, dried meat, and manioc flour, occasionally augmented by game, fruit, molasses, and fish. The average Mexican's diet consisted of maize, beans, squash, and *chiles*, with small amounts of eggs, pork, meat, and cheese, with the corn tortilla as an essential staple. Women shucked corn and soaked the kernels in water with small bits of limestone, which loosened the sheath of the corn, imbued it with calcium, and increased its amino acid content. The latter created proteins from the mix of corn and beans, crucial in a diet that lacked meat. Next, the women beat the corn in the grinding bowl for hours. Finally, small pieces of the resulting dough were worked between the hands—tossed, patted, and flattened—until they were no thicker than a knife blade, after which they were thrown on a steaming-hot griddle (*comal*). The combination of maize tortillas and beans (tucked inside the folded tortilla) was not only delicious, but also provided almost all of the eater's required daily protein. (The more prosperous could afford to obtain more of their protein from meat, mostly pork.) Squash, which is 90 percent water, supplied badly needed liquid in an arid land and filler (fiber) to make meals more satisfying. Chiles were added to the beans as the source of crucial vitamins A, B, and C. The capsaicins in chiles, the chemical elements that make chiles "hot," killed bacteria that caused intestinal disorders. Water or pulque was drunk with the meal, and lump sugar provided a sweet. The urban poor took few meals at home for there was no place in their crowded rooms for cooking appliances. Instead, they purchased inexpensive food from vendors and ate it on the street.

The diet of the middle class, while also modest, was more varied and nutritious. In a respectable house in Rio de Janeiro, residents woke to a cup of strong coffee. Later in the morning they ate bread and fruit. The afternoon meal consisted of hot soup, then a main course of fish, black beans sprinkled with manioc flour, rice, and perhaps vegetables and, on occasion, well-cooked meat or stewed or roasted chicken. Two favorite dishes that took hours of preparation were *feijoada,* which required black beans to be soaked overnight and cooked for a long time with fatty pork, and cod (*bacala*), which was soaked for 20 hours and then baked. Desserts were sweets, such as fruit glazed with a paste made from guavas and sugar, or candy made from egg yolks, egg whites, and sugar, and was accompanied by highly sweetened strong coffee.

In Mexico City, breakfast started with a hot drink—chocolate for the adults or corn gruel (*atole*) for the children—and then toast, biscuits, or pastries with coffee and milk. At 11 A.M., chocolate or atole was drunk again, but this time flavored with anisette. The large meal, served in mid-afternoon, consisted of bread, soup, a roast, eggs in chile, vegetables, and beans flavored with pickled onion, cheese, and sauce. Dessert was honey with grated orange on a toasted tortilla. A light dinner in the evening consisted of a spicy sauce (*mole*), stewed meat, and a lettuce salad. A small staff served the meals.

For wealthy Mexicans, food was plentiful, varied, and rich, and meals were leisurely. At 8 A.M., the well-to-do partook of a small cup of chocolate with sweets. Two hours later, they ate a hearty breakfast of roasted or stewed meat, eggs, and beans (boiled soft and then fried with fat and onions). Dinner was served at 3 P.M. It began with a cup of clear broth, which was followed by highly seasoned rice or some other starch; a meat course consisting of beef, mutton, pork, fowl, or sausages; various vegetables and fruits; and dessert. After such repast a siesta was in order. At 6 P.M., families enjoyed a warm drink of chocolate during the cooler months or a cold, sweet beverage in summer. Cigars and conversation or a walk followed. Wealthy families ate "light" supper at 10 P.M. consisting of roasted meat, salad, beans, and sweets. Domestics served all meals on elegant china and silverware with tablecloths and napkins.

Clothing

Differences in dress between the affluent and poor were as striking as the differences in their diets. Rich urban women conformed to the latest fashions from France, often adding traditional Spanish garb, such as the *mantilla* (a shawl, usually made of lace, worn over the head). European diplomat Brantz Mayer described one woman in church in

Mexico in the 1840s: "She wore a purple velvet robe embroidered with white silk, white satin shoes, and silk stockings; a mantilla of the richest white blond lace fell over her head and shoulders, and her ears, neck, and fingers were blazing with diamonds." The dandies who frequented the fashionable spots in Mexico City might wear a "French cutaway suit, American patent leather shoes and an English stovepipe hat." The more sedate wore broadcloth suits and silk hats.

Few Mexicans, of course, could afford rich silk and woolen apparel. Travel writer Frederick Ober described mestizo dress in the early 1880s: "In the warmer regions he wears (on Sundays) a carefully plaited white shirt, wide trousers of white or colored drilling, fastened round the hips by a gay girdle, brown leather gaiters, and broad felt hat, with silver cord or fur band about it." Ranchers wore "open trousers of leather ornamented with silver, with white drawers showing through, a colored silk handkerchief about the neck, and a *serape*—the blanket shawl with a slit in the centre . . . ." The women "seldom wear stockings, though . . . feet are often encased in satin slippers; they have loose, embroidered chemises, a woolen or calico skirt, while the *rebozo*—a narrow but long shawl—is drawn over the head, and covers the otherwise exposed arms and breast."

Poor Mexicans dressed in simple, practical clothes. They went barefoot or wore sandals (*huaraches*) made simply from rawhide or plaited fibers. Despite the laws that demanded they wear pants and hats in public, Indian men usually wore only a breechcloth. Other rural Mexicans wore cotton shirts without collars and buttons and pants with long legs that covered their feet. Belts were strips of rawhide or cloth. The serape, a brightly covered woolen blanket, was an all-purpose garment that protected its wearer from the elements. The one common luxury among poor men was a straw hat. Rural women's apparel was no fancier than that of men. Indian women often wore only a few yards of cloth wrapped around their bodies. Rebozos were used similarly to serapes, protecting women from the elements and providing modesty. When folded the right way, the rebozo also was used to carry small children. Other women wore a scarf bound at the hips with a girdle that extended to the feet, accompanied by a broad mantle that covered the upper part of the body. This wool garment had with openings at the head and arms and was often ornamented with colorful embroidery. Wealthier Indian women wore a white petticoat with embroidery and ribbons. Some girls wore simple white cotton dresses with the head, neck, shoulders, and legs below the knees left bare. Women also wore heavy earrings and necklaces of cut glass. Their feet bore the same sandals worn by men or nothing. For the most part, women went without head coverings. Both men and women often carried rosary beads.

Shelter

As in the case of diet and clothing, housing, too, sharply differentiated the classes. The wealthy lived in opulence. In larger cities, houses of the affluent often had two stories. The ground floor in these buildings was for shops or other businesses, while the second floor was the family home. The house of Vicente Riva Palacio, well-known soldier-statesman, had 50 rooms. One entered through an impressive stairway leading to the living quarters.

The stairs and the floors of the corridors were made of the finest Italian marble. Tropical plants decorated the halls, and an aviary was filled with singing birds. Of the numerous rooms, there were three parlors, a grand salon, and two smaller salons. There was also an impressive private chapel adorned with luxurious drapes and beautiful religious ornaments. Mirrors and massive sideboards took up the walls of the dining room, measuring 100 by 50 feet. On these shelves were thousands of pieces of china, crystal, and silver. The brass bedsteads in each of 30 bedrooms bore an elegant bedspread of velvet, silk, lace, and crochet; hand-stitched linens; and canopies. The large living room, whose ceilings were 30 feet high, contained furniture decorated with gold trim, fabulous mirrors and chandeliers, and rich carpets. The family had its own 200-seat theater. Maintaining this remarkable establishment required 35 servants.

Guillermo Prieto, a noted social critic, described the typical middle-class home in Mexico City, which was considerably more modest:

> A steep stairway led to a corridor paved with red varnished millstones. (The middle class usually lived on the second floor . . . because of the flooding that periodically afflicted the city, and the servants occupied rooms on the first floor.) The corridor was embellished with cages filled with stuffed birds, squirrels, wind chimes, and earthen crocks packed with stored foods and vegetables. Landscapes . . . adorned the walls. Comfortable chairs and couches . . . furnished the principal chamber. . . . In the bedroom were a large bed of fine wood, easy chairs, and wardrobes. The small children of the family slept in the halls. Those of a small family slept with their parents in curtained compartments of the main bedroom. The dining room contained a washstand holding towels, soap, straw, and a scouring stone for scrubbing. Colored vegetables, pots and pans, and jars lined the kitchen walls . . . with strips of garlic and pepper for a festive air.

In contrast to the domestic comfort enjoyed by the urban well-to-do, housing for farmers in the countryside was little more than a hut. Because wood for construction or fuel was prohibitively expensive in these deforested or arid areas, neither lumber nor bricks were practical building materials. (Wood was too costly to use in ovens to bake bricks.) Consequently, in temperate climates, country people constructed their huts with adobe made from sun-baked straw and mud blocks. In the highlands, where wood was more plentiful and affordable, houses consisted of brick (or stones plastered with mud rather than mortar) walls and a flat roof of beams laid close together and covered with finely washed, carefully stamped clay. In the tropics, farmers built their huts with saplings and leaves held together with mud. Occupants drove hewn logs into the ground to support the beams and roof and used bamboo sticks for the walls. The normal hut measured 20 by 15 feet and contained one room with no windows and a floor of packed earth mixed with ashes. Doorways (without doors) provided ventilation and light. Roofs were commonly made either with thatch or by laying rows of poles across the tops of walls that were covered with 1 or 2 feet of dirt and a layer of pine boards. Where it was colder, roofs were covered with shingles. Native vegetation, such as palm leaves or straw, served as roofing material in the tropics.

The kitchen area, where a fire burned continuously, was outside or in a separate, smaller building. The metate for tortillas was beside the fire. Huts had no furniture. Mats known as *petates* served as sleeping pallets. Better-off rural dwellers might have a bed consisting of four mounds of clay crossed with rough boards. No one could afford bedding or mattresses. Men and women slept in their clothes, wrapped in serapes and rebozos in cold weather. Because most people owned only the clothes they wore, there was no need for chests or closets. Pottery and baskets stored food and whatever other possessions the family owned. The only decoration in the hut was a picture of the Virgin of Guadalupe or a saint. Most regions were warm enough that homes did not require heating—and even if heat was needed, no one could afford it. The more prosperous rancheros lived in slightly less simple abodes. They might have a few pieces of furniture, such as a bench, a table (perhaps with low stools for seating), and board beds with mats and skins for pillows.

Poor people in Mexico City lived in rooms rented in crowded tenements (*vecindades*). Because the city endured periodic flooding, ground-floor rooms were continually damp. Badly ventilated, filthy, and crowded, the vecindades were breeding grounds for disease. Apartments lacked cooking facilities, which meant most of the poor took all their meals from street vendors. Not everyone was fortunate to have a roof over his or her head. Joel Poinsett, the United States Minister in 1824, estimated that 20,000 people slept on the streets. In Buenos Aires, most of the poor lived in small, ugly houses on the outskirts of the city. About a quarter of the residents in 1887 lived in tenements (*conventillos*), where they and their many children inhabited tiny rooms piled high with garbage and filth. In Rio de Janeiro, many of the new immigrants and internal migrants lived in crowded slums known as *corticos*. As in Mexico City the fashionable suburbs sprang up on the periphery, while the core of the city became the ever more crowded home of the poor.

Entertainment

Statistics and anecdotal evidence depict everyday life in nineteenth-century Latin America as being unpleasant or even miserable (if one were poor or a slave), but people found ways to enjoy themselves. The church, family, drinking, and gambling provided the most common entertainment for people of all classes. Solemn church masses were great spectacles, offering the best entertainment of the time, a theater of rites and rituals, resplendent priests, and majestic music. While no parish in the capital or anywhere else duplicated the magnificence of the great cathedral in Mexico City, many churches elsewhere stirred and inspired the people. Even in a modest village chapel, a visiting clergyman might put on a good show despite the lack of an opulent setting.

Religious fiestas took up a large number of days; in Aguascalientes, Mexico, for example, in the 1860s, there were 40 per year. These occasions provided both solemn consideration and joyous fun. Cities, towns, and villages prepared carefully for these celebrations by repairing and cleaning the streets, so that the processions that marked the special days were fit for the event. The Palm Sunday march represented Jesus' entrance into Jerusalem. On Good Friday, the crucifixion procession took place. Repentant sinners paraded through the roads half-naked and wearing crowns of thorns.

Mexico City celebrated Corpus Christi in unusual splendor. The archbishop conducted mass in the great cathedral in the Zócalo after which he led a grand parade from the church through adjacent streets, walking under a canopy of white linen, decorated with a red border. Everyone who was anyone—presidents, generals, cabinet ministers—appeared in full regalia. The procession was a time to show off. The wealthy displayed their fine clothes, perhaps imported from Paris. The surrounding homes were decked out with carpets, flowers, flags, and streamers. And a vast crowd of costumed people of different races and colors watched as the spectacle passed before them.

One of the most important holidays in Mexico was the Day of the Dead, celebrated in late October and early November. The celebrants burned massive numbers of candles and consumed large quantities of food. Poor Indians expended years of earnings in remembrance of departed loved ones. The night of the last day of October, families decorated their homes with flowers and candles and set out a colorful mat on which they lay a feast to lure the dead children back. The next day, the family repeated the ritual, adding dishes too hot for children, such as turkey mole and tamales. On this day, liquor also was offered. The Day of the Dead celebrations indicated that Mexicans knew death well and did not fear it.

Drinking was an important aspect of religious celebrations and, perhaps, for many, a crucial method of alleviating the pain of daily life. Alcoholism became a serious problem among the poor, however, as the alienation of urban life and industrialized working conditions became widespread at century's end. Pulque was the alcoholic beverage of choice. The *maguey* (agave) cactus has leaves of up to 10 feet in length, 1 foot wide, and 8 inches thick. After some years, it sends a giant flower stalk 20 to 30 feet high, on which grow greenish yellow flowers. The plant dies after it blooms. Just before it is about to emit its stalk, the Indians cut into the plant to extract the central portion of the stem. The incision leaves only the thick outside rind, forming a natural basin 2 feet deep and a foot and a half in diameter. The sap that would feed the stem, called *aguamiel* (honey water), oozes into the core and is extracted. A small amount is taken to ferment for 10 to 15 days. This becomes the *madre pulque,* which acts as a leaven inducing fermentation in the aguamiel. Within 24 hours it is pulque. As one draws off the pulque, one adds aguamiel to the mix. A good maguey yields 8 to 16 liters of aguamiel a day for as long as 3 months. Although the pulque has a lumpy consistency, tastes something like stale buttermilk, and smells like rotted meat, it is quite nutritious, and many believe it helps digestion.

Another popular diversion was gambling, which many observers of the time believed was a Mexican obsession. Cockfighting was a passionate outlet for gamblers and necessitated considerable preparations. Handlers bred and selected the cocks (roosters) carefully, fed them strictly, and trained them assiduously. The event required an arena 6 feet in diameter fenced in by 3-foot boards with benches around it. From the gallery, spectators urged on and bet on their favorites. The spectacle of the birds was bloody and brutal. The brave cocks exhausted themselves, but would not quit until one of the two contestants lay dead. Money then changed hands.

Of the different types of entertainment available in Mexico during this period, bull-fighting was the most famous. Thousands frequented the Sunday afternoon spectacles in Mexico City. Although it was a sport shared by all classes, one's status was made clear by virtue of seating. The wealthy sat in the shade, while the masses suffered the searing sun. The spectacle proceeded in traditional stages: The bull entered to have *picadors* and *matadors* goad and tease him with lances and red cloaks. These men had to be agile to avoid death on the animal's horns. Then, amid trumpet sounds, the bull's tormentors stuck small lances into his neck. The bull, snorting, thundering to no avail, attacked anyone and anything. Finally, the chief matador emerged, accompanied again by trumpets, to do battle armed with his red cloak and long blade. After some flourishing, the matador plunged his weapon between the bull's shoulder blades and into its heart, putting the animal out of its misery.

CONCLUSION

Life in Latin America during the first seven decades of the nineteenth century was enormously difficult for all but the wealthiest classes. The huge majority of Latin Americans struggled in poverty. Most people resided and worked in the countryside, either on large estates, in communal villages, or on small farms. A small percentage found employment in mining camps. As the century progressed, growing numbers of the populace migrated to the great cities in hopes of creating a better future for themselves. Inept and corrupt governments, war and banditry, and stagnant economies tormented nearly everyone, most profoundly, of course, the poor.

In the face of such dauntingly difficult lives, Latin Americans sought to preserve their customs and traditions. The best means at their disposal was to defend local governance. As we learned in Chapter 9, political and economic instability ironically allowed the lower classes to maintain their autonomy, at least in the countryside, for several decades after independence. Political centralization and economic development during the latter half of the century, however, undermined local prerogatives and eroded the practices of everyday life that had been sustained for centuries. New forms of work emerged, and modernization made life worse, rather than better, for most of the population.

LEARNING MORE ABOUT LATIN AMERICANS

Arrom, Silvia. *The Women of Mexico City* (Stanford, CA: Stanford University Press, 1985). Pathbreaking study of the changes in the conditions for women during the nineteenth century.

Barickman, B. J. *A Bahian Counterpoint: Sugar, Tobacco, Cassava, and Slavery in the Recôncavo, 1780–1860* (Stanford, CA: Stanford University Press, 1998). Explores economics and society in the Brazilian northeast.

Beezley, William H. *Judas at the Jockey Club and Other Episodes of Porfirian Mexico* (Lincoln, NE: University of Nebraska Press, 1987). Explores popular culture at the end of the century.

Burns, E. Bradford. *The Poverty of Progress: Latin America in the Nineteenth Century* (Berkeley, CA: University of California Press, 1980). Classic argument against the European notion of progress.

Calderón de la Barca, Frances. *Life in Mexico* (Berkeley, CA: University of California Press, 1982). Sometimes biting observations by foreign diplomat's wife.

Fowler-Salamini, Heather, and Mary Kay Vaughn, eds. *Women of the Mexican Countryside, 1850–1990* (Tucson, AZ: University of Arizona Press, 1994). Essays on the social history of women in everyday life.

Francois, Marie Eileen. *A Culture of Everyday Credit: Housekeeping, Pawnbroking, and Governance in Mexico City, 1750–1920* (Lincoln, NE: University of Nebraska Press, 2006). Details the struggles of everyday people.

Graham, Sandra Lauderdale. *Caetana Says No: Women's Stories from a Brazilian Slave Society* (New York: Cambridge University Press, 2002). The lives of a woman slave owner and a woman slave.

Graham, Sandra Lauderdale. *House and Street: The Domestic World of Servants and Masters in Nineteenth-Century Rio de Janeiro* (Austin, TX: University of Texas Press, 1992). A study of lower-class women who worked as domestics.

Johns, Michael. *The City of Mexico in the Age of Diaz* (Austin, TX: University of Texas Press, 1997). Mexico City, warts and all.

Mattoso, Katia M. de Queirós. *To Be a Slave in Brazil, 1550–1888* (New Brunswick, NJ: Rutgers University Press, 1986). The most thorough analysis of what it was like to be a slave in Brazil.

Stein, Stanley J. *Vassouras: A Brazilian Coffee County, 1850–1900* (Princeton, NJ: Princeton University Press, 1985). Classic study of a coffee plantation.

Wasserman, Mark. *Everyday Life and Politics in Nineteenth Century Mexico: Men, Women, and War* (Albuquerque, NM: University of New Mexico Press, 2000). A lively rendition of what life was like in nineteenth-century Mexico.

11

ECONOMIC MODERNIZATION, SOCIETY, AND POLITICS, 1880–1920

THE PERIOD FROM 1880 to 1920 was a time of momentous changes in the world economy. Railroads, steamships, telegraphs, and telephones made it possible for people, goods, ideas, and money to move rapidly across oceans and international boundaries. In Western Europe and the United States, most people now lived in cities and earned their livelihoods in industry rather than agriculture. The population of these areas grew in both numbers and affluence, creating demand for a wide range of agricultural products, such as beef and grains for consumption and cotton and wool for wear. New industries required minerals, such as copper for electric wire, and other commodities, such as petroleum for internal combustion engines. Large corporations emerged to provide the capital, technology, and administrative know-how in a global process of economic modernization.

These transformations had especially profound economic, political, and social consequences in Latin America. Beginning in the 1870s and continuing to the 1920s, Latin America experienced an extraordinary export boom. The construction of thousands of miles of railroads and the refurbishment of seaports eased the flow of products from Latin American mines and fields to waiting North Atlantic markets. Europe and the United States not only provided expanding markets but also new technologies and capital to facilitate the extraction of agricultural and mineral resources. Economic growth brought a measure of prosperity, but it was unequally distributed. Workers in the region's mines and nascent industries experienced harsh working conditions and often received scant compensation for their contributions to the growing economies. Poor farmers, usually indigenous peoples who still held their land communally, often lost their holdings to large estates that sought to increase their acreage in order to produce more agricultural commodities for export. Aided and abetted by national governments, who looked unfavorably on collective landholding as an impediment to progress, land expropriations created a large class of landless rural people, whose customs and mores had for centuries revolved around collective and individual landownership. Meanwhile, as the region became more closely tied to the world economy, it became exceptionally vulnerable to fluctuations in overseas markets. The resulting boom and bust cycles wreaked havoc in many countries. Major depressions in the world economy in the 1890s and again in 1907 sparked political conflict in various Latin American countries.

Export-led modernization brought enormous political and social changes to Latin America. Emerging from the violent decades that followed independence, many nations experienced long periods of political stability, dominated by land-based upper classes ruling through rigged elections or dictatorships. This political stability was vital to the modernization process, but economic development generated forces that disrupted the status quo. The export boom created two new, crucial social classes—an urban middle class and an urban industrial working class—whose demands for equality and equity eventually brought an end to the rule of the large landowners. The export economy expanded the size and role of governments, which needed a growing number of white-collar workers who obtained middle-class status. These workers formed one component of the new middle class. Economic opportunities in boom times created an entrepreneurial group of small-scale businesspeople, who also joined the ranks of the middle class. This middle sector commonly formed the foundation of rising political parties.

Meanwhile, railroads, mining, food processing, and other new industries stimulated by the export economy required growing numbers of workers. In some countries, massive immigration—made possible by rapid development of railroads and steamship lines—helped fill the demand. The new export economies needed large numbers of unskilled workers, but the new technology also required many workers with specialized skills. Workers of all ranks, but particularly those who were highly skilled, organized labor unions and joined political parties in search of improved living and employment conditions.

Workers' grievances joined with those of dispossessed farmers to form an increasingly volatile political climate. The crisis, known in some countries as the "Social Question," intensified after 1900. Those who ruled struggled to maintain their position. Some upper classes grudgingly made concessions to the middle and lower classes, while others stubbornly refused. During the first two decades of the twentieth century, many cities and mining regions witnessed violent protests against upper-class oppression, but only in Mexico did these protests lead to revolution. Almost everywhere, however, the rule of large landowners drew to a close.

Export-led development brought with it not only profound economic and political dislocations, but wrenching social changes as well. The old ruling classes faced the

TIMELINE

1876
Porfirio Díaz takes power in Mexico

1888
Abolition of slavery in Brazil

1889
Empire overthrown by military in Brazil

1891
Chilean civil war ousts President José Manuel Balmaceda; parliamentary rule begins

1910
Mexican Revolution begins

1912
Sáenz Peña Law in Argentina extends male suffrage

1912
Foreign investment in Latin America reaches US$8.5 billion

1916
Election of Hipólito Yrigoyen as president of Argentina

1917
Mexican Constitution

1919
Semana Trágica in Buenos Aires

erosion of the patriarchal norms that underlay their positions of power. The urbanization, industrialization, and migration that accompanied export-led development undermined traditional gender roles and family structures that cast fathers and husbands as the heads of families and men as the sole actors in the political sphere. Women's positions in the family, the workplace, and the public arena changed. Feminism rose to demand that women be recognized as important contributors to the construction of modern nations. Women sought equality under the law, both inside and outside the family. Not only was the public rule of the upper classes under attack, but the private basis of their position as well.

Economic change notwithstanding, the core of the political struggle remained control over everyday life. Urbanization and industrialization merely shifted the locations, altered some of the methods employed, and broadened some of the goals. In the countryside, struggle continued much the same as it had before against the intrusions of central authority. To country people, modernization and centralization meant a widespread assault against their culture and traditions.

ECONOMIC MODERNIZATION

After nearly a half-century of stagnation with interludes of export boom, much of Latin America entered into a period of economic growth from the 1880s through World War I, resulting from the influx of new technologies and capital, mostly from abroad, and the advent of domestic peace. Massive new railroad networks were both the products of modernization and the engines of further economic development. They also facilitated national consolidation in ways unimaginable before 1880.

Exports

The development of export agriculture and industry was at the core of the economic, social, and political transformations of the era. The export boom displayed several notable characteristics. First, most nations concentrated on one or two export commodities. Second, the booms were not sustainable, for the most part, for more than a decade or two at a time. International markets for primary products were cyclical, and busts inevitably followed booms. Third, the question of who actually benefited from the expansion of exports is subject to unending debate. Finally, linkages between the export economy and domestic sectors of the Latin American economies were not consistent. As a result, the growth of exports did not necessarily stimulate overall economic development.

The industrialized nations of the North Atlantic (Great Britain, France, Germany, and the United States) greatly increased their population and general prosperity after 1850. Annual income per capita doubled. The market demand for agricultural staples, such as grain, meat, and wool, exceeded locally available supplies, while increased affluence stimulated demand for more "exotic" products, such as coffee, cacao, sugar, and bananas. Simultaneously, technological advancements in agriculture and industry created additional demands for primary materials. New farming techniques required fertilizers, for example. Intensifying industrialization created a need for mineral ores such as lead, silver, gold, tin, zinc, and copper. The invention and widespread use of the internal combustion engine expanded demand for petroleum. Technological improvements in metallurgy and mining made it possible to extract minerals from previously unusable sources and cut down on the bulk and cost of ore shipments. New railroads and communications and the introduction of steamships facilitated the transportation of raw materials. The new ships reduced the Buenos Aires to Europe route to weeks. Refrigerated shipping made it possible to send even fresh meat and other delicate commodities across the ocean.

Latin American nations possessed the natural resources to help satisfy the North Atlantic market for food and minerals. The industrialized nations supplied capital, technological expertise, and administrative organization to extract and transport these commodities. A vast inflow of foreign investment stimulated the expansion of exports. By 1912, foreign investment in Latin America reached $8.5 billion, of which railroads accounted for $2.9 billion. The largest other sectors of investment were in government obligations (bonds), mining, and public utilities.

Great Britain accounted for the largest share of foreign investment in Latin America, nearly $5 billion. Between 1900 and 1914, the British doubled their holdings in the region. The British were a notable presence in Chilean nitrate mining and Mexican petroleum. U.S. capital was second in importance to the British and concentrated in Mexican railroads and mining, Cuban sugar production, and Central American plantations and railways. Between 1900 and 1914, U.S. investment in Latin America quintupled. Mexico received the most capital, more than $1 billion. U.S. investors mostly sought export industries. Before 1914, the third largest source of foreign investment was Germany. Germans invested heavily in Argentina, Brazil, and Mexico (more than $100 million in each). World War I, however, broke most of Latin America's commercial and financial ties with Germany.

Growing demand in the North Atlantic economies, transportation improvements, and massive foreign investment all combined to increase Latin American exports enormously. Some of this growth began as early as the mid-nineteenth century, but the pace accelerated greatly after 1880. Between 1853 and 1873, Argentine exports grew sevenfold. By 1893, they had doubled again. Brazilian coffee exports more than doubled in the years between 1844 and 1874 and quadrupled between 1874 and 1905. Colombian, Costa Rican, and Venezuelan coffee exports also increased spectacularly. Total Mexican exports rose nearly 700 percent from 1878 to 1911. Bolivian tin exports jumped by 1200 percent from 1897 to 1913.

The burgeoning export economy had important positive effects. In 1916, Argentina's per capita national wealth stood at approximately 10 percent less than that of the United States, but 62 percent higher than that of France. By 1914, Argentina's per capita income exceeded that of Spain, Italy, Switzerland, and Sweden and compared with that of Germany, Belgium, and the Netherlands.

The Downside of Export-Led Modernization

Despite overall growth, export-led modernization proved a mixed blessing for Latin Americans. The rise in per capita income was statistically impressive, but the numbers masked the fact that this wealth was not equitably distributed. Wealthy landowners became fabulously rich, while the situation of the rest of the population remained the same or deteriorated.

Moreover, few Latin American nations were able to sustain steady high growth. Only Argentina and Chile expanded their exports at a rate averaging more than 4 percent from 1850 to 1914. Argentina averaged more than 6 percent, a truly impressive accomplishment. The other nations had spurts of growth followed by long periods of stagnation. By World War I, however, exports seemed to reach a ceiling, because either the products of these nations dominated the world market to such an extent that little room for growth remained or severe competition had arisen and market share inevitably fell.

Latin America's vulnerability to world market fluctuations was exacerbated by the fact that most nations continued to rely on a limited number of export commodities. To be sure, in the first decade of the twentieth century, there were a number of efforts to diversify from the model of one or two raw material exports, but concentration of exports persisted. In five Latin American nations (Bolivia, Chile, Cuba, El Salvador, and Guatemala) in 1913, one commodity comprised more than 70 percent of exports. In five more nations (Brazil, Ecuador, Haiti, Nicaragua, and Panama), one product accounted for more than 60 percent of exports. And in three others (Costa Rica, Honduras, and Venezuela), one commodity accounted for more than 50 percent. The most diversified export nations were Argentina, Colombia, and Peru. Argentina was the most successful at diversification, exporting grains (wheat, linseed, rye, barley, and maize) and livestock (chilled and frozen beef, lamb, wool, and hides).

Most Latin American export economies became dependent on a handful of consuming nations and therefore found themselves vulnerable to economic fluctuations in those countries. Four markets, the United States, Great Britain, Germany, and France, together accounted for 90 percent of the exports in 10 countries and more than 70 percent in 18. Only Argentina avoided this heavy dependence on the four markets.

The foundation of Latin American trade was the shipment of primary commodities in return for manufactured goods. Historians have long debated the equity of this system. Some have maintained the terms of trade were unfair because manufactured goods constantly rose in price while commodity prices declined. This is difficult to determine conclusively, however, because the statistics for trade and prices are not very reliable and those that are available do not show firm trends. The advantage, however, was not always with the industrialized nations.

The impact of export-oriented development strategies is also heatedly argued among historians and economists. Advocates claim that these strategies stimulated the other sectors of the economy, particularly industrialization. Some export commodities require processing, such as butchering and chilling meat, tanning hides, and milling flour. Sugar production, as we have seen, is as much an industrial as an agricultural enterprise. Exports drove the construction of railroads and other transportation. At the same time, however, export commodities often drained the nation of resources, leaving little or nothing for other economic activities. In nations where capital was chronically scarce, precious few resources trickled from the export machine. Some export economies, notably petroleum drilling, operated in enclaves without enhancing the overall economy.

The rapid rise of the various export economies of the region did not necessarily lead to development of the nonexport economy. Industrialization, the usual measure of economic modernization, did not automatically derive from increased primary exports. In general, the nations with the most varied export product base were the most likely to develop. Those economies that relied on one product were the least likely to develop.

Finally, export booms inevitably ended. Agricultural commodities wore out the soil, causing production gradually to decline. This was particularly the case for coffee in Central America, Venezuela, and Haiti around 1900. Bananas were vulnerable to disease and natural disasters. More important, world market demand was fickle. For example, demand for Brazilian rubber skyrocketed at the turn of the century, creating fabulous fortunes, only to fall precipitously when competitors from Southeast Asia flooded the market and, later, chemists invented a substitute.

Railroads

Railroads were, perhaps, the greatest technological agents of change during the nineteenth century, and as such they provide a good illustration of the benefits and drawbacks of modernization. They were the "backbone" of the export economy, bringing unparalleled prosperity to some regions and unmitigated misery elsewhere. The expansion of the railways was spectacular (see Table 11.1). The railroad system of Argentina increased from 1600 miles in 1880 to 21,200 miles in 1914. Mexico had less than 400 miles of railroads in 1880, but by 1910 it had constructed nearly 15,000 miles of track.

Railroads provided inexpensive transportation for agricultural commodities, minerals, and people. The rail networks opened up new lands for cultivation. In Argentina, they made it possible to cultivate grains on the rich soil of the Pampas and to push livestock raising farther and farther south into the semiarid region of Patagonia. Brazilian planters spread coffee cultivation to the vast interior of São Paulo. Railroad transportation facilitated the recovery of the Mexican mining industry.

The new transportation systems brought together nations torn by regionalism. They enabled governments to exert their authority in previously autonomous areas. What once were months-long journeys for armies now took only days, and former day trips now took only hours. Railroads enabled people to travel farther and at less cost than ever before.

TABLE 11.1

Railways in Latin America, 1880–1920 (Number of Miles)

	1880	1900	1920
Argentina	1,600	10,400	21,200
Brazil	2,100	9,500	17,700
Chile	700	8,300	13,000
Peru	1,100	2,700	5,100
Latin America	7,200	34,500	62,900

Source: Copyright © 2000 Frederick Stirton Weaver. Reprinted by permission of Westview Press, a member of the Perseus Books Group.

Walking to the mines of northern Mexico from the center of the nation was an impossible dream, but the railroad carried passengers to potentially better lives for minimal expenditure. It also created truly national markets for the first time.

Despite the obvious benefits they generated, railroads also were a symbol of unwanted modernization, one that people frequently resisted. In Mexico during the last quarter of the nineteenth century, there was violence in almost every region where tracks were laid for the first time. It was not unusual for people anywhere in Latin America to throw rocks at the train cars as they passed, so hated were the engines of progress. The railroads disrupted old patterns of landholding. Their presence raised the value of land. In areas where indigenous people owned lands collectively and individually and grew subsistence staple crops, government officials and large landowners forced them off their properties. The greedy landowners then converted production to commercial crops, which they sent to urban and international markets by means of the railroads. This process created a large, landless class of poor rural people, and thus a pool of inexpensive labor, and cut the total production of staple crops, which in turn caused the prices of basic foodstuffs to rise. The subsequent inflation undermined the living standards of both the middle and working classes.

MODERNIZATION AND SOCIAL CHANGE

The economic and technological transformations described in the preceding section triggered great changes in Latin American society. First, improved diets and medical care, coupled in many countries with a steady stream of immigrants, brought a substantial increase in population, most particularly in urban areas. Second, new social classes arose, complicating the social hierarchy and political agendas for the region. Third, discontent mounted in the countryside. Finally, people were on the move—from rural areas to cities and mining camps, from overseas to Latin America, from one country to another. All these changes had a profound impact on the daily lives of men, women, and children throughout Latin America.

Population Increase

As we saw in Chapter 9, the decades following national independence were pervaded by warfare throughout Latin America. These conflicts cost many lives, and the population growth that many areas had experienced in the late colonial period came to a halt. By the 1880s, however, the populations of Latin American nations began to grow once more. The population of Argentina doubled between 1895 and 1914, from 3.9 to 7.8 million. Brazil's population went from 10.1 million in 1872 to 30.6 million in 1920. Cities exploded. The population of Buenos Aires went from 178,000 in 1869 to nearly 1.6 million in 1914. Other than Hamburg, Germany, it was the fastest-growing city in the Western world. Lima, which because of the War of the Pacific and subsequent civil wars, did not begin to grow until the 1890s, jumped from 104,000 in 1891 to 224,000 in 1920. Guayaquil, Ecuador, grew from 12,000 to 90,000 between 1870 and 1920.

New Classes, New Voices

The increase in population and the development of industry created both a bigger, more complex middle sector and an industrial working class, while at the same time providing opportunities for women. Each of these groups would in turn seek to add their voices the political discourse begun in the decades after independence.

There had been from colonial times a *gente decente* (decent folk) that comprised light-skinned people who did not work with their hands. In great part their status depended on their race. Few Indians, blacks, or mulattos found acceptance into the middle class (although there were, of course, exceptions). The new middle class that arose from the export boom and industrialization was quite varied. In Buenos Aires, the mostly immigrant middle class operated small businesses, such as bakeries, breweries, print shops, and retail shops. The number of small-scale manufacturers doubled from 1853 to 1914. These remained vulnerable to the fluctuations in economic conditions. The depression of 1907, for example, devastated small-scale entrepreneurs in northern Mexico, erasing a decade of gains. Oftentimes the middle class depended on the goodwill and good fortune of their bosses, not necessarily their own merits. Proprietors of small businesses rarely had any other assets other than their own skills. In the cities few middle-class people owned property.

White-collar employees occupied the most complicated and difficult position among the middle classes. Not always earning income sufficient for full-fledged middle-class status, they, nonetheless, sought respectability. They lived precariously on the edge of ruin, fearing above all the prospect of falling back into poverty. In Lima in 1908, the census revealed that half the 6600 white-collar employees were white, 25 percent were mestizo, and 15 percent Asian. Only 1 percent of white-collar employees in Lima were women. According to D. S. Parker, they were "marginal figures at best. With no family connections, they were only capable of moving into the lowest rung of the commercial ladder. Poorly paid for long hours, ruthlessly exploited, and lacking any job security, their highest realistic expectation was to receive a steady pay check and to wear a clean shirt."

The rapidly emerging industrial working class was also quite diverse. In mining, its members ranged from unskilled peons, who carried 200-pound sacks of ore up rickety ladders from deep tunnels to the surface, to experts in explosives. On the railroads, common pick-and-shovel men toiled with locomotive engineers. In meat packing there were unskilled meat carriers and skilled butchers. Although in Argentina meat-packing plants were large enterprises, thousands of small workshops manufactured an enormous variety of products. European immigrants comprised from one-half to two-thirds of the workers. The number of workers in Lima, Peru, rose from 9500 in 1876 to more than 44,000 in 1920, and in Callao, Lima's port, their number doubled between 1908 and 1920. Women and children comprised one-fifth of the working class employed.

Expanding literacy rates among the middle classes and some sectors of the working classes gave these groups greater access to information about national affairs and emboldened them to demand a voice in political debates. In Brazil, to cite one example, only 19.1 percent of all Brazilian men and 10.4 percent of all women were literate in 1890. By 1920, literacy had improved to 28.9 percent for men and 19.9 percent for women. Literacy was much higher in the cities. By 1920, 65.8 percent of the men and 54.5 percent of the women in São Paulo and Rio de Janeiro had learned how to read and write.

The emergence of these new middle-class and working-class groups added new voices to the political debates in Latin America by the early twentieth century. A growing number of these voices were female. Although women comprised a tiny percentage of white-collar employees, they entered the urban workforce and gained access to at least a rudimentary education in unprecedented numbers. As factory workers, operators of small businesses, and heads of households, they acted independently of traditional family ties and increasingly sought equal treatment in both private and public spheres. Feminists among them asserted their equality with men, while insisting on their differences as well. They used the regard society had for them as females to establish their role in the public sphere and their position as working women to campaign for societal reforms. Feminism called for a redefinition of the traditional notions of the home as women's space and the street as forbidden. At stake were the long-held values of honor and the double standard. They challenged the basic structure of the family, seeking to end the legal subordination of women and the illegality of divorce. Ultimately, women sought to obtain suffrage. Initially, however, they focused on securing equality under the law and better health care for women and children. Their active voices changed the nature of political discourse in the modernizing nations of Latin America.

Rural Discontent

Although the emergence of middle and industrial working classes had limited impact in rural areas, other disruptive trends affected people living in the countryside. Generally, conditions for rural working people deteriorated. In central Mexico, for example, wages had stagnated while purchasing power declined. In Mexico, land expropriations by politicians and large landowners left many rural dwellers landless, who toiled either for

Slice of Life   A Chilean Mining Camp

LIFE IN THE MINING camps of Brazil, Chile, Mexico, and Peru was difficult, dangerous, and expensive. Spanish and Portuguese colonial enterprises had little success in attracting voluntary labor to the camps without substantial monetary inducements or coercion. The indigenous peoples steered clear of the mines as much as possible. The advent of a freer labor market and the introduction of modern technology during the nineteenth century did not improve the living and working conditions. As one observer noted, "Labor in the copper mines of the nineteenth century was harshly disciplined, intense, and brutal."

Chilean copper mines were small and totally lacking in modern technology. Mine owners had no capital, suffered poor transportation, and lacked a dependable labor supply: Who would want to work in a copper camp? The mines were usually isolated, accessible to the outside world only by several days of hard travel through rugged terrain. Most were located in the mountains, which were buffeted by inhospitable weather.

The miners were treated abominably. The physical labor was arduous and included working with heavy hammers and chisels and carrying 200-pound sacks of ore up rickety ladders. Charles Darwin observed that the miners were "truly beasts of burden." Miners had little time for meals, working from dawn until dusk. Adding

Mining camp. The work was backbreaking and dangerous.

insult to injury, armed guards patrolled the camps, and if miners were caught stealing ore, they were subject to corporal punishment.

Conditions changed somewhat during and after World War I, when copper prices rose because of increased demand. After the war, large international corporations invested in the copper industry. They brought in new technology, such as the widespread use of dynamite. The big companies paid relatively high wages and provided better living conditions than the small Chilean operations. This was not saying much, however.

Better wages were offset by the skyrocketing cost of living in the camps. And slightly improved working conditions did not change the fact that life in the mines was unendurable: The mine tunnels were hell-like, either unbearably hot from the venting of underground gases or cold and wet. Copper dust swirled in the air, making it nearly impossible to breathe and causing rampant respiratory disease. Miners were often injured or killed by cave-ins, falls, asphyxiation, and dynamite explosions. Housing for single workers was makeshift; in the smaller camps, it usually consisted only of tents. Often, 20 men were packed into one room. Families fared no better, residing without ventilation, electricity, or light in hovels made of wood and aluminum boards. There was no heat, and the cold was unbearable. Two families often shared two-room, dirt-floored apartments in the barracks.

The mines recruited workers from the southern agricultural regions, especially the Central Valley, where the concentration of landholding pushed landless people to seek work in the mines and cities. *Enganchadores* (less-than-honest recruiters) haunted the bars and plazas, buying drinks for hungry, desperate men, getting them drunk, and convincing them to sign work contracts. The following morning, these men woke up, hung over, only to find themselves on a train bound for the north, often having been advanced money from the enganchadores that had to be worked off. Because the mining companies needed workers who were at full strength to do the arduous work, they often rejected men supplied by these recruiters.

Agricultural labor went back and forth between the farming regions and the northern mines, and levels of turnover in the labor force were high. Many rural workers spent a year in the mines to earn the relatively high wages and then returned home to pay their debts or settle on a plot of land. Others migrated to the mines during the agricultural off-season to accumulate enough money to buy their own land. Still others worked just long enough to amass some cash and then left without notice. The companies did not always pay departing workers what they were owed. In 1917, El Teniente employees averaged only 18 to 20 days' work. The high job turnover had numerous causes, including the harsh working conditions; exhaustion, injury, and illness; and racial discrimination, especially from foreign supervisors employed by the large companies.

Women moved in and out of the camps, working as domestic servants, preparing and selling food and alcohol, and working as prostitutes. Women came to the camps mostly independent of men, looking to earn and save money, perhaps to start again elsewhere. They ran their own households, raised children, and struggled mightily to make ends meet. Formal marriage was infrequent, because life at the mines was too transient.

Both men and women resisted the efforts of large foreign companies to institute labor discipline. Mobility and independence were highly valued by the workers and widely opposed by the companies. It took decades to instill the industrial work ethic into rural workers.

Workers and bosses frequently clashed over control of aspects of everyday life. This struggle was a microcosm of the relationship between the upper classes and lower classes throughout Latin America during the nineteenth century.

Questions for Discussion

Compare the lives of Chilean miners to those of Argentine gauchos. What were the social and economic processes that gradually limited their independence? How did the miners assert their control over their own lives?

small remuneration on the great estates or abandoned their villages to labor in the mines and cities or across the U.S. border. The ownership of land was concentrated among the upper classes. At the same time, in some areas, such as northern Mexico and the Argentine Pampas, the number of owners of small farms increased. In the Mexican north, small holders were a vocal and prosperous group that deeply resented unfairly high taxes and government centralization.

In Argentina, rural conditions for farm tenants, gauchos, shepherds, and seasonal laborers varied. Landowners no longer recognized any traditional, patriarchal obligations to look after the welfare of their employees, in return for which they had received both labor and loyalty. As in Mexico, there was a sector of small farmers, mostly tenants, who increased their numbers and prospered. By the 1910s, however, many tenants, chronically in debt to suppliers, lived in desperate conditions.

In both rural Argentina and Mexico, the onslaught of centralization grew more intrusive, because landowners and governments sought not only to extend their control to local governance but also to modernize owner–labor relations. This meant that the ruling classes attempted to transform age-old customs and traditions that lay at the core of rural society. Regional autonomy remained strong in Argentina, but rural society changed to suit the needs of the estancieros. In Mexico, however, where the traditional village structure remained strong despite unending assaults by the national government, rural protests led to revolution in 1910.

Mass Movements of People

Latin American leaders, even before independence, had dreamed of populating their vast nations with immigrants from Europe as part of their effort to modernize their economies. For the upper class and intellectuals, disdainful of their indigenous and mestizo brethren, an influx of Europeans was the way to "get rid of the primitive element of our popular masses." Domingo Sarmiento, the liberal ideologue who was president of Argentina (1868–1874), claimed that only mass immigration could "drown in waves of industry the Creole rabble, inept, uncivil, and coarse that stops our attempt to civilize the

TABLE 11.2

Destination of European Emigrants to Latin America, c. 1820–1932

Country	Number of Immigrants
Argentina	6,501,000
Brazil	4,361,000
Cuba	1,394,000
Uruguay	713,000
Mexico	270,000
Chile	90,000
Venezuela	70,000
Peru	30,000
Paraguay	21,000

Source: Copyright © 1998, The Regents of the University of California.

nation." Despite the fervent wishes of upper classes almost everywhere, few Latin American countries attracted many immigrants. Five nations, Argentina, Brazil, Uruguay, Cuba, and Mexico, drew the preponderance of the new arrivals.

From 1860 to 1920, 45 million people left Europe to go to the Western Hemisphere (see Table 11.2). Massive immigration occurred in Argentina, Brazil, and Cuba. From 1904 to 1914, on average, 100,000 immigrants a year found their way from Italy and Spain to Argentina. Much of the new middle and working classes derived from the immigrant and migrant population. The export economies demanded labor and, consequently, Peruvian cotton and sugar industries brought in Chinese coolies, the construction of the Panama Canal drew British West Indians, and the Dominican Republic exploited Haitian workers for plantations. By the beginning of the twentieth century, then, an increasingly diverse population demanded a say in the affairs of Latin American nations.

POLITICS IN THE AGE OF MODERNIZATION

The spectacular growth in Latin America's national economies in the late nineteenth and early twentieth centuries was accompanied by an equally impressive degree of political stability that stood in marked contrast to the recurring political upheavals that had occurred during the first few decades after independence. Political stability fostered economic growth by guaranteeing a safe climate for domestic and foreign investment. Economic growth, in turn, gave the ruling classes the tools they needed to maintain order—professionalized and better-equipped armies to repress dissidents and sometimes act as arbiters of political disputes, railroads to carry troops quickly to the scene of any potential disorder, and jobs to keep the middle classes happy. The philosophy of positivism was the ideological underpinning of the ruling classes during this era.

Developed by Frenchman Auguste Comte (1798–1857) and infused with social Darwinism by Herbert Spencer (1820–1902), positivism emphasized reason, science, order, and progress, which fit nicely into the efforts of the Latin American upper classes to modernize their nations.

The political stability of the age of modernization assumed a variety of forms. In Argentina and Brazil, ranchers and planters played a dominant role in national politics. Chile demonstrated a fair degree of democracy, while in Peru an "Aristocratic Republic" held sway. The long dictatorships of Porfirio Díaz (1876–1911) in Mexico and Antonio Guzmán Blanco (1870–1888) in Venezuela brought a measure of peace and prosperity at least for those who enjoyed the favor of the regime in power.

The rise of the new middle and urban working classes and the widespread encroachments on traditional rural politics and society undermined this stability. In 1910, Mexico burst into revolution that tore it apart for nearly a decade. In other countries, political parties representing the new classes and labor unions formed to contest upper-class rule. By the first decade of the twentieth century, the challenges to the ruling classes were profound.

A Modernized Military

Latin American military establishments reflected the transformations of the times. In Argentina, Brazil, Chile, and Peru, upper classes sought to modernize and professionalize the armed services. Latin American governments imported European consultants to update and professionalize their militaries. These foreign missions inculcated a sense of separateness, nationalism, and impatience, which reconstructed the military in a way that ultimately made it the major threat to democracy in the region. The military was a crucial ally of the upper classes, for the two groups envisioned similar futures of order and economic development. As the social pressures from below increased, self-proclaimed professional, apolitical, incorruptible military officers came to despise civilian politicians. Concurrently, middle-class people entered the armed services as a route toward upward mobility. As a result, Latin American militaries were integral participants to the struggles over the "Social Question."

The revamped militaries recreated their officer corps through education at special military academies and a career system based on merit. The new career routes were meant to keep the young officers away from politics. Technology changed the military, as it did society as a whole. Railroads, cannons, rifles, machine guns, and telegraphs altered warfare. Ironically, professionalization took place when the region was at peace. After the War of the Pacific, there were no more external wars until the Chaco War between Paraguay and Bolivia in the 1930s. Nonetheless, militaries expanded their role in society and politics.

Isolated and confident (though untested in most cases), Latin American militaries set themselves up as arbitrators of their nations and saw themselves as saviors of their fatherlands. One Argentine army officer wrote in 1911: "The army is the nation. It is the external armor that guarantees the cohesive operation of its parts and preserves it from shocks and falls." No constitutional guarantees, moreover, could dissuade the military from its duty to ensure that governments responded to the needs of the nation. But the military was far from unified. As in the upper classes, there were divisions between those who those who wanted to crush all dissidents and those who were willing to compromise with the new urban classes. In Chapter 12, we will see how these disagreements evolved as the militaries asserted more power and influence.

The Rule of the Ranchers and Planters: Argentina and Brazil

A pattern emerged across Latin America in which export-dominated economies experienced successive booms and busts, with the downturns leading to political unrest and sometimes rebellion. This pattern was evident in Argentina and Brazil during the depression of the 1890s, though none of the resulting rebellions overthrew the existing order. The large landowners of Buenos Aires and the Pampas and the coffee planters of Brazil who dominated politics in their respective nations from the mid-nineteenth century until the 1920s were willing to concede very little, if anything, to the new groups. In Argentina, the large landowners accommodated only the middle classes, while harshly repressing the urban working class. The Brazilian upper class stubbornly refused any compromise. Eventually, it would split over tactics toward the new classes.

General Julio A. Roca dominated Argentine politics at the end of the century, first through puppets from 1892 to 1898 and then as president from 1898 to 1904, using a combination of patronage and force. He advocated economic growth financed through foreign investment in the export sector. Eventually his support base among landowners split into two factions, one that supported him and his hard line toward the lower classes and the other that sought progressive reform. Fortunately for the upper classes, the new classes also divided. The middle class took refuge in the Radical Party (Unión Cívica Radical), while the working class divided its allegiance among various leftist parties centered in Buenos Aires.

The Radical Party challenged the rule of the landowners, staging two revolts during the 1890s. In response the upper classes consented to expand voting rights to all males through the Sáenz Peña Law of 1912. The Radicals changed their violent tactics and triumphed in the presidential election of 1916 with Hipólito Yrigoyen (1916–1922, 1928–1930).

The Buenos Aires working class divided into anarchists and socialists. The anarchists sought to obtain better conditions for workers by means of the general strike. In 1910, a government crackdown against threatened demonstrations at the nation's centennial broke the movement. Argentine socialists were moderates, who supported democracy and sought primarily to raise living standards by raising wages and lowering prices. They also advocated women's suffrage. Neither anarchists nor socialists made more than a passing mark on Argentine electoral politics. Nonetheless, they frightened enough of those in power into making some concessions to the lower classes.

Yrigoyen proved a masterful politician, building a formidable political machine founded on patronage. However, the Radicals, never in control of both houses of Congress, were neither able nor inclined to implement extensive reforms. Yrigoyen confronted his greatest crisis in 1919, when strikes in Buenos Aires led to widespread violence. The Radicals sided with the upper classes and crushed the unions in what became known as the Tragic Week (*Semana Trágica*). This instance of the middle class siding with the upper class in confrontation with workers set the pattern for the next century of politics in Latin America.

In Brazil, the emergent classes were weaker and the upper classes stronger than in Argentina. Regionalism remained a major force, with state governments more influential than the national government. In the 1880s, Brazil experienced two enormous political and economic shocks. First, the monarchy proclaimed the abolition of slavery on May 13, 1888. Then, on November 15, 1889, the army overthrew the Empire, thus beginning the First Republic (1889–1930). Thereafter, a fragile alliance of state upper classes ruled Brazil until this arrangement broke down in 1930 at the outset of the Great Depression.

At first, the military ruled. The Republic's first two presidents were military officers. Eventually, large landowners took the reins of power, sharing control with state-level alliances of local political bosses, known as colonels, who presided over the rural hinterlands through a strict system of patron–client relations. The colonels' clients obligated themselves to vote as ordered in return for patronage and protection.

An alliance of São Paulo coffee planters and Minas Gerais cattle barons controlled the national government. By agreement, the major states, Minas Gerais and São Paulo, alternated their representatives in the presidency. (This agreement was the so-called *café com leite* alliance.) Of 11 presidents during the First Republic, 6 came from São Paulo and 3 from Minas Gerais. A third state, Rio Grande do Sul, muscled its way into the mix after the turn of the century. Brazilian states exercised control over their own finances and militaries. The State of São Paulo had a well-equipped state militia with as many as 14,000 men. State governments could even contract foreign loans. The coffee planters openly used government for their own economic gain, relying on the national and state governments to buy their surplus crops. Brazil's slower industrialization delayed the development of pressure from below for a decade or two after other Latin American nations confronted the social question.

Democracy in Chile

Chile's landed upper class ruled until 1920. But it, too, was vulnerable to the downturns of the export economy. As in Argentina and Brazil, the depression of the 1890s brought unrest. President José Manuel Balmaceda (1886–1891) encountered unparalleled rancor because to many Chileans he symbolized the corrupt, coercive system so long in power. Balmaceda's opposition, which sought to hold free elections and modify the balance of power, stalemated Congress in 1890, virtually paralyzing the national government. When the president closed Congress (which was legal), it established a rival government, and its forces defeated Balmaceda in an 8-month-long civil war.

During Chile's so-called Parliamentary Republic from 1891 to 1920, Chilean politics reached an impasse. The government's inability to meet the demands of the emerging classes led to recurring crises during the 1920s. The working class increased in numbers as people moved into the mines and cities from the countryside. Inevitably, they sought ways to protest their brutal labor and living conditions through unions. In the 1890s, there were riots in the nitrate fields, where conditions were unimaginable. Conflict worsened in the first decades of the new century. Disturbances in Santiago in 1905 cost the lives of 60 people. There were economic depressions in 1907–1908 and after World War I. The worsening economic crisis led to terrible strikes in 1919; one in Santiago involved 50,000 workers. Arturo Alessandri emerged in 1920, promising to accommodate the demands of the new classes, and won election to the presidency. The upper class continued to be unwilling to compromise, creating a political stalemate. Reformist military officers, impatient for change, overthrew Alessandri in 1924. Only then was the impasse broken, but only temporarily.

The Aristocratic Republic: Peru

Thirty or 40 families, consisting of large landowners and businesspeople tied closely to the export sector, dominated Peruvian politics at the turn of the century. These upper-class families often were more familiar with Paris than with the Peruvian countryside. Racist, as well, they viewed Indians and castas as barbarians. Nonetheless, from the mid-1890s until 1919, Peru experienced an era of relative peace and stability, known as the "Aristocratic Republic." Like everywhere else, however, the inevitable downturns eventually brought discontent and unrest.

The War of the Pacific (1879–1883) left the nation's economy and politics in ruins. Exports fell sharply. Andrés Avelino Cáceres, a hero of the War of the Pacific, brought some order to Peruvian politics and government finances from 1885 to 1895, first as president and then through puppet rulers. His successor Nicolás de Piérola (1879–1881, 1895–1899) presided over a considerable measure of development, by expanding exports of agricultural commodities and minerals. However, increased agricultural exports caused landowners to expand their territory at the expense of individual and communal landholdings, which created widespread unrest.

During World War I, Peru experienced rebellions in the countryside, uprisings of Chinese immigrant laborers, and protests by university students. Social unrest exploded in 1919 with huge strikes in Lima and Callao. The presidential election in 1919 returned to power former president Augusto B. Leguía (1908–1912, 1919–1930), who ruled for the next 11 years. His solution to the nation's economic problems was an extensive program of public works construction that was devised to provide employment.

Dictatorship: Mexico

In Mexico, dictator General Porfirio Díaz ruled for 35 years (1876–1911), in conjunction with the landed upper class, the military, and a cadre of professional bureaucrats. Building his regime on a shrewd combination of consensus and coercion, Díaz wove an intricate web of alliances among once fragmented regional upper classes. He bound them together using the revenues generated by his export-based economic strategy. Don Porfirio, as he was called, was a masterful politician who was simultaneously admired and

LATIN AMERICAN LIVES

EVARISTO MADERO (1829–1911), PATRIARCH OF THE NORTH

In 1910 a 37-year-old rancher and industrialist from the northern state of Coahuila, Mexico, Francisco I. Madero, led a political movement against the long-term regime of Porfirio Díaz, setting off what was to become the Mexican Revolution. Defying enormous odds, he overthrew the dictator and became president. Not 2 years after his victory, he fell to assassins' bullets. The martyred Madero achieved perhaps the highest rank in the pantheon of Mexico's heroes.

Sometimes forgotten is the fact that Francisco I. Madero was the scion of one of the richest families in Mexico. The Madero, based in Parras, Coahuila, and Monterrey, Nuevo León, were at the fulcrum of the crucial network of northern entrepreneurs who were crucial to the Mexican economy from the mid-nineteenth century through the Porfiriato, Revolution, and postrevolution. Evaristo Madero, its patriarch, built a great empire through shrewd entrepreneurship and familial and political connections. In 1910, the *El Paso Morning Times* referred to him as a "Mexican Croesus." He had a personal fortune estimated at US$20,000,000. The Madero were important cattle raisers, cotton growers, and guayule producers in the Laguna region of Coahuila, and were involved with many industrial and banking concerns, among which was the largest Mexican-owned mineral smelting operation in the nation. Family members reportedly owned 7 million acres of land, with holdings in Chihuahua, Coahuila, Durango, San Luis Potosí, and Zacatecas.

Despite their vast economic resources, the Madero's influence in politics was limited by the patriarch's difficult relations with dictator Díaz and his representative in northeastern Mexico, General Bernardo Reyes. The family's ambiguous relations with Díaz at times thwarted its economic interests. Subsequently, family members stood at the forefront of local and statewide opposition to the national regime during the 1890s and the first decade of the twentieth century. Eventually, this led to Francisco I. Madero's seemingly quixotic campaign for the presidency in 1910.

The patriarch of the family, Evaristo, was born in the late 1820s. He began his career as a freighter along the recently drawn border between Mexico and the United States in the years after the war between the two nations. At first he operated mule and wagon trains in Coahuila, soon moving on to trading contraband silver bullion, wool, and hides across the border in return for dry goods and manufactures. Evaristo Madero earned a fortune in border trade, in particular generating enormous profits from Confederate cotton during the U.S. Civil War in the 1860s, when the Union Navy blockaded southern ports, leaving only outlets through Mexico to export to markets in Europe. In his illicit trade, Madero benefited from the protection of Santiago Vidaurri, then the political boss of Nuevo León and Coahuila. Evaristo used the income from his mercantile business to buy land and expand into industry and banking. His first investments were a huge ranch in Coahuila that included an old winery, then a number of flour mills, and a textile mill. From the late 1860s to the 1880s he bought large haciendas in the Laguna region.

The Madero relied heavily on their family connections. Evaristo Madero had 18 children, and between them his children, grandchildren, and great grandchildren numbered 124. Many married into prominent families. His first marriage in 1847 brought him his brother-in-law and long-term business partner Antonio V. Hernández. Also important were his son Francisco's marriage to Mercedes González Treviño, a member of a family of important landowners and politicians in Nuevo León, and his daughters' marriages to Lorenzo González Treviño, Melchor Villarreal, and Viviano Villarreal. He also had marriage ties to prominent Monterrey families such as Zambrano and Sada Muguerza. With nine sons and numerous sons-in-law, he had a substantial pool of managers to succeed him.

Evaristo was governor of Coahuila from 1880 to 1884, when Porfirio Díaz, whose rebellion in 1876 he had opposed, allied with rivals to force him out. The Madero family retained local influence in Parras and continued to compete in state politics but was unable to reestablish itself at the top. Despite maintaining cordial relations with the científico faction within the national regime, the Madero found themselves badly disadvantaged by a series of decisions made by the old dictator during the first decade of the twentieth century. This quite likely led to considerable disgruntlement among family members toward Díaz and may very well have led to Evaristo's grandson's revolution. Evaristo died in 1911 before Francisco I. became president.

Questions for Discussion

Do you think that there was a link between the Madero family's exclusion from political power in Coahuila by Díaz and Francisco I. Madero's opposition to the regime? What is more important in causing revolutions, the desire for political access or for economic gain?

feared. He was a war hero, recognized as one of the commanders at Puebla, where Mexican troops won a great military victory against French invaders on May 5, 1862. (The *Cinco de Mayo*, or Fifth of May, is a national holiday in Mexico.) Díaz was often magnanimous in victory, when it was to his political advantage. He could be equally ruthless, however. When, early in his regime, a subordinate asked him what to do with captured rebels, Díaz told him to "kill them in cold blood." His rural police, the *Rurales*, kept order in the countryside. (One practice was to shoot prisoners, even those guilty of minor offenses, while allegedly trying to escape.)

During Díaz's rule, Mexico's economy grew spectacularly. Domestic peace and the end of foreign invasions combined with burgeoning markets for Mexican agricultural commodities and minerals and the inflow of international capital to cause unprecedented economic expansion. The Díaz government oversaw the investment of $1 billion in U.S. capital and a ninefold increase in trade from 1877 to 1911 and sponsored the construction of more than 10,000 miles of railroad.

Despite peace and prosperity, however, Mexico's economy and politics had a dark underside. As did other export economies, Mexico endured periodic booms and busts. There were downturns during the mid-1880s, the early 1890s, and from 1907 to 1909.

"The Liberal Party under the regime of Porfirio Diaz" (1910).

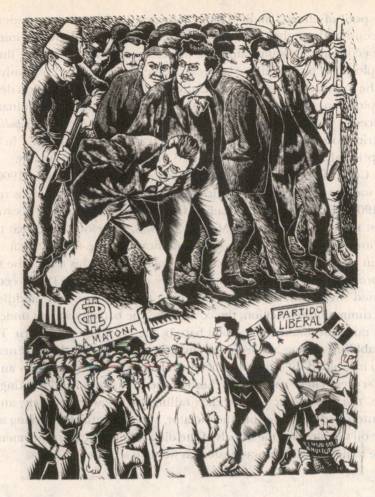

The booms brought prosperity, but the busts caused widespread suffering among the urban and rural working class. Economic depressions caused political disruptions by undermining the conditions of the emerging working and middle classes and by unbalancing the delicate system of political arrangements between Díaz and regional upper classes. Díaz's web of political alliances depended on his ability to reward cooperation with jobs, tax exemptions, subsidies for businesses, and other benefits. The economic downturn in 1907 allowed him insufficient resources to pay for cooperation. Ungrateful upper-class allies looked for opportunities to free themselves from the dictator.

While the economic crisis undermined his support among the upper classes, the countryside had reached the point of rebellion. Improved transportation and widened markets for agricultural commodities both in Mexico and abroad had sharply increased land values. Political officials and large landowners, particularly in the mid-1880s and in the decade after 1900, undertook to expropriate the lands of small owners and the communally held lands of Indian villages in order to expand both their landholdings and the pool of cheap, landless labor. As a result, there was an undercurrent of agrarian discontent throughout the dictatorship. This discontent evolved into crisis in 1907, when the economic downturn and the upper classes' land grabbing limited the alternative employment possibilities of landless people in rural areas. Previously, they had found jobs in the mines, the cities, and the United States, but the depression deprived them of these employment opportunities. The Díaz dictatorship also had eliminated elections to local offices by creating a system of appointed district leaders (*jefes políticos*). Some of these district bosses proved extraordinarily intrusive, meddling even in private matters. Not surprisingly, country people protested this loss of local autonomy.

Coinciding crises helped bring down the dictatorship after 1900. The most immediate was the furor over Díaz's succession. Díaz was 74 when he was reelected as president in 1904. His vice president, Ramón Corral, was given the post because he was one of the most unpopular officials in Mexico and was, therefore, no threat to Díaz. None of the obvious successors dared to show ambition, despite the fact that if Díaz was reelected again in 1910 at 80, few expected he would live out his term. The second crisis was the depression of 1907, which erased many of the gains of Díaz's economic miracle and ruined the businesses of the emerging middle class. The middle class had suffered discrimination in taxation, the courts, and the banking system under Díaz's regime, and this rampant unfairness was laid bare by the economic downturn. The last crisis was the squabbling among and eventual division of the upper classes. Enemies of the dictator, who had bided their time and been content to be bought off, saw an opportunity to even old scores. These combined crises left the urban and rural working classes with little to lose, the embryonic middle class falling back toward poverty, and the upper classes uninterested in supporting the dictator, at best, or quietly working against him, at worst. The oil that greased the wheels of the dictator's political arrangements evaporated. It was time to fight, and Díaz was ousted, as we shall see later.

MODERNIZATION AND RESISTANCE

The situations described above specifically caused the disintegration of the Mexican dictatorship, but similar conditions existed generally throughout Latin America during the early part of the twentieth century. The export boom presided over by the upper classes disguised inherently unfair societies everywhere, because the prosperity accrued to only a small minority. The new middle classes were extremely vulnerable to economic downturns and saw their modest gains erode during the depression following the turn of the century and the inflation of World War I. The mines and new factories paid pitiful wages and offered miserable working conditions for new migrants from the countryside and immigrants from abroad. Workers agitated not only for better compensation and working conditions but also against the regimentation that domestic and foreign employers tried to impose upon their daily lives. Meanwhile, rural people lost their lands and livelihoods to the forces of the export economy. Some migrated in search of better opportunities elsewhere, but others stayed where they were and revolted in an attempt to regain or retain their landholdings and their control over their daily lives. National leaders in a number of countries grappled with the question of how best to draw indigenous peoples into the new capitalist nation-state. Resistance then was inevitable in the face of the intrusion of the world market and national authorities.

Indigenous Peoples

Many Latin Americans of the upper class and urbanized middle classes regarded the indigenous population as a serious impediment to national progress. Positivists in Mexico shared this view, and the Díaz regime alternated between ignoring and trying to exterminate indigenous peoples. Apaches in the north of Mexico were at times subject to bounties on their scalps. Conversely, some of the victorious factions in the revolution that overthrew Díaz adopted a conscious policy of glorifying the nation's indigenous heritage. Archaeologists and historians rediscovered the great cultures that had existed in Latin America before the arrival of the Europeans, while the brilliant muralists of the 1920s and 1930s illuminated the Indian past.

The place of indigenous peoples also provoked much discussion in Peru, where the humiliating defeat in the War of the Pacific caused a reevaluation of the nation's priorities and policies. Peruvian intellectuals concluded that Indians required "reform." Fired by the 1889 novel *Aves sin nido* by Clorinda Matto de Turner, which exposed the harsh exploitation endured by Indians in a small Andean town, a new movement, *indigenismo,* resolved to rediscover Indian Peru. U.S. archaeologists rediscovered Machu Picchu, the long-lost Incan city, further fueling interest in pre-European Peru. After World War I, the indigenismo movement shifted from willingness to study Indians to a more revolutionary stance. A few envisioned a new nationalism that glorified the Indian past. A second strain of indigenismo arose from José Carlos Mariátegui, the noted Marxist intellectual, who tied indigenismo to socialism. He advocated radical land reform to end the centuries-old oppression of Indians by the hacienda system.

Resistance in the Countryside

Not everyone accepted the notion that modernization and economic development were good, as is illustrated by the Latin Americans who threw stones at passing railroad cars. The first, and perhaps most crucial, source of opposition to modernization arose in the countryside. During the first half of the nineteenth century, political disruptions and inadequate transportation kept land values down. As we observed in Chapter 9, after mid-century, Liberals, following the models of England and the United States, attempted to create a class of small farmers that they believed would form the basis for both capitalism and democracy. Their efforts to break up the landholdings of the Catholic Church and communal indigenous villages backfired, however, because politicians and large landowners inevitably ended up with much of this property. A number of nations, notably Argentina and Mexico, gave away vast tracts of public lands to the politically well connected, which concentrated landholding even further.

Unlike the peaceful, political attempt to create social equity described above, country people sometimes violently resisted modernization. Two such movements erupted in Brazil. The first occurred in Canudos, an estate in the northern part of the state of Bahia, where Antônio Conselheiro and his followers set up a community in 1893. Located deep in the backlands, it grew into a considerable city of 20,000 to 30,000 people. The local upper class—and eventually the national government—viewed Canudos as a threat. Several military expeditions were sent to Canudos in an effort to oust the residents and break up the community, but the residents defeated the soldiers. Finally, in October of 1897, the federal army destroyed the city and slaughtered its last 5000 residents. The events were made famous by the book *Rebellion in the Backlands* by Euclídes da Cunha. Another movement, the *Contesdado,* took place in the border area between the states of Paraná and Santa Catarina in southern Brazil. The rebellion began in 1911, led by José María, who his followers regarded as a saint. The processes of modernization in rural and urban areas had alienated many of the people who joined the movement, including small farmers who had been thrown off their lands as railroads spread across the country and railroad workers who were abandoned to unemployment when their contracts expired. Despite the deaths of their leaders, including José María, rebels continued to fight until late 1915. Meanwhile, widespread banditry swept Brazil during the period of the Canudos and Contesdado rebellions. Many of the poor dark-skinned people who made up the majority of the rural population had lost their lands or ended up on the wrong side of local political disputes, and they filled the bandits' ranks, having few other options.

The Mexican Revolution

Nowhere was the impact of the rapidly developing export economy dominated by foreign investors clearer than in Mexico, where a diverse coalition of profoundly discontented people waged a revolution of unprecedented duration and cost. In 1910, a multiclass alliance of dissidents from the upper class, middle-class people who had suffered financial ruin in the depression of 1907, country people whose lands the upper class had expropriated, and unemployed workers rallied around Francisco I. Madero, a disaffected, wealthy landowner, who toppled Porfirio Díaz from power. As we have learned, the depression of 1907, the uncertainty of succession, and the deteriorating state of the army and police had badly weakened the Díaz regime. In the spring of 1911, the coalition ousted Díaz, who prudently embarked on a comfortable retirement in Paris, never to return to Mexico. But the consensus among Madero's followers soon crumbled as landowners and landless country people clashed over land reform and the middle and lower classes disagreed over the importance of property rights. Dormant regionalism, suppressed temporarily by Díaz, reawakened as well.

In 1913, supporters of Díaz took advantage of the disintegration of the revolutionary coalition and the resurgence of regionalism to briefly reestablish the old regime without Díaz. General Victoriano Huerta, Madero's most important military commander, took over the reins of the counterrevolutionary movement, betraying Madero and ordering his execution. Others then formed a loose partnership of revolutionary movements to defeat Huerta in 1914. Their leaders included Venustiano Carranza, another alienated northern landowner; Pancho Villa, a bandit-businessman from Chihuahua (also in the north); and Emiliano Zapata, a village leader from the state of Morelos (just south of Mexico City). This alliance did not last even as long as Madero's. Carranza, representing the dissident landowners, clashed with the *Zapatistas* (followers of Zapata) who advocated wide-ranging land reform. Villa and Carranza disliked each other intensely. Villa and Zapata allied since they both stood for the lower classes. The three factions set upon each other in a brutal civil war that lasted until 1917. In those 3 years, there was virtually no functioning government in Mexico.

By 1917, however, Carranza emerged triumphant with the brilliant assistance of his best general, Álvaro Obregón, another northerner. Carranza owed much of his victory to his ability to win over the working class and some rural people with promises (later unfulfilled) of reforms. Carranza also appealed to members of the middle class because he defended private property rights and offered political patronage. The revolutionaries promulgated the Constitution of 1917, which provided for extensive land reform, workers' rights, and other wide-reaching reforms. Carranza then split with Obregón over the extent to which the government would implement the provisions of the constitution. Obregón, who favored reforms, overthrew Carranza in 1920 and made himself president. Meanwhile, Zapata and Villa continued guerrilla warfare until 1919 and 1920, respectively. Mexico's bloody struggle had lasted a decade and cost the lives of between 1 and 2 million people. The revolution also devastated the nation's economy. It would be well into the 1930s before most economic indicators recovered to 1910 levels.

CONCLUSION

In 1920, middle-aged and elderly Latin Americans could look back on the enormous changes that had occurred in their lifetimes. Those who lived in the cities saw signs of "progress" all around them—streetcars, automobiles, modern office buildings, banks, and factories. In the more fashionable parts of towns, they could marvel at the lavish homes and other symbols of the upper classes' conspicuous consumption. More people could read and write than ever before. Outside the cities, railroads crisscrossed the countryside, although they were concentrated along routes that served the new export economies. Large estates and modern farm machinery produced crops for sale in nearby cities and overseas markets (while small farmers, however, found it increasingly hard to produce the subsistence crops they needed to support themselves and their families).

With the notable exception of Mexicans, this generation of Latin Americans had seen fewer wars than their parents or grandparents, but only the most naïve among them would have predicted that this peace would last indefinitely. Some of them had witnessed massive strikes by urban workers in the turbulent aftermath of World War I.

How Historians Understand   WHY DO PEOPLE REBEL?

The era from 1880 to 1920 was a tumultuous one for Latin America. Emergent working and middle classes jostled for a place in politics, economy, and society. Upper classes struggled to maintain their positions. Country people sought a return of the protection they had enjoyed under the Catholic monarchs of the Iberian empires. Technological innovations disrupted society at all levels. The international movement of ideas, people, and money reinvented the ways that men and women worked, lived, and interacted. Yet, despite all these upheavals and rapid changes, only in one country, Mexico, did the people rise up in revolution. It is an enduring and important question in Latin American history as to why only the Mexican the lower and middle classes allied to destroy the old regime.

Most people in Latin America had lived with a (sometimes considerable) degree of day-to-day oppression. The daily struggle to subsist consumed their days; they had little time or energy to plan, let alone carry out, a rebellion. At some points in history, however, individuals have ignored survival in order to rise up against their oppressors (though such occurrences are rare). Historians have almost universally failed to discern what causes such rebels to risk everything.

In the case of the Mexican Revolution, as in any social revolt, historians and sociologists have numerous questions: Why did some groups or individuals rebel and

Ordinary people from central and southern Mexico rose up against Porfirio Díaz in 1910.

others did not? Why did some country people, such as permanent residents on the haciendas, remain uninvolved, while northern small landowners led the overthrow of Porfirio Díaz? Why did some large land-owning families join the revolution, while others fought it to the death?

Most difficult to answer, perhaps, is the question of why individuals participated in uprisings, because very few sources exist to give scholars insight into individuals' motivations. Historians researching the Mexican Revolution have compiled many oral interviews and discovered criminal court records, both of which reveal personal stories. But these sources are not available for all regions or eras.

Of all the groups that rose in rebellion against Díaz in 1910, the most elusive have been country people. Everyone concedes that rural people were central to the Mexican Revolution, but there is disagreement as to why exactly they revolted. Did country people fight to restore their lost lands? Did they resist the encroachments of centralized government on their local prerogatives? Do people risk their lives for land or religion or local autonomy? It is extremely difficult for twenty-first–century historians to penetrate the worldview of late nineteenth-century rural dwellers.

Historians and social scientists have formulated various theories, based on such factors as rising expectations, class conflict, moral economy, and mob behavior, to try to understand why people rebel. The paucity of evidence, however, has made it impossible for scholars to validate or confirm any of these theories of motivation. Analysts have tried to circumvent the lack of direct evidence (also called *primary sources,* such as accounts of participants' actual words) by examining the possible grievances, the economic circumstances, and the political crises that might have alchemized discontent into revolution. Thus, historians build circumstantial cases without proof of causality.

Perhaps the most convincing and plausible attempts to understand the mental and emotional states of various revolutionaries have appeared in the works of fiction written during and after the Mexican Revolution. The works of such authors as Mariano Azuela (*The Underdogs*), Martín Luis Guzmán (*The Eagle and the Serpent*), and Carlos Fuentes (*The Death of Artemio Cruz*) give insights into the rebels' reality through the imagined conversations and thoughts of their characters. The novelists often portray the revolutionaries as petty, greedy, and murderous, with few heroes among them. (For instance, Azuela's Demetrio Macías was less than admirable.)

How, then, do historians obtain an accurate picture of the revolutionaries and their motivations? It is unlikely that we ever can: Pieces of the puzzle will always be missing.

Questions for Discussion

Without benefit of an extensive written record to which to refer, how do you think historians can understand the thinking of working-class and country people? How can the twenty-first–century historian "get into the heads" of people who lived decades, even centuries, in the past?

Rural discontent was in evidence everywhere as well. Intellectuals and some political figures began to carve out a more active role for indigenous peoples, and women began to demand changes in the home, the legal system, and society as a whole. In Chapter 12, we shall see how Latin Americans met these and other serious challenges in the coming decades.

LEARNING MORE ABOUT LATIN AMERICANS

Azuela, Mariano. *The Underdogs*. Trans. Frederick H. Fornoff (Prospect Herights, IL: Waveland Press, 2002).

Dore, Elizabeth, and Maxine Molyneux, eds. *Hidden Histories of Gender and the State in Latin America* (Durham, NC: Duke University Press, 2000). Essays on women, the state, and society.

Gwynne, Robert N., and Cristobal Kay, eds. *Latin America Transformed: Globalization and Modernity*, 2nd ed. (New York: Arnold, 2004). The impact of vast change in the twentieth century.

Haber, Stephen, ed. *How Latin America Fell Behind: Essays on the Economic Histories of Brazil and Mexico, 1800–1914* (Stanford, CA: Stanford University Press, 1997). Essays that attempt to account for the lack of Latin American economic development.

Hart, John Mason. *Revolutionary Mexico: The Coming and Process of the Mexican Revolution* (Berkeley, CA: University of California Press, 1987).

Knight, Alan. *The Mexican Revolution*. 2 vols. (Durham, NC: Duke University Press, 1994). The best history of the Revolution in English.

Lavrín, Asuncíon. *Women, Feminism, and Social Change: Argentina, Chile, and Uruguay, 1890–1940* (Lincoln, NE: University of Nebraska Press, 1995). Traces the feminist movement in the Southern Cone.

Poniatowska, Elena. *Las Soldaderas: Women of the Mexican Revolution* (El Paso, TX: Cinco Punto Press, 2006).

Wasserman, Mark. *Everyday Life and Politics in Nineteenth Century Mexico: Men, Women, and War* (Albuquerque, NM: University of New Mexico Press, 2000).

Weaver, Frederick Stirton. *Latin America in the World Economy* (Boulder, CO: Westview Press, 2000). An overview of the role of external economic factors in Latin American economic development.

12

BETWEEN REVOLUTIONS:
THE NEW POLITICS OF CLASS AND THE ECONOMIES
OF IMPORT SUBSTITUTION INDUSTRIALIZATION,
1920–1959

THE ERA FRAMED by the end of the Mexican Revolution (1910–1920) and the beginning of the Cuban Revolution (1959) continued, augmented, and refocused the conflicts and dilemmas of Latin America's politics and economy, which emerged from the transformations experienced in the preceding four decades. Battered by recurring crises—two world wars and a debilitating depression—and the exigencies of the superpower confrontation we know as the Cold War, Latin America struggled to answer the questions raised at independence and discussed in Chapter 9: Who was to govern (and for whom) and how were they to govern? Latin American upper classes fiercely resisted the strident demands of the middle and urban working classes, whose rise we studied in Chapter 11. Refurbished and reformed militaries established themselves as crucial participants in politics, mostly as conservatives, but on occasion as moderate and even radical advocates of social justice. For the most part, however, the upper classes allied with the military against labor organizations and popularly based political parties, the primary advocates of the lower classes. Armed forces anointed themselves as the ultimate arbiters of civil society, intervening periodically when differing versions of democracy faltered.

The profound changes brought about by urbanization and incipient industrialization altered relationships not only between classes but also between men and women. Women entered the public political and economic arenas, forcing readjustments to traditional patriarchy. Old notions of women's role, sexuality, and honor underwent important transformations. During this period, women fought for and eventually won suffrage.

Constant battles between moderates and hard-liners in the upper classes and militaries were reflected in the rise and fall of democracy and dictatorship. Many members of the upper classes and allied military officers realized the necessity of altering the economic and political systems, at least so as to minimally satisfy the demands of the lower and middle classes for better living and working conditions and for electoral and economic fairness. Compromise was difficult because the ruling classes of most nations were no longer homogeneous, making consensus virtually unattainable, and intransigent elements of the upper class—military alliance were unwilling to make concessions. The most notable divisions arose because export economies had created a brash new class of industrialists and entrepreneurs whose interests were not always in harmony with the landowning class. The militaries were divided as well, usually between old-line upper-class senior officers and up-and-coming middle-class junior officers.

The lower classes strove for their voice in politics and the economy by joining labor unions, though these mostly served skilled workers. With expanded male suffrage, workers were valuable allies for rival middle- and upper-class political parties. Left political groups, such as the Socialists and Communists, experienced only modest success. With the exception of the brief Socialist Republic proclaimed in Chile in 1932 and Chile's and Cuba's popular front (alliances of Left and center political parties) governments of the late 1930s and early 1940s, none of the leftist parties ever shared national power. The working class more commonly attached itself to a rising political leader, such as Colonel Juan Perón (1946–1955, 1974–1976) in Argentina, who traded concessions, such as wage increases, for support. A number of other democratic leaders and dictators also relied on the support of the middle and lower classes. Thus, populism, comprised of cross-class alliances brought together by a charismatic leader advocating social reform, dominated the politics of the era.

The struggle for control over their everyday lives continued to be at the center of lower-class demands. Although the increasing migration of people to the cities muted somewhat the demands for local autonomy in the countryside, they remained at the core of Mexican politics into the 1940s (and perhaps longer). The strength of regionalism forced even dictators like Juan Perón in Argentina and Getúlio Vargas in Brazil to ally with provincial and state political bosses, who obtained the support of the people of the countryside by defending local customs and traditions.

At the same time, important sectors of the national ruling classes came to realize that they could not obtain their goals of modernization without national governments becoming more active in the economy. The prolonged economic crisis of the 1930s strengthened and expanded governments' role. Concerned with the industrial base of national security, the new industrialists and organized labor joined elements of the military to institute extensive tariff protection for domestic manufacturing. The resulting resurgent drive for modernization became known as import substitution industrialization.

Nonetheless, exports fueled the economies of Latin American nations throughout all the crises. The plight of the region depended on the booms and busts of the international markets for agricultural commodities and minerals. Political instability or stability and the choice between dictatorship and democracy often (though not always) derived from the status of the economies of the individual nations.

THREE CRISES AND THE BEGINNINGS OF INTENSIFIED GOVERNMENT INVOLVEMENT IN THE ECONOMY, 1920–1945

As we observed in Chapter 11, the export boom from the 1870s to the 1910s stimulated industrialization, mainly in the form of processing agricultural commodities. The boom ended after 1920, however, when three great crises—the two world wars and the Great Depression—disrupted international trade and capital markets for prolonged periods (1914–1919, 1929–1941, and 1939–1945). Latin American upper classes reassessed their nations' reliance on exporting commodities and importing consumer goods.

The Aftermath of World War I

World War I revealed the extreme uncertainties and costs of the booms and busts associated with economic reliance on exports. The war should have stimulated exports and benefited the region, as European countries placed their economies on a wartime footing. Instead, the war exposed Latin America's vulnerability to temporary stoppages in the flow of goods and capital back and forth across the Atlantic Ocean. During the early part of the war, the demand for Latin American commodities plummeted. Government revenues dropped sharply, which led to government deficits. When the demand for strategic materials finally rose, other factors, such as the rising cost of imports, mitigated the benefits. Latin American exports earned high prices, but only for a short period.

This brief boom proved detrimental to Latin American agriculture in the long term, because many farmers tried to respond to the temporary increase in demand by borrowing money to increase the amount of land under cultivation. When Europe recovered its agricultural capacity and the rest of the world regained access to European markets, these farmers faced ruin. The most startling case of this agricultural boom and bust was the Cuban "Dance of the Millions." In 2 years, sugar prices soared from 4 cents to more than 20 cents a pound, only to plunge to prices even lower than where they had begun. In anticipation of booming demand and prices, Cuban sugar growers greatly expanded landholdings and production, only to confront disaster when prices dropped.

With competition from abroad cut off by the war, domestic manufacturing seemingly had unprecedented opportunities. Unfortunately, machinery and capital

TIMELINE

1914–1918
World War I

1919–1930
Augusto B. Leguía, dictator of Peru

1924
Young military officers overthrow President Arturo Alessandri in Chile

1929–1941
Great Depression

1933
Cuban Revolution ousts dictator Gerardo Machado

1937
Getúlio Vargas overturns his own government and establishes the Estado Novo

1938
Lázaro Cárdenas expropriates foreign oil companies in Mexico

1939–1945
World War II

1946
Juan Perón elected president of Argentina

1952
Fulgencio Batista returns to Cuba as dictator

were not available. The United States furnished an alternative market, but during the war it could not supply Latin America with all the needed industrial equipment, materials, and capital.

Despite the lessons of the world war and the nasty, though brief, depression in 1920 and 1921, Latin American economies remained export oriented throughout the decade. Unfortunately, overall international trade grew far more slowly than it had in the previous decades. From 1913 to 1929, the volume of trade rose an average of only 1 percent per year. To make matters worse, Latin American nations confronted harsh postwar competition for this stagnant global market. It was nearly impossible to increase market shares of primary commodities because there were other, often cheaper, producers elsewhere. Latin American nations were already operating at high efficiency, so they could not significantly decrease costs.

Circumstances were right for the development of modern manufacturing. Urbanization had brought together a relatively more affluent population that demanded consumer goods. The expanding middle and laboring classes furnished a growing market. Improved transportation and communications expanded the market to the countryside. Domestic manufacturing, however, could not compete successfully against its external rivals unless protected by government. Internal markets were simply too small to obtain economies of scale.

The Great Depression

As the 1930s began, Latin American economies remained highly concentrated on a few export commodities sent to a handful of markets. For 10 countries (Bolivia, Brazil, Colombia, Cuba, the Dominican Republic, El Salvador, Honduras, Guatemala, Nicaragua, and Venezuela), one product in each accounted for at least 50 percent of the exports. Four nations, the United States, Great Britain, Germany, and France, provided 70 percent of the trade. This concentration put the region in serious jeopardy when the century's worst economic crisis hit.

The worldwide Great Depression wrecked havoc with Latin American economies. Between 1928 and 1932, export prices tumbled by more than half in 10 countries. Mineral producers in Bolivia, Chile, and Mexico were hit the worst, as both unit volume and prices declined. Argentina's exports fell from about $1.5 billion in 1929 to $561 million in 1932. The Cuban sugar industry was all but ruined.

Recovery from the depression began between 1931 and 1932. The fastest recoveries, where the gross domestic product (GDP) rose 50 percent or more from 1931 to 1939, took place in Brazil, Mexico, Chile, Cuba, Peru, Venezuela, Costa Rica, and Guatemala. Argentina, Colombia, and El Salvador came back more slowly, with their GDPs increasing 20 percent in these years. The countries worst off were Honduras, Nicaragua, Uruguay, Paraguay, and Panama. Real GDP in Colombia exceeded its predepression level in 1932. The same was true for Brazil in 1933, Mexico in 1934, and Argentina, El Salvador, and Guatemala in 1935, while Chile and Cuba, where the depression was most severe, recovered later in the decade. Honduras, solely dependent on bananas, did not regain its

Slice of Life   COLOMBIAN COFFEE FARM IN 1925

COFFEE IS PRODUCED in two distinct ways: on plantations (fazenda in Brazil, *finca* or hacienda elsewhere) and on small, family-operated farms. Two nations, Costa Rica and Colombia, are particularly known for the latter. Between 1920 and 1950, small producers came to dominate Colombian coffee production. Small holdings required, as one historian observed, a "lifetime struggle in which ingenuity, hard work, and a good measure of luck . . ." were crucial elements.

The small operators did not always own their own property. On the huge plantations in the older coffee regions, permanent workers (*arrendatarios*) obtained the right to farm a small parcel on which they grew corn, yucca, plantains, and sugarcane and raised fowl or livestock. In return for the use of the land, the worker undertook an obligation to labor ranging from a few days to nearly a whole month on the plantation, depending on the size and quality of his plot. The coffee estates also employed temporary workers, small farmers from other areas, contracted for harvest and paid according to the amount of coffee beans they picked. Temporary labor weeded the groves as well. A third type of worker, the *colono,* contracted to open up new lands for coffee production, clearing the land, planting new trees, and caring for them for 4 years. The colono then sold the trees to the plantation owner and renounced all rights to the land. The colono also cultivated food crops between the trees for family subsistence.

In the newer coffee regions, small- and medium-sized family farms predominated, the latter operated by sharecroppers or renters. The sharecroppers received half the harvest in return for caring for the trees and processing the beans. They received only one-third, however, if they did not dry and depulp the beans. Although some medium-sized farms were worked with the help of sharecroppers, these operations mostly relied on family labor.

Small farmers had to adapt to the environment and the family's limited resources. The topography of Costa Rica and Colombia made it impossible to use mechanized machinery, so farmers used axes and fire to clear the land and hoes to weed it. Colombian farmers planted their crops in vertical rows on the severely steep slopes so they could weed standing upright. (Weeding bent over is excruciating work.) The farmers planted using a *barretón,* a heavy wedge-shaped implement with an iron tip and a long, straight wood handle that the farmer poked into the soil. The farmer then placed corn or a coffee seedling into the resulting hole in the ground. Clearing was done with a *peinilla* or *machete.* They planted food crops between the rows of coffee trees not only to provide sustenance for themselves but also to help prevent erosion. Shade trees, such as plantain, also were planted to inhibit erosion and provide leaves that were used as fertilizer for the coffee trees. Shade also slowed the growth and ripening of the coffee beans, so that they matured at the proper pace. Pigs and fowl wandered in the fields, eliminating insects and supplying fertilizer. Family farms grew many crops, but the smallest farms concentrated on subsistence staples such as plantains, bananas, manioc, corn, and beans. Corn was grown on the least fertile land.

The work of growing coffee was hard and long. Men usually did the heavy work of clearing, planting, and weeding. Women and children helped with the harvest, including depulping, washing, fermenting, drying, and selecting. Once this process was complete, women and children were responsible for putting the coffee beans into burlap sacks and transporting the sacks by mule or horse, on difficult trails, to coffee towns, where the coffee was sold to merchants and traders.

Farm families lived simply. Corn, eaten in soups and bread, was the staple of their diet. It also was fed to the fowl and pigs, which, in turn, were eaten by the family on special occasions. The usual meal was soup and then some kind of starch with small bits of salted beef or pork purchased in town. The farmers also bought most of their vegetables. Many farmers grew citrus and mango trees and, in the warmer zones, sugarcane. From this sugarcane, they produced brown sugar cakes called *panelas* and the molasses that was later fermented and distilled to yield *aguardienté* or rum. These provided sweets and alcoholic beverages.

To survive, the families had to be frugal and self-sufficient. They usually produced most of what they needed, except for some of the men's clothing (pants, shoes, and boots). Poor children wore little or no clothing. The women made baskets, mattresses, and candles.

Small-farm coffee growers lived in houses consisting of bamboo walls, thatch roofs, and dirt floors. Washing was done in local rivers and streams. Human waste was dropped in the fields; this unsanitary practice fouled water supplies and resulted in the transmission of intestinal diseases, including intestinal parasites, which were common.

In Colombia, small producers engaged in constant, often violent, competition with their neighbors. The prevalent *clientelist* politics, in which country people owed allegiance to local political bosses, usually powerful landowners, forced them to participate in partisan wars, such as *La Violencia*. It had been the hope of Latin American liberal politicians during the nineteenth and twentieth centuries that small farmers would form the bedrock of a democratic society, as they had in some parts of Europe and the United States. In Colombia, however, they were at the heart of conflict.

Questions for Discussion

Compare the lives of Colombian coffee farmers with other small farmers, such as cassava growers in Brazil. Why was violence so integral a part of conditions in the countryside? Was violence a result of the local loss of autonomy?

precrisis GDP until 1945. The recovery of external trade in the 1930s was at least partly the result of a shift away from markets in Great Britain and the United States to those in Germany, Italy, and Japan.

The depression acted much like World War I in that it impeded the flow of imports to Latin America. But again, manufacturing did not necessarily flourish. Low productivity, the result of shortages of cheap power, the lack of skilled labor, the lack of credit, obsolete machinery, and overprotection (tariffs that were too high), hindered industrial development. The depression also shut off the flow of capital into the region from Europe and the United States. The only way for Latin American countries to modernize, therefore, was through some form of government intervention. National governments established agencies such as CORFO (Chilean National Development Corporation) in Chile to foster industrialization that the private sector was unable or unwilling to undertake.

World War II

World War II hit Latin America harder than the depression and previous world war. The British market shrunk when it went on war footing, and the British blockade of Europe cut off recently expanding continental European markets. U.S. programs such as Lend-Lease and the Export-Import Bank never replaced the shortfall in either finance or commerce. Some of the lost market was made up with inter–Latin American trade.

The drop in U.S. and European imports after 1939 should have provided impetus for further Latin American industrialization, but wartime inflation eroded real wages and purchasing power. Nonetheless, industrialization expanded in several nations. The United States fostered industry by supplying technical assistance. Governments established nonconsumer industries, such as the Volta Redonda steel works in Brazil. Latin American nations accumulated tremendous reserves from the sale of exports during the war, which led to inflation. Very few workers' wages and middle-class salaries could maintain their real earnings in the face of rising prices. Those who had assets, on the other hand, saw them appreciate. This increase in the cost of living had created social unrest by the end of the war.

PEACETIME ECONOMIES

Peacetime solved few of the region's problems. First, as in the aftermath of the World War I, Latin America suffered from the decline of U.S. purchases of primary products and the elimination of the cooperative mechanisms for funneling technical assistance and capital into Latin America. Second, to make matters worse, the inter–Latin American markets gained during the war were lost as cheaper European and U.S. products flooded Latin America. Latin American nations were further disadvantaged because their governments did not devalue their currencies, making their exports more expensive abroad. Third, the United States, confronted by the threat of Soviet communism, turned its attention to rebuilding Europe, so U.S. government resources were no longer available, and Latin America had to rely on insufficient private sector capital investment. Fourth, slow European recovery (until the advent of the Marshall Plan for European recovery in 1948) limited potential markets. (The outbreak of the Korean War (1950–1954) sent prices up again, but only briefly.) Fifth, Latin American nations faced a dilemma as to how to spend the large foreign exchange reserves they had built up during the war before those reserves were eroded by inflation. Some, like Argentina, repaid external debt. Argentina also purchased its foreign-owned railroads. Mostly, however, Latin American governments spent the reserves, setting off a wave of inflation.

Facing dismal market opportunities and with only limited resources available from abroad, Latin America turned inward in the late 1940s. Most governments instituted tight restrictions on imports, both to end the spending spree and to protect domestic manufacturing. Postwar depression in Europe erased traditional markets with no prospects for quick recovery. Latin America shared only minimally in the vast postwar expansion of international trade. The growing consensus among government officials and intellectuals was that Latin America could no longer rely on the export model. Some nations sought to diversify their exports, others adopted the policies of import substitution industrialization (ISI), and another, smaller, group attempted both. These goals proved illusive. In the most advanced countries (Argentina, Brazil, Chile, Colombia, Mexico, and Uruguay), the easiest steps toward industrialization were already taken. The next stage was to be far more demanding in terms of capital and technology. Domestic enterprise was unable or unwilling to risk capital. This left the field open to either multinational corporations (which were eager to enter protected markets) or state-owned companies.

Unfortunately, the ISI strategy for development was critically flawed. Domestic manufacturers were hard pressed to compete with multinational companies, because the former were so highly protected by tariffs that they were extremely inefficient. To make matters worse, the small size of domestic markets meant there were no economies of scale. Often, domestic manufacturers operated at less-than-full capacity. They could not compete outside their home countries. Moreover, industrialization was itself import intensive; it needed capital goods available only from abroad. Foreign exchange paid for technology, royalties, licenses, and profits, creating a further drain of scarce capital. With the exceptions of Brazil and Mexico, the 1950s were a time of economic stagnation in the region. Meanwhile, the developed nations were on the path to unprecedented prosperity, leaving Latin America behind.

DICTATORS AND POPULISTS

The Social Question remained preeminent in Latin American politics throughout the years of world wars and economic crises. The constant conflict and negotiation among the upper, middle, and lower classes (at least the organized elements) and between genders defined political parameters. The region's nations alternated between limited democracy and dictatorship, for the most part, but not always, in correlation with the booms and busts of the world market. Good times allowed democracy to function; bad times increased conflict between classes and led to the imposition of coercive governments by the upper class allied with the military.

During the 1920s a wave of popularly elected leaders prepared to make concessions to the new aspiring classes and the changing circumstances of women. Unfortunately, both Hipólito Yrigoyen, the head of the Radical Party in Argentina, and Arturo Alessandri in Chile eventually fell victim to military coups. Augusto B. Leguía in Peru and Gerardo Machado in Cuba turned from populism to dictatorship when economic depression eroded their support.

The 1920s and 1930s were troubling times for the traditional social order. The upper and, to some extent, the middle classes feared their societies were coming apart as challenges by the lower classes increased. Perhaps the greatest uncertainties evolved from the transformation of women's roles. Women worked in visible urban settings in factories and offices. They organized and staged strikes. The new "free" woman—sexually active, cigarette smoking—was not the reassuringly pliant, passive mother of old. As in the case of those who were agitating for the improvement of working- and middle-class conditions, however, feminists found it difficult to obtain their goals in the face of resistance from the male hierarchies that composed the government and religious and financial establishments. Feminists' major objective, to obtain equality in law, was not achieved until the 1930s, and suffrage (the right to vote) took even longer.

E' coisa certa e patente
Que toda "élite,, elegante
Adopta unanimamente
O "Guaraná Espumante.,;

E não contente com isso,
A gente chic se mata
Para gosar o feitiço
Dos finos bonbons do "Lacta,,,

Modern women in Brazil.

Women's organizations received assistance from liberal and populist political parties. A handful of liberals viewed changing laws to reflect women's new roles to be part of the modernization process crucial to societal development. Women were active participants in the multifaceted campaigns for social reform all over the region. They sought not only the right to vote but also better working, sanitary, and health conditions for everyone. As Latin American governments haltingly involved themselves in public welfare, women made these activities their own as social workers and teachers.

In both Argentina and Peru, the upper classes, through populist leaders Yrigoyen and Leguía, shared power with the middle class. As long as the export economy stayed strong and the national government did not attempt far-reaching reforms, this tension-filled alliance held. The Great Depression of the 1930s, however, put the upper and middle classes into competition for rapidly shrinking resources. Ultimately, the upper classes used coercion (by the police, thugs, or the military) to maintain their status. In Chile, politicians could not reach consensus about the Social Question. As a result, the younger elements of the military twice intervened to force reforms that would improve conditions for the middle and lower classes.

The 1920s

In Argentina, the Radical Party alliance between the middle class and elements of the landowning upper class dominated the country's politics during the 1920s. A major accomplishment was the 1926 enactment of the law of women's civil rights, which provided that women had all the rights of men, thereby removing gender limits to the exercise of all civil functions (but, crucially, not the vote). Heavily reliant on government patronage to bolster their support, the Radicals required prosperity to generate the revenues to pay for their strategy. The economic downturn that began in 1928, however, sharply curtailed the ability of the Radicals to provide patronage employment for their followers. In September 1930, the military, overthrew Yrigoyen, who had won a second term in 1928.

Yrigoyen's case clearly illustrates that populist politics succeeded only when government revenues were sufficient to fund patronage and that the precarious alliance between the upper and middle classes disintegrated rapidly when the two groups had to compete for scarce resources or when their interests clashed. Their ties, forged from their mutual fear of the lower classes, proved unstable. When there was conflict, the side with the strongest links to the armed services, most often the upper classes, won out.

Peruvian politicians, like Argentina's Radicals, sought to find answers to the Social Question by appealing to the middle class and by adopting a vast program of patronage. Former president Augusto B. Leguía (1908–1912, 1919–1930) returned from exile in 1919 to topple the "Aristocratic Republic." With strong backing from middle- and lower-class voters, he proclaimed *La Patria Nueva* (the new fatherland). He proposed a stronger interventionist state, which would modernize and grow the economy, financed by foreign investment and increased exports. The center of his administration was a massive program of public works. He rebuilt Lima into a beautiful modern city and constructed nearly 10,000 miles of roads. Leguía's plan was successful until 1930, when the depression sharply limited the funds available.

Leguía focused on the middle class and country people as his bases of support. To appeal to the former, he vastly expanded the government bureaucracy and the educational system, quadrupling the number of public employees and doubling the number of students. Leguía took advantage of growing unrest in the Indian countryside, where indigenous peoples and landlords were at bitter odds, to undermine landlords whom the president regarded as impediments to his drive to centralize power. The end of Leguía's efforts to forge an alliance with country people came when the army and local authorities killed 2000 small farmers and landless residents during two uprisings in 1923. Like Yrigoyen and so many after him, Leguía learned that populism was only as successful as its economic program. Leguía could not survive the crisis of the depression. He was ousted in August 1930.

The Chilean upper classes, unlike some of their counterparts in Argentina and Peru, steadfastly refused concessions to the middle and lower classes. As a result, Chile's Parliamentary Republic (1891–1920) simply did not work. Social unrest escalated as the government was unable to ameliorate the economic crisis and hardship brought on by the World War I. Strikes tore apart the northern nitrate region. Out of the turmoil of the late 1910s rose veteran politician Arturo Alessandri Palma. Drawing support from the working class, promising sweeping reforms, and professing an interest in women's issues, Alessandri won the presidential election of 1920. For 4 years, however, he was unable to overcome congressional opposition to his program. Impatient junior officers, led by Major Carlos Ibáñez del Campo and Major Marmaduke Grove Vallejo, seized the government in 1924. In 1925, their administration decreed a law that extended the property rights of married women; they also penned a new constitution that restored strong presidential rule (lost in the 1890 civil war). Ibáñez took office as president in 1927, and his foreign loan–financed spending spree brought a measure of prosperity. The impact of the Great Depression, however, was especially harsh in Chile, which was heavily dependent on mining exports. Massive street demonstrations forced Ibáñez to resign in mid-1931.

In Cuba, populism also evolved into dictatorship in response to the depression. The 1920s were plagued by the terrible collapse of sugar prices in 1920, and a two-decade-old tradition of ineffective, corrupt government, exacerbated by the Platt Amendment to the Cuban Constitution of 1902, which had installed the United States as the island's protector. Gerardo Machado became president in 1925. Like other populists he initiated a massive foreign loan–financed public works program. But in 1929, sugar and tobacco prices crashed, and the ensuing crisis wore away Machado's popularity. His regime thereafter was increasingly brutal. He lasted until August 1933, when a coalition of students and military officers forced him out of office.

In Argentina, Peru, Chile, and Cuba, leaders with reform programs had emerged, supported by the urban middle and working classes. Yrigoyen, Leguía, Ibáñez, and Machado encountered difficulties when economic depression limited their ability to provide employment in government and build public works projects. All turned to

How Historians Understand

RECONSTRUCTING THE *SEMANA TRÁGICA* (TRAGIC WEEK) IN ARGENTINE HISTORY

Class conflict, as we have seen in Chapters 11 and 12, was always just beneath the surface in Latin America. And as we will see in Chapter 14, the political outcomes of these confrontations depended to a considerable extent on the middle class. When the demands of the lower classes threatened the middle class (which they nearly always did), its members sided with the upper class–military alliance against workers and country people.

One of the first instances of this was *Semana Trágica,* which occurred during the "red scares" (Communist scares) after World War I. The middle class panicked, believing the government had lost control over the lower classes. But class conflict was not the only factor in the horror, it also focused on the festering prejudices Argentines felt toward the vast wave of new European immigrants that had poured into their country over the preceding half century. In particular, it exposed Argentine anti-Semitism, for much of the violence Argentines committed was against the Jewish community.

The events began in December 1918 with a strike in a metallurgical factory in Buenos Aires. As the month wore on, the single factory strike spread throughout the city. It continued into January of 1919. Fueling the tension, rumors flew about plots

Jewish synagogue in Buenos Aires in the early twentieth century.

from abroad, and the badly frightened urban middle and upper classes believed the government had "lost control" of the situation and allowed a communist conspiracy to run amok. This led to violent reprisals from the upper classes, carried out by vigilantes who formed militias to protect their neighborhoods from the workers. President Hipolito Yrigoyen sent police and the army to subdue the strikers.

The situation culminated horribly in the Semana Trágica, which lasted from January 10 through 14. Many upper-class Argentines blamed Jews for the troubles. The upper classes identified Jews with the Left, because most Jewish immigrants in Buenos Aires had come from Russia, where a Communist revolution had recently (1917) taken place. Acting on their fears, groups of vigilantes took to the streets. Allied with the police, they attacked Jewish neighborhoods, arresting people and destroying property. The Argentine Navy played a crucial role in encouraging, arming, and leading these middle- and upper-class vigilante groups.

In mid-January, the government finally brokered an agreement that ended the strike and the conflict. In light of the universality of the anti-Left riots of the post–World War I era (the Palmer Raids in the United States, for example), historians paid little attention to the anti-Semitic aspect of the event. Later, Argentina, like most of the world, closed its doors to Jews fleeing Nazi Germany during the 1930s. Again, because the situation was commonplace, historians found this unremarkable. Many did comment, however, on the military rightist regime's affinity for Germany during World War II; Argentina had steadfastly refused to declare war against the Axis powers until the last day of the conflict.

Anti-Semitism reappeared publicly during the dire crisis of the 1960s and 1970s. The military governments (1966–1973 and 1976–1983) fired Jews from positions of prominence. In the early 1970s, rightist paramilitary groups killed Jews suspected of Left sympathies. When the army instigated the "Dirty War," Jews bore the brunt of the violence disproportionately. The harrowing story of newspaper publisher Jacobo Timerman's imprisonment and torture was, perhaps, the least daunting, for many Jewish young people filled the rolls of "the disappeared ones."

Looking back through the context of Argentina's growing anti-Semitism over the course of the twentieth century, historians are reevaluating the initial assessment of Semana Trágica, which too easily dismissed the tragedy.

Questions for Discussion

Given the propensity of Argentines, particularly of the Right, for anti-Semitism in times of domestic strife, should historians look for patterns within that society? Are the Argentine Right's acts, some decades apart, indicative of wider aspects of the country's history that historians should explore? Why did the Argentine middle class turn on the lower classes in the period after World War I? Why do people in crisis look for scapegoats? Why were Jews convenient scapegoats in 1919 Argentina?

coercion. Each of these leaders lost the confidence of the middle and working classes and was toppled by the military.

Mexico's situation differed from these other cases because its middle class, allied with workers and country people, had won the revolution and controlled the national government. The new ruling group, comprised of middle-class northerners (from the state of Sonora in particular), did not share power with the upper classes because it was ruined by the civil war. The main problems facing the revolutionary regime were rebuilding the economy, satisfying the demands of the victorious revolutionaries, and unifying an army fragmented by regional and personal loyalties.

From 1920 until the mid-1930s, Mexicans struggled to balance reconstructing their nation's economy after a decade of destructive civil war against satisfying the various revolutionary factions. Middle-class demands for equal and fair access to education, employment, and economic opportunities were, perhaps, the easiest to meet. The middle class sought, in particular, the expansion of government to provide them with jobs.

The needs of country people and urban workers, however, encountered more government resistance because they threatened private property rights, of which their middle-class allies were the firmest advocates. Landless villagers had fought in the revolution to regain the lands stolen from them and their ancestors by hacendados. The Constitution of 1917 guaranteed the return of these lands. Nonetheless, the revolutionary government redistributed land only when politically necessary, because government leaders feared that land reform might undermine private property rights and decrease agricultural production and thereby impede economic recovery. Moreover, during the 1920s a new landowning class, many of them ex-revolutionary military officers, emerged

LATIN AMERICAN LIVES

ELVIA AND FELIPE CARRILLO PUERTO

ELVIA CARRILLO PUERTO (1876–1967) and her brother Felipe Carrillo Puerto (1874–1924) were, respectively, among the foremost feminist and radical leaders of the postrevolutionary era in Mexico. Elvia once said that "I want ... women to enjoy the same liberties as men ... to detach themselves from all the material, sensual, and animal, to lift up their spirituality and thinking to the ideal ... to have a more dignified and happier life in an environment of sexual liberty and fraternity." As the radical governor of the state of Yucatán (1922–1923), Felipe carried out the most extensive redistribution of land outside of Morelos. In their brief time in power, the siblings created the most progressive state government in postrevolutionary Mexico in terms of women's rights.

Elvia and Felipe Carrillo Puerto were 2 of 14 children born in the heart of the *henequen* region. (Henequen was used to make twine.) Their father was a small merchant. Both lived and worked during their formative years among the poor Maya of the region, learning their language, customs, and traditions.

Elvia Carrillo Puerto was a feminist, an activist, a politician, an administrator, and a teacher for the first two-thirds of the twentieth century. She was a controversial figure in Yucatán as the governor's sister, and her activities defined Yucatán feminism during the 1920s. Married at 13 and widowed at 21, she scandalized Yucatán's traditional society by living with men to whom she was not married, as well as marrying three times. When her brother was killed during a rebellion in 1924, she had to flee the state and returned only once during the next 40 years.

Elvia worked as a rural schoolteacher to support herself and her son after her first husband died. She saw firsthand the horrors of poverty and malnutrition in the countryside. She was well read (Marx, Lenin, and others), especially for a woman of her status and time. She joined the movement against the dictator Porfirio Díaz in 1909 and continued her work as a teacher and organizer through 1915. In 1912, she organized the state's first feminist league. In the late 1910s, she moved to Mexico City, for a short time sharing a house (1921–1922) with her brother, who was then a deputy in the federal congress. She married again, divorcing in the early 1920s and remarrying in 1923. In 1921, Elvia was the first woman elected to a seat in the state congress of Yucatán. After her exile from Yucatán, Elvia held a series of administrative posts in the capital. She continued to organize feminists, founding a succession of important feminist groups.

Felipe, as the governor of Yucatán, led one of the failed "Laboratories of the Revolution" during the 1920s, only to be killed in a brief rebellion that failed nationally but succeeded in Yucatán. As a youth, Felipe was a small landholder, mule driver, trader, and railroad conductor. During the 1910s, he spent time with Emiliano Zapata's agrarian movement in Morelos before attaching himself to General Salvador Alvarado, the socialist governor of Yucatán. Felipe took over the Socialist Party of the Southwest, the governing political party of Yucatán, when Alvarado left the state in 1918. Felipe encouraged the people to become involved in politics, and he advocated Mayan culture and history. Felipe, however, was too radical for the so-called Sonoran Dynasty made up of presidents Álvaro Obregón and Plutarco Elías Calles. They readily abandoned him during the revolt by army officers, led by Adolfo de la Huerta, in 1923.

The Carrillo Puerto siblings symbolized the unfulfilled promise of the Mexican Revolution at its turning point during the 1920s. A series of local and state radical initiatives all fell victim to the harsh practicalities of rebuilding a war-ravaged nation and the hard-eyed greed of the victorious generals. Elvia, however, who lived into the late 1960s, never gave up her dreams of women's equality.

Questions for Discussion

In some ways, the careers of the Carrillo Puertos were microcosms of the failures of both the Mexican Revolution and Mexican feminism. Why did both movements fail? Or, do you think that one or the other did not fail? Do you think that the Carrillo Puertos had the same goals as their constituents in the latter's battle for control over their everyday lives?

to oppose the implementation of land reforms. The revolutionary regime was willing to allow industrial labor to organize as long as the unions affiliated with the Regional Confederation of Mexican Workers (CROM). Presidents Álvaro Obregón (1920–1924) and Plutarco Elías Calles (1924–1928) balanced reconstruction and reform and survived a series of major rebellions. Obregón won reelection in 1928, but an assassin's bullet killed him before he took office. Calles ruled from behind the scenes, as three puppet presidents filled out the 6-year term until 1934. He solved the problem of the fragmented army by founding (1929) and building a new political party, the National Party of the Revolution (PNR), which brought together the disparate factions and wayward generals.

Brazil's middle and lower classes were the politically weakest in Latin America in 1920. Nonetheless, the old order fell apart when it experienced the depression. The power-sharing arrangement among the upper classes of the largest states gradually broke down during the course of the succeeding decade. When the upper classes of São Paulo (the other participants were the states of Rio de Janeiro and Minas Gerais) refused to alternate out of the presidency in 1930, their action set off a rebellion. Plummeting coffee prices added to the crisis. A coalition of dissident regional upper class, disgruntled mid-rank army officers, and disparate members of the urban middle class revolted to overthrow the old republic. Out of the uprising, Getúlio Vargas, governor of Rio Grande do Sul and the defeated presidential candidate of 1930, emerged to rule Brazil for the next 15 years.

Depression and War

To meet the crisis of the Great Depression of the 1930s, most of Latin America turned from democracy to military dictatorship or to civilian dictatorship with strong military support. The major exception was Mexico, which, instead, constructed a one-party regime. A number of important experiments took place during this period, such as the *Concordancia* in Argentina, the Socialist Republic in Chile, the *Estado Novo* in Brazil, and the revolutionary administration of Lázaro Cárdenas in Mexico. Almost all were short lived, and although each aimed to end conflict between classes, only Cárdenas's reforms succeeded.

Leftist ideologies, such as socialism and communism, often flourished as intellectual exercises, particularly among university students, but they were no match for upper-class and military opposition. More eclectic, and at times relatively radical, leftist political parties, such as the American Popular Revolutionary Alliance (APRA) in Peru and the National Revolutionary Movement (MNR) in Bolivia, proved more enduring and influential. In the short term, local variations of rightist ideologies, most importantly corporatism and fascism, had greater impact, but quickly receded.

By 1932, the moderate military, led by General Agustin Justo (1932–1938), formed an alliance (known as the Concordancia) comprised of old-line conservatives, independent Socialists (primarily from Buenos Aires), and, most importantly, anti-Yrigoyen Radicals. The new conservative alliance confronted the depression by balancing the budget, paying the foreign debt, encouraging exports, and discouraging imports. The Justo administration introduced Argentina's first income tax, which substantially cut the government's reliance on trade taxes for revenues, and established a central bank, which gave the government unprecedented influence on the management of the economy. The depression did not hit Argentina as hard as it did other Latin American nations, and, as a result, the upper-class regime was relatively benign. The moderate Concordancia continued to govern when Roberto M. Ortiz took over as president in 1938.

In Chile during the 1930s, the upper classes made concessions to urban workers and women but were unwilling to accommodate demands for land reform in the countryside. For a year and a half after the fall of Carlos Ibáñez, Chileans stumbled from one government to another. One of these was the Socialist Republic, led by Marmaduke Grove, which lasted for 100 days in 1932. Former president Arturo Alessandri won a new term in 1932. By 1935, Chile had recovered from the economic crisis, which allowed Alessandri to make overtures to the lower classes. He permitted extensive labor union organization and instituted a very effective process of mediating employer–employee disputes. A law in 1934 expanded women's freedoms and property rights, though men still maintained legal authority in the family. Alessandri cracked down hard in the countryside. Pedro Aguirre Cerda, the candidate of a coalition of center and Left parties known as the Popular Front, captured the presidency in 1938. His administration established the National Development Corporation (CORFO).

Brazil's social ferment and economic crisis led it to dictatorship. Like the postrevolution Mexican government during the same period, Brazilian dictator Getúlio Vargas (1930–1945) obtained the support of white-collar and industrial workers. He was unable to create a wide political consensus, however, instead ruling by decree. Vargas's appeal to the masses was more show than substance. Three years after winning election as president by vote of a constituent assembly (1934), Vargas engineered a coup against his own government to prevent new elections and established the *Estado Novo* (New State) in 1937. At this point, he no longer made even a pretense of having popular support.

In Peru, various forms of populism failed because the military remained steadfastly opposed. Sánchez Cerro represented the same middle class that had formed the core of Leguía's following. His "Conservative Populism" promised to restore the old social and economic structure, but at the same time offered the lower classes land reform, social security, and equal rights for Indians. After a bitter election campaign in 1931 against APRA's Víctor Raúl Haya de la Torre, Sánchez Cerro survived 16 terrible months of civil war and economic crisis until he was assassinated. General Oscar Benavides (1933–1939), a former provisional president (1914–1915), took over. Despite issuing a general amnesty, he engaged in a continuing struggle with Haya's followers in APRA. Peru recovered more quickly than other nations in the region from the depression, as exports surged beginning in 1933. Benavides cancelled the 1936 elections when it became apparent he was losing and ruled as dictator for the next 3 years. Modest conservatives inclined toward slightly expanding the role of government served as presidents from 1939 to 1948. Like Brazil, Peru experienced short periods of stability, but the Social Question remained unanswered.

Mexico experienced the most far-reaching reforms and consequently the longest era without upheaval. By 1934, the Mexican Revolution (set forth in detail in the Constitution of 1917) had seemingly reneged on its promises. Seventeen years after revolutionary victory, however, the country's new president, Lázaro Cárdenas, finally implemented long-awaited reforms. His major accomplishment was to redistribute 49 million acres of land to 15 million Mexicans, one-third of the population. As we discussed in Chapter 11, rural Mexicans had fought the revolution for land, and Cárdenas fulfilled Emiliano Zapata's promises to return these lands to the lower classes. As a result, the president bestowed an aura of legitimacy on the postrevolution regime that lasted for half a century. The Cárdenas administration more than doubled the average wage of urban workers. In 1938, Cárdenas expropriated the foreign-owned petroleum companies operating in the country when they refused to obey a Supreme Court order to increase the wages of their employees. In addition, the president undertook major efforts in public health and education. He also reorganized the official party in 1938, transforming it from a loose alliance among revolutionary generals, regional bosses, and labor leaders into an organization responsive to four major sectors: labor unions, rural organizations, the military, and government bureaucrats (middle class). Cárdenas did not, however, fulfill his promise to amend the Constitution to ensure equal rights for women.

Reform reached its acme in 1937. Land redistribution had disrupted food production, worsening conditions for the lower classes. Cárdenas had gone as far as he could, for there was enormous opposition among the postrevolution upper class to any further radical policies, and the nation did not have sufficient resources to carry out further reform.

During the 1950s, the Revolution moved to the center and shifted to policies for economic growth and produced the second great Mexican economic miracle (the first occurred under Porfirio Díaz). Mexico flourished as the official party consolidated its support among the middle class by providing large numbers of jobs in the government bureaucracy and government-operated businesses and free education at the fast-expanding National University (UNAM).

In all of Latin America, only in Mexico was the ruling group substantively responsive to the demands of the middle and working classes. Country people and the urban middle class obtained the land and opportunities for which they had fought so long and hard. As a result, Mexico prospered until the 1960s and maintained unparalleled political stability.

Cubans rose up in popular rebellion against Gerardo Machado in 1933. The victorious revolutionaries, comprised of a coalition of university students, noncommissioned military officers (sergeants, corporals), and political opponents of Machado, encountered strong disapproval from the U.S. government. Sergeant-stenographer Fulgencio Batista emerged from the plotting and violence as the power behind the scenes. Batista used methods similar to those of other populist leaders of the era, appealing to the working class from which he had come. He won election as president in 1940 and led the island through World War II. He retired peacefully and moved to Florida in 1944. Cuba, like Mexico, had achieved a measure of stability through concessions by a government run by the middle class (with a few leaders from the lower classes as well) to the needs of the middle and working classes.

Argentina became the setting for the most notorious populist regime in the Americas during the twentieth century, when the charismatic Juan Domingo Perón and his wife Evita Duarte de Perón emerged from a series of wartime political crises. The two towered over postwar Argentine politics. Perón, though the military ousted him in 1955, was a major influence until his death in 1974. *Peronism* was the most important example in Latin America of an alliance between a dictator and the lower classes. Perón built a base of support among organized labor, known as the shirtless ones (*descamisados*), in 1943 and 1944. Military hard-liners pushed him out of the government in 1945, but a massive demonstration by workers in October of 1945 rescued him, and he won the presidential election in 1946. Unlike Yrigoyen and Leguía, both of whom drew support from the middle sectors, Perón's politics was based on the urban working class with strategic allies among conservative bosses in the provinces. Perón repaid the working class for its support, greatly improving working conditions and benefits. The president opened the way for massive government involvement in business enterprise with the establishment of one state agency for marketing all of the nation's agricultural exports and of another that administered industries confiscated from German citizens during the war. His government also operated shipbuilding and steel firms. He nationalized the railroads and telephone service. After 1950, however, postwar prosperity ended as stagnation and inflation tormented the economy. Like the other populists, Perón found that he was unable to pay for his programs in times of downturn and lost support. In response, he shifted his strategy from popular appeal to repression, generating bitter opposition from the middle and upper classes. Nonetheless, he maintained his hold on the masses, overwhelmingly winning reelection in 1951. The economy stagnated, inflation rose, and his regime grew increasingly harsh, leading to a military coup in 1955.

A unique aspect of Perón's rule was the crucial role played by his wife Eva Duarte de Perón, a former actor. Evita, as she was known, exerted enormous influence through her Eva Perón Foundation, which funded medical services and provided food and clothes for the needy. She had come from the lower classes, and she became Perón's connection to them. Unfortunately for Perón, Evita died in 1952.

Peacetime Politics

The first major revolutionary movements to arise from the ashes of World War II took place in Guatemala in 1945, when a group of young, reformist military officers overthrew the long-running dictatorship of Jorge Ubico (1930–1945), and in 1951 in Bolivia, when a coalition of country people, miners, and the middle class, under the banner of the National Revolutionary Movement (MNR), toppled the conservative government backed by landowners, industrialists, and the military. The Bolivian Revolution implemented widespread land reform, destroying the traditional landowning class; nationalized the tin mines, the producers of the nation's major export; enfranchised all males and females; and virtually eliminated the military.

More common was a profound shift to the Right, as the upper class–military alliance, in the midst of the international Cold War between the communist Soviet Union and the capitalist United States, struck hard against the threat of communism in Latin America. Anti-Left dictators arose in Chile, Colombia, Cuba, and Venezuela in the early 1950s.

After a number of years under the rule of Left and Left-center coalitions, in 1948 Chile turned to former dictator Carlos Ibáñez, who took advantage of widespread discontent to bring together an odd coalition of Socialists, feminists, the middle class, and deserters from various parties to win the election of 1952. Unable to build consensus, he repeated his earlier policies of repression. His major innovation was to vastly intensify and broaden government involvement in the economy, establishing a central bank and also state enterprises in major industries such as sugar, steel, and petroleum. Colombians looked to Conservative General Gustavo Rojas Pinilla, as dictator of Colombia, who tried to bring peace to a nation wracked by civil war, but he could not survive through an economic downturn. Fulgencio Batista returned to rule Cuba in 1952, overthrowing a corrupt, democratically elected regime, and presided over a measure of prosperity on the island until the late 1950s. Batista, like Ibáñez and Rojas Pinilla, used harsh repression to govern instead of his earlier appeal to the masses. A young lawyer, Fidel Castro, led a rebel band in the mountains of southeastern Cuba, which gradually attracted support and allies among the middle class and workers in the cities to defeat Batista's army in late 1958. Reformers alternated with dictators in Venezuela. A group of officers, calling themselves the Patriotic Military Union, overthrew the president of Venezuela in 1945, but the Democratic Action Party (AD), led by Rómulo Betancourt, outmaneuvered the officers and installed a civilian government. Three years later, Marcos Pérez Jiménez took the reins as dictator until 1958, when the military overthrew him and returned Venezuela to democracy. In Brazil, GetúlioVargas joined Batista and Ibáñez as former presidents, once discredited, who returned to power. He won election as president in 1950 mainly because of the support given him by the working class of the big cities. Economic stagnation and inflation, however, badly eroded real wages and drastically undermined his base among workers. Amid a scandal over his role in the attempted assassination of a political rival, Vargas killed himself on August 23, 1954. Ironically, his death at his own hands prevented a military coup and paved the way for the continuation of civilian rule under Juscelino Kubitschek (1955–1960).

In each of these cases, neither populism nor coercion succeeded in establishing social peace. Reform was possible only in times of economic boom. Populism disintegrated during economic downturns. Efforts to win the support of the middle and lower classes through public patronage and concessions to labor unions required booming economies to pay for them. Coercion was unsustainable without some concessions to the middle and lower classes. The upper classes and military were willing to make only superficial accommodations. The basic unfairness and unjustness of Latin American society remained.

FAILURE OF THE LEFT AND RIGHT

The major populist experiments all failed in the long term. Their success, as we have seen in the cases of Yrigoyen's Radical Party and Perón's movement (known as *peronismo* or *justicialismo*), were tied closely to the fortunes of their nations' export economies and the unbending opposition of the hard-line elements of the military and upper classes.

Perhaps the most auspicious failure of populism in Latin America was that of the American Popular Revolutionary Alliance (APRA) in Peru. Victor Raúl Haya de la Torre founded APRA in 1924. He gained support among labor unions and the middle class. APRA's program consisted of opposition to U.S. imperialism, unification of Latin America, internationalization of the Panama Canal, nationalization of land and industry, and solidarity for oppressed peoples. Although its leadership was middle class, the party extolled the Indian past and sought to adapt the majority of Peruvians, who were Indians, into modern life. Haya believed that socialism was not possible in Peru, with its tiny industrial working class. He envisioned, instead, the middle class leading a cross-class alliance.

With the upper classes and military adamantly opposed to Haya, he was never to gain the presidency, though APRA was often an influential force in Peruvian politics. After losing in the election in 1931, Haya led an unsuccessful revolt, which led to the party being outlawed. Haya moved APRA to the center during the 1940s, ending its plotting and eliminating its anti-imperialist rhetoric to the point of exhibiting a favorable attitude toward the United States. During much of the 1940s and 1950s the government banned APRA.

The most successful and extensive social reforms in Latin America took place in Bolivia. Bolivia's National Revolutionary Movement (MNR) sought to create a strong centralized state with middle-class leadership of a cross-class alliance. In 1943, the MNR helped Major Gualberto Villaroel overthrow a conservative military government. Villarroel, in turn, fell in 1946 without accomplishing much reform. Conservative governments followed until 1951, when the MNR, which adopted a much more radical program, won the presidential election with its candidate Victor Paz Estenssoro. After the military intervened to prevent Paz's victory, the MNR rose in rebellion in 1952 allied with organized labor. The MNR carried out extensive land reform; nationalized the tin mines, which produced the nation's most important export; and enacted universal suffrage without literacy requirements. For the first time in centuries, the Indian population had access to land and politics. After these initial radical transformations, the MNR balanced the rival interests of small landowners, who had become conservative when they received land, and tin miners, who sought more radical changes. The MNR maintained its power until it was overthrown by the military in 1964.

The APRA failed in Peru and the MNR succeeded in Bolivia because the APRA alienated the military, which remained unalterably opposed to it, while the MNR initially defeated the Bolivian military. Just as importantly, the MNR, unlike the APRA, enjoyed a cross-class alliance between the middle and urban and rural lower classes.

Women's Suffrage

Industrialization and urbanization transformed the place of women in society. As we have seen, women always worked, whether inside or outside the home, and were often single heads of households in the nineteenth century. At times, women were crucial participants in politics, as in the military aspect of the Mexican Revolution from 1910 to 1920. The white upper-class men who controlled governments had to find satisfactory ways to recognize the realities of these transformations. This required a reassessment of such concepts as public and private space, honor, and gender (see Chapter 13).

Latin American feminists of the early to mid-century (the first wave of Latin American feminism) were comfortable with defining themselves as mothers and wives, emphasizing their childbearing and nurturing capacities. They did not seek to gain equality with men but rather to eliminate laws and conditions that impeded their traditional roles. They also used their status as mothers and teachers to further their argument for their participation in the public sphere. Feminists' early successes included revising civil codes to eliminate the legal inequality of married women and raising

Acción Femenina in 1922.

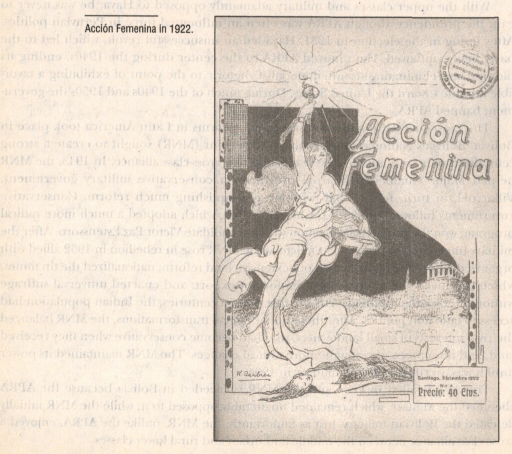

TABLE 12.1

Women's Enfranchisement

Nation	Year	Nation	Year
Ecuador	1929	Argentina	1947
Brazil	1932	Chile	1949
Uruguay	1932	Bolivia	1952
Cuba	1934	Mexico	1952
El Salvador	1939	Honduras	1955
Dominican Republic	1942	Nicaragua	1955
Panama	1945	Peru	1955
Guatemala	1945	Colombia	1957
Costa Rica	1945	Paraguay	1961
Venezuela	1947		

important social welfare issues. Because elections were meaningless in many Latin American nations, suffrage was not an important issue to feminists until the 1920s. Furthermore, not all feminists agreed on the value of women participating in the corrupt male world of politics. In fact, some doubters believed that the female vote would be overwhelmingly conservative and thus impede their progress. Thus, prior to World War II women obtained suffrage in only four Latin American nations (see Table 12.1).

CONCLUSION

Import substitution economics and populist politics dominated the era from 1920 to 1959. Latin American ruling classes sought to industrialize and modernize their nations, while maintaining the political status quo. The urban middle and working classes simultaneously looked to better their living and working conditions and to have a meaningful say in government. In the countryside, small property owners and landless workers wanted either to maintain what they had or to acquire lands previously stolen from their ancestors by the greedy upper class and to defend their control over their local traditions and values.

Import substitution, which protected Latin American manufacturing from foreign competition, did not succeed in stabilizing economic conditions, despite the opportunities for improvement afforded by two world wars and the depression. Most Latin American countries were too poor to constitute markets extensive enough to enable domestic industries to achieve economies of scale. The capital required for industrialization was available from only three sources: domestic private credit, domestic public funds, or foreign investment. Given the high risk involved with such enterprises, domestic private capital was unwilling to invest. Although Latin American banking had emerged by 1900, it had only a scattered impact on import substitution industrialization (ISI).

Foreign investment was unavailable through much of the period because of the world wars and economic crises. As a consequence, Latin American upper classes had to turn to domestic public funds, expanding the role of government in economic enterprise. Both public and private capital, however, relied almost entirely on the export sector to generate revenues for investment. And as we have seen, the export sectors were subject to booms and busts and therefore unreliable.

As for the Social Question during this era, the answer seemed at times to be populism, with its cross-class alliances. Charismatic leaders such as Yrigoyen and Perón, who were willing to distribute patronage and other economic benefits to their loyal followers, enabled years of social peace. The price was high: sham elections and loss of institutional independence for popular organizations. More importantly, populism, like ISI economic policies, was built on sand. It relied on booming exports to pay for the public works, expanded bureaucracy, and higher wages and benefits. When export booms ended, populism often deteriorated into oppressive dictatorship.

The struggles of ordinary Latin Americans remained much the same as they had since independence. The upper classes, as always, sought to maintain their wealth and power and were reluctant to share either. Those at the bottom of the economic scale fought to preserve their control over their everyday lives: to feed, clothe, and shelter their families and to maintain their local values and traditions.

The inability of Latin American economic policies and politics to lead to development and to answer the Social Question intensified societal tensions. When combined with the threatening specter of the Cold War struggle between communism and capitalism, these tensions would produce the conditions that in turn created two decades of tyranny and civil wars.

LEARNING MORE ABOUT LATIN AMERICANS

Bergquist, Charles. *Labor in Latin American History: Comparative Essays on Chile, Argentina, Venezuela, and Colombia* (Stanford, CA: Stanford University Press, 1986). Places workers at the center of Latin American politics.

Besse, Susan K. *Restructuring Patriarchy: The Modernization of Gender Inequality in Brazil, 1914–1940* (Chapel Hill, NC: University of North Carolina Press, 1996). Traces the changes in gender relations in the first half of the twentieth century.

Caulfield, Sueann. *In Defense of Honor: Sexual Morality, Modernity, and Nation in Early Twentieth Century Brazil* (Durham, NC: Duke University Press, 2000). Explores the role of public honor in gender relations.

Chant, Silvia, with Nikki Craske. *Gender in Latin America* (New Brunswick, NJ: Rutgers University Press, 2003). Excellent overview.

Craske, Nikki. *Women and Politics in Latin America* (New Brunswick, NJ: Rutgers University Press, 1999). Another insightful overview.

Dore, Elizabeth, ed. *Gender and Politics in Latin America: Debates in Theory and Practice* (New York: Monthly Review Press, 1997). Provocative essays.

Dore, Elizabeth, and Maxine Molyneux, eds. *Hidden Histories of Gender and the State in Latin America* (Durham, NC: Duke University Press, 2000). A collection of essays on the nineteenth and twentieth centuries.

Fraser, Nicholas, and Marysa Navarro. *Evita: The Real Life of Eva Perón* (New York: W.W. Norton & Company, 1996).

Gwynne, Robert N., and Cristobal Kay, eds. *Latin America Transformed: Globalization and Modernity*, 2nd ed. (New York: Arnold, 2003). Examines changes from all angles.

Krauze, Enrique. *Mexico: Biography of Power* (New York: Harper Collins, 1997).

Levine, Robert M. *Father of the Poor: Vargas and His Era* (New York: Cambridge University Press, 1998). A short, comprehensive biography.

13

PEOPLE AND PROGRESS,
1910–1959

IN THE ERA FROM the 1910 to 1960, Latin America underwent a vast transition from rural, agriculturally based traditions to urban middle- and working-class "modern" life. This transformation manifested not only in the politics of popular organizations and upheavals but also in all aspects of everyday life, such as employment, housing, food, popular entertainment, and art. The prolonged processes of altering gender roles, begun in the nineteenth century, continued. The struggle by common people for control over their everyday lives, particularly in the countryside, became as much cultural as political, though no less intense as a result.

Change, as always, was contested. In the countryside, especially, people resisted transformations of their long-held values and practices. Interestingly, not only rural dwellers, who would seem to most benefit from change, struggled against modernity, but also many members of the upper classes, the nominal promoters of change. The latter looked on mass popular culture as vulgar—the products of the slums—and regarded with suspicion the repercussions of migrations and industrialization. The wealthy and powerful were torn between their goals to transform their nations and the lower classes and their worries about whether they could control these changes.

The transition from countryside to city and from rural agricultural to urban industrial worker or middle class did not transform the attitude of the upper classes toward the lower, whom the rich and powerful continued to fear. The wealthy, as we have seen in previous chapters, grappled with the Social Question in politics and economics and allied with the armed services and the middle class to control the masses. This seeming contradiction was reflected in a Brazilian saying: "The social question is a question for the police." It was not enough, however, for the upper classes merely to maintain their control over the lower classes through government coercion. The wealthy tried mightily to force all aspects of social life and culture to conform to their need to rein in the urban lower classes. They sought to transform immigrants and migrants into a quiescent proletariat loyal to the nation (sometimes known as the *patria,* or fatherland). Moreover, they attempted to exert similar influence over the transformation of gender roles, particularly the place of women, in the rapidly changing urban society. Through the state, Latin American upper classes sought to shape the families, relationships, homes, leisure time, and tastes of workers to maintain their (male) hegemony (patriarchy). This meant potentially massive intrusions into local and personal prerogatives.

The movement of people from the countryside to the cities was and continues to be the most crucial process in Latin America. In 1950, 61 percent of the population was still rural. But from 1950 to 1960 alone, nearly 25 percent of rural Argentines abandoned the countryside for the cities; 29 percent of Chilean country people and 19 percent of Brazilian rural folk did the same. They left their homes because neither land nor jobs were available to them. Increasing concentration of land ownership severely limited their opportunities to obtain their own plots. "Land reform" projects distributed only marginally productive properties and did so without the opportunity to obtain credit to purchase equipment and make improvements. Burgeoning populations added to the pressures on the accessible land. Making matters worse, large landowners required fewer year-round laborers because of technological innovations and changes in crops. Many export commodities needed only seasonal workers, at planting and harvest. In contrast to the deterioration of conditions in rural areas, cities offered more employment, better opportunities for education—and therefore upward mobility—and improved health care. However miserable the living conditions in the slums of the cities, they were infinitely better than in the countryside, and however limited the possibilities in the metropolises, they were shining rays of hope compared to the darkness obscuring economic opportunities for the poor on large estates and in villages.

Even in the cities, of course, everyday life remained a constant struggle, as it had in the nineteenth century. Most Latin Americans continued to be poor and uneducated. Literacy rate for those older than 15 years of age was 50 percent. Only 7 percent of the people possessed a secondary education. As for work, if anything, it became harder. Large companies rather than small, family-operated workshops now employed most industrial workers. Impersonal bureaucracies replaced personal relations. City streets, noisy and smelly, polluted and unsanitary in the previous century, deteriorated further. The vast influx of people from the countryside and from abroad increased the pressures on existing facilities and public works beyond the breaking point. Like the Europeans and North Americans before them, Latin Americans who advocated modernization cared little that their relentless drive for economic development decimated their forests and pastures and polluted their water and air.

The contrasts between rich and poor, and the ironies they generated, were striking. Latin American upper classes during the first half of the twentieth century rebuilt the cores of the largest cities to emulate London or Paris. Governments built the Teatro Nacional (now the Palacio Nacional de Bellas Artes) in Mexico City and the Teatro Colón in Buenos Aires and constructed the elegant avenues of Rio de Janeiro and the Avenida de Mayo in Buenos Aires. While resplendent buildings and gleaming boulevards appeared in the cities' centers, however, more and more people crammed into the decaying tenements in the vast tracts of the city untouched by renovations.

SOCIALIZATION IN THE FACTORY AND THE MINE: PROLETARIANIZATION AND PATRIARCHY

Conditions in rural areas had deteriorated steadily for the lower classes since independence, and life for farm tenants and other workers was as precarious as in the preceding century. Work on the farms and ranches, if available at all, remained as hard and as badly paid as ever. Employment was erratic or seasonal. It was impossible to do more than scratch out the barest living. Most rural workers faced lifelong indebtedness to their bosses or landlords. At a ranch in the northwestern part of the state of São Paulo, in Brazil, in 1929, for example, 50 laborers rose at 4 A.M. to eat a breakfast of bread and coffee, after which they cleared fields to plant pasture for cattle. The men ate lunch at 8 A.M. and consumed their third meal consisting of beans, rice, and pasta at 2 P.M. Their toils did not end until dusk. Although the food was plentiful, no more was provided after the early dinner. Famished at the end of their long day, workers purchased additional food—perhaps cheese and bread or candy—from the ranch store, buying it on credit to be charged to their salaries. On Chilean estates, tenants were provided with a house and a small parcel of land in return for their labor. But the landlord could change the arrangements at a moment's notice and evict or move the tenants. Protest was futile, for the police and military were at the service of the landowner. In short, conditions for rural workers had not changed at all since the nineteenth century.

Living in any one of thousands of small villages in Peru or Mexico was little better. The villages were often isolated, reachable only over muddy or dusty potholed roads hours from any city. There was no electricity. Many of the inhabitants of the Indian and mestizo villages, especially women, spoke only their Indian language, such as Quechua and Aymara in the Andean nations or Nahuatl in Mexico.

It was nearly impossible to feed a family on the produce of small, individually owned plots, despite the families' modest meals—Andeans, for example, ate simple stews of potatoes, other vegetables, and, in good times, shreds of chicken, beef, or pork, accompanied by wheat or barley bread. As a result, country people sought work on neighboring estates and farms, in mines, and in cities. The movement of people from place to place was continual from the mid-nineteenth century on. Country people in Chile, for instance, often left their farms for short periods to work in the mines, drawn by high wages and the possibility of saving enough to buy their own land. After a few months, when the farmer-miner had accumulated enough money, he returned to his own parcel of land or to the estate where his family members were tenants. Manuel Abaitúa Acevedo, who first traveled to Chile's El Teniente copper mine in 1924 from his home in an agricultural town, was typical of the early migrants, who traveled back and forth between farm and mine. Initially, Abaitúa Acevedo worked 9 months in the mine before going home. The next year, he mined for 4 months, and in the following 2 years, 1 month each. In 1928, he worked in the mine for 5 months. His dream, of course, like that of others in his situation, was to someday save enough money to buy his own land.

Rural working conditions improved somewhat early in the twentieth century, in large part due to the arrival of two machines that had significant impact on country life. First, in Mexico, the *molino de nixtamal,* which ground soaked maize kernels into damp flour to make tortilla dough, revolutionized the everyday lives of women, allowing them to escape the centuries-long practice of grinding corn by hand, which required hours and hours of work. Second, the sewing machine, many of which operated through foot power rather than electricity, facilitated home piecework production, thus permitting women to work and tend to their families, and forming the basis of the cottage clothing industry. Sewing machines also eased the transition from wholly traditional to more western-style, modern clothing. (Access to electricity and the radio would have enormous effect on rural life, as well, but they were not universally accessible until the 1950s. Only 40 percent of the residents of Huaylas, a village in Peru, for example, had electricity in 1963.)

Despite these improvements, however, rural life in the first half of the twentieth century was so difficult that vast numbers of country dwellers left their homes and migrated to the mines and cities in hopes of finding better work. These women and men bravely left their villages and estates in order to improve their situation by entering the unfamiliar culture of mining camps and urban landscapes and acquiring new skills. When necessary—and it often seems to have been—they moved from job to job.

The history of María Elisa Alvarez, a Medellín textile worker, illustrates this situation. Alvarez arrived in Medellín, Colombia, at age 16 after toiling on a coffee plantation for 5 years. She had also sold cured tobacco, sweets, and produce on the streets of her hometown. In the city, Alvarez worked in domestic service for a year and then went to the textile mills. She worked there for a few months and then labored at a small dyeing shop and a local hospital. Having learned enough as a nurse's assistant to care for a patient, she gained employment caring for the invalid son of a wealthy family. After quitting because the son was unpleasant, she obtained employment in the factory she had worked in years before and then found a position in another mill, where she stayed until retirement.

Migrants from the countryside, such as Alvarez, arrived in the cities or mining camps only to face a long process of socialization and accommodation. The very sights, sounds, and smells were different, and as if this weren't disorienting enough, the newly migrated workers became immersed in struggles over their customs, traditions, and demeanor with their employers.

The conflicts between laborer and company are evident in the histories of two important industries, textile manufacturing in Medellín, Colombia, and copper mining in Chile. In both cases, companies required a reliable body of workers, but this proved difficult. Medellín textile workers were known for being uncooperative and mobile.

Slice of Life   VILLAGE LIFE IN PERU

HISTORIAN FLORENCIA MALLON conducted extensive research in the villages of the neighboring Yanamarca and Mantaro Valleys, in the central highlands of Peru, that illuminates the lives of rural people. The land is fertile and well watered by the Yanamarca and Mantaro rivers. The area lies on the major transportation routes to both important mining regions and the tropics, which meant that the mines furnished a market for the area's livestock and produce.

At the beginning of the twentieth century, the region was predominated by small- to medium-size farms, the proprietors of which enlisted the help of family labor to grow alfalfa, wheat, and vegetables. In the higher altitudes around the valley, people raised livestock and grew potatoes and quinoa. The holdings were much larger in this area. They drew labor from local villages.

Some proprietors owned plots in three zones: the humid lowlands located in the center of the valley, the valley slopes, and the flat lands on the other side of the mountains. This practice, of course, replicated the ancient Incas' approach to farming and commerce. To illustrate how the country people diversified, Mallon tells us the story of Jacoba Arias, an Indian who spoke only Quechua, from Acolla in the Yanamarca Valley. She owned 14 hectares (2.47 acres = 1 hectare) divided into small parcels scattered in different growing regions. She had 40 sheep, three teams of oxen, six bulls, and one cow. These animals provided the family with milk, cheese, meat, and lard, as well as wool for Arias's family's clothes. She also owned three mules, which allowed her to engage in small-scale commerce.

Farming the valley's slopes was no easy task. The environment often changed radically even within a single plot, resulting in variations in soil and climate. Farmers had to intimately understand their land and to meticulously adapt their methods and crops to it, according to the soil composition, the temperature, and the amount of sunlight and rain. Families also adjusted to the needs of the farm and the capabilities of their members. Young children and the elderly tended the livestock because these duties required less arduous work. No time was wasted. The shepherds, for instance, spun wool thread while they watched the flock.

Family farmers diversified their economic activities to make ends meet. Agricultural work was seasonal. Everyone participated in planting and harvest. Spinning thread, weaving, and household chores were major year-round tasks. Some men, usually those who were young and single, worked in the mines or as muleteers, transporting goods, during the off-season. Others made handicrafts, such as shawls, hats, ponchos, blankets, or woodcarvings. In good years, there was an agricultural surplus that could be used for purchasing extras, perhaps coca and alcohol. In bad years, the family was required to sell handicrafts or even some livestock.

Agriculture was a risky enterprise under the best of circumstances. An early frost, hail, or too little or too much rain could bring disaster. Because family size was not planned, inheritance eventually divided up the land into such small plots that no single family could subsist on them. Some families augmented their property's produce by working the farms of other owners in return for splitting the harvest between them. Some families tended other livestock owners' animals in return for half the newborn sheep or cattle. Another arrangement included cooperation between a farming household and a livestock-raising household: The latter's sheep fertilized the fields of the former, and the two families tended to and shared the crops.

Godparenthood enhanced cooperation among local families. On the occasions of a baby's first haircut, baptism, marriage, and roofing of a new house, children obtained six godparents, who, tied with the bonds of affection and respect, looked out for them in difficult times. Usually, one of the families was better off, but the arrangement worked to the benefit of both families because the wealthier had access to labor (and perhaps political support), while the less affluent could expect assistance in case of poor harvests or conflicts.

Governance in each village in the region consisted of two or more administrative units with their own officials. These entities oversaw community projects such as cleaning the irrigation ditches or planting community fields. There were also *cofradías,* religious lay brotherhoods, that sponsored the local saint's celebrations. Each of these organizations had a mayordomo to administer the celebration. He had to pay for the expenses not covered by the income from cofradía lands. The people of the community came together in these shared tasks. There was, of course, always conflict, ranging from petty arguments to more serious disputes over landownership.

Questions for Discussion
Compare village life in Peru with that of village life in Mexico. Why do you think the upper classes so mistrusted villagers even though the former need the latter's support in the politics of the nineteenth and twentieth centuries? Which of the villages in Peru and Mexico were more successful in retaining their autonomy over time?

At the El Teniente mine in 1922, an exasperated foreman fired close to 100 employees for "disobedience, laziness, fighting, insolence . . . leaving the job, carelessness, sleeping on the job, gambling, thieving, and incompetence." Companies sought to transform rambunctious and itinerant country bumpkins into passive, stable, productive workers. Workers resisted mightily. With the new century came critical changes in labor relations and market conditions, technology, and gender relations. In response to these changes, large companies attempted to control workers' lives to an extraordinary extent.

First, labor strikes during the mid-1930s in Medellín led company owners to formulate new strategies to instill stronger discipline into their unruly workers. Second, firms had grown larger and more bureaucratic, so owner families no longer supervised their operations from the factory floor, which, in turn, meant that they no longer fostered personal relations with their employees. Third, large looms capable of weaving much more cloth at one time began to be commonly used in textile mills. These new machines increased productivity, but—together with the industry's attempt to keep women "in their places"—caused a drastic shift in the gender makeup of the workforce. Bosses believed the looms were best operated by men, which resulted in a large number of women employees being fired. Medellín's textile and clothing factories, like most in Latin America, had heavily employed women through the 1930s, but by the end of the 1950s men far outnumbered women textile workers.

These transformations left employers struggling to reacquire control over the workplace during the 1940s by devising a new, two-pronged strategy: on one hand, providing desirable benefits for their employees, and on the other hand, seeking to influence all aspects of their employees' lives.

The first part of this strategy included improving working conditions and keeping salaries relatively high. The corporations that owned the mills and mines hoped that good pay would ensure a steady supply of able laborers, but it soon became clear that high pay would not persuade workers to abandon their freedom of movement or reform their behavior. Repressive tactics also were tried, but they proved to be equally ineffective at creating a body of compliant, respectable workers.

This led industries to the second part of the strategy: to influence every aspect of their employees' lives. Thus, corporations adopted paternalistic (fatherly) practices, making workers' lives more comfortable—and the job more attractive—by providing bonuses for attendance, establishing social and cultural organizations, setting up schools, and offering inducements to form traditional nuclear families.

As a result, Colombia's mill workers were paid well and were provided with such amenities as cafeterias that served subsidized meals and were surrounded by landscaped patios. The companies subsidized housing and grocery stores and paid for medical care, chapels, and schools. Similarly, in Chile, the foreign-owned mining companies sought to ensure a stable, resident, skilled labor force by offering workers schooling, movies, libraries, organized sports, and clubs—the last of which were to substitute for labor unions—in hopes of simultaneously attracting and altering them.

The Chilean state became involved in the socialization of workers during the 1930s in order to incorporate the middle and lower classes into the new conception of the nation. The government sought to build a citizenry of disciplined and responsible people. This, of course, coincided exactly with the goals of the foreign copper companies. Thus, both the government and the corporations were vested in successfully implementing new responsibilities for the lower classes, who were to be "disciplined, educated, and responsible [in order to] fulfill the demands of citizenship for the national community." Workers, nonetheless, wanted to rule their own lives. Miners resented attempts to control them by both the companies and the unions, and they continued to get drunk, play cards, and fornicate.

The efforts made by the Chilean government and mining companies, as well as by the Colombian textile industry, to reform workers quickly became the aggressive reassertion of traditional, patriarchal definitions of gender roles.

With the encouragement of the Chilean state, the mining companies, for instance, created a masculinized culture of work. The difficulty and danger of the labor was to be overcome by the sense of dignity. Pride was to overwhelm the dehumanization that accompanied modern mining.

Masculinizing work was one-half of the process; the other half was reemphasizing women's traditional roles. Latin American culture at the time—like most cultures—viewed female workers as a threat to the "proper" relationship between men and women, because when women earned wages, they redefined narrow definitions of gender. Further, owners believed that patriarchal and paternalistic authority could not be maintained in the factory if it no longer functioned in the family setting—that is, if employment in mills or mines provided women with the means to be independent of the authority of fathers, husbands, brothers, and sons.

Crucial to patriarchal beliefs and authority is the notion of female "virtue," specifically virginity. If women worked only when they were (theoretically) virgins—and the comforting assumption was that all unmarried women were—the factory maintained its patriarchal standing as "father" figure. So, mills and mines stopped hiring married women and single mothers. This way, women were allowed to work only while awaiting marriage, rather than working as independent females who would provide for themselves and potentially remain unincorporated into the family system.

Thus, in the midst of modernization, women's status in the mines and mills was altered to conform to centuries-old beliefs, but practicalities stood in their way. Women in the mining camps played a large part in helping the camps function. Women worked as domestics, as petty traders, and in the bars and brothels (which they sometimes owned) that sprouted like mushrooms around every camp. Like the men, many of these women hoped to save some money and move on. They usually came to the camps alone and often entered into sexual and domestic arrangements with men.

The foreign companies that owned the mines believed that this transient and unruly population of women, especially prostitutes, in the camps added to the instability and lack of discipline among the miners by adding to and exacerbating the problems caused by rampant alcohol use and gambling. Thus, the companies sought to regulate the sex lives of the workers and the women in the camps. The mine managers even went so far as forcing men and women found alone together either to marry or to leave their jobs. During the 1930s, some companies offered a monthly bonus and an extra allowance to workers who had families and were willing to formalize their relationships. This induced many couples to enter into civil unions and legitimize their children.

In addition, the companies sought to "civilize" the women in the camps, as they did the men. Company-sponsored programs, for instance, taught housekeeping skills to wives. Especially important in these lessons were the pointers in managing money and making ends meet, because the companies feared that poverty would tear apart the nuclear families they were trying so hard to create. As for single women who became pregnant or had abortions, the companies' solution was simple—the women were fired.

All of these policies, programs, and attempts to reinforce traditional gender roles succeeded in creating a stable mining workforce during the 1930s and 1940s. They could not, however, eliminate the difficult working conditions in the mines. And, what neither the companies nor the state anticipated was that their efforts to masculinize the work culture would generate not only an increased sense of pride on the part of male workers, but an equal increase in their disdain for authority.

Therefore, the miners never became entirely passive. Union activity continued, as did women's economic activities. Women sold food and beverages from their homes, took in laundry, and brought in boarders. Some even operated as female bootleggers (smugglers of illegal alcohol). Worst of all, some married women managed to obtain a degree of economic independence through their involvement in the informal market sector.

The ways in which the companies' tactics failed is well illustrated by the story below.

Ana (Nena) Palacios de Montoya worked as a domestic in Medellín when she met Jairo, who would become her husband. He was a driver for the local textile factory and used his contacts to obtain a position for her in the factory. Palacios de Montoya loved working in the mill. With funds cobbled together from yearly bonuses, mill loans, and the help of friends, she and her husband bought land and built a house. She gradually built her dream home, adding to the original structure as the family saved enough money for more construction. Amazingly, she managed to marry and have a child without being discovered and fired from her job. The bosses obtained two good workers, and their employees earned a good life—but, precisely contrary to the companies' efforts, Nena and Jairo clearly maintained their independence.

A Miner's Day at El Teniente

Work at the copper mines paid better than any other occupation in Chile. By the mid-1940s, miners earned 50 percent higher wages than from any other employment. Despite this, mines frequently experienced labor shortages until the relative stabilization of the workforce during the 1930s. When demand for labor grew, the companies dispatched unethical recruiters (*enganchadores*) to the rural areas. These recruiters got farmers drunk and told them about all the money to be made in the mines. When the desperate, drunken men "agreed" to become miners, the enganchadores had them sign contracts (which they could not read) and then loaded them onto a train headed to the mines. The farmers woke up, hung over, only to find themselves at a mine miles away from their villages, contractually bound to their new employers, and in debt to the recruiters, who often advanced them funds on their wages—which, of course, had to be repaid by working in the mines. If the farmers protested or tried to leave, the threat of police intervention persuaded them to cooperate. Despite these recruiting practices, turnover was a continual problem.

Regardless of how they had arrived at a mine, however, most miners' lives were similar to the description of the daily work at El Teniente, described below.

At four or five o'clock in the morning, a Chilean copper miner would rise and have breakfast at a cantina or the house of a family. By six, he was on his way to the train, completely enclosed and dark, that would take him up to the mine. When he arrived, the miner reported to the foreign supervisor, who recorded his time of entry. A giant elevator then transported the miner and some 600 of his fellow workers to the different levels of the mine, where they joined their teams, which consisted of 15 people, and began work in the tunnels.

The lead miners entered the designated tunnel first, laying pipes and tubes that brought in compressed air and water for the drills. As the miners drilled, the machines sprayed water on the work site to prevent dust from filling the cavern. (Despite this precaution, the tunnels were perpetually filled with so much dust that the miners could see only 5 or 6 feet ahead.) Dynamite was inserted into the drilled holes—a delicate, highly skilled process—and the walls were blown up, creating access to the veins of ore. Other team members then lay rails in the tunnels for cars that hauled in timbers to support the shaft's walls and ceiling, and then hauled out the ore. Once a vein was accessed, miners began the grueling work of chopping the ore out of the rock walls. The ore was loaded into the railcars, which were pushed to and emptied into chutes that carried it to the concentrating plants.

Mining was brutal work in terrible conditions. Foremen, under relentless pressure from the companies to increase productivity, pushed the workers hard. Miners learned these varied skills—all of which were dangerous and required enormous strength—on the job. When they exhibited proficiency, they moved on to better positions, though some refused to take the most dangerous assignments. A few became foremen. Work in the concentrating mills also required a great deal of skill and was even more dangerous than work in the tunnels, because the refining process released toxic fumes. There was never sufficient protective equipment, so the miners who labored in the plants inevitably acquired silicosis, a respiratory disease. Concentrating plant workers were lucky to survive a dozen years.

Living conditions in the El Teniente mining camp were generally abhorrent. Lodgings for families had no electricity, light, or ventilation. ". . . [T]he barracks for single workers [were] so awful as to be irrational." Miners with their families lived in two-room apartments in barracks buildings. Often, two families shared one apartment. A member of a family consisting of nine children and parents wrote: ". . . [W]e women had the bedroom because there were six girls and three boys, so in the big bedroom there were only women, in the other were my father with the boys, and in the other the kitchen." The company did not allow electric heaters or irons, so families used small wood- and kerosene-burning stoves, but both were expensive. There were common taps for water and toilets.

The worst disadvantage of living in the camps, perhaps, was the extraordinarily high cost of living, which badly eroded the real value of the nation's highest wages. Food was especially expensive, which meant that workers' and their families' nutrition suffered. Monopoly prices were at the heart of the problem. Miners often resisted the difficult conditions. New miners often skipped work after a few days to recover from their aches and pains. Ultimately, because miners were in perpetually short supply, they had the advantage of being able to find another job if the work environment was unacceptable.

URBANIZATION AND SOCIAL CHANGE

The transformations sweeping through Latin American society during the first half of the twentieth century were nowhere more apparent than in the growing cities of Latin America. They were particularly evident in the conditions of the middle class and attitudes toward women.

The Cities

Latin American cities were overcrowded, unsanitary, overrun by epidemic diseases, and teeming with uneducated migrants from the countryside and abroad. At the beginning of the century, the upper classes in Rio de Janeiro, Buenos Aires, and other cities determined to dramatically alter their metropolises' physical and social space while simultaneously inculcating moral values in the masses. Urban redevelopment, electrified public transportation, and massive population growth transformed the cities economically, spatially, and culturally.

The divide between the wealthy and the lower classes widened and grew more obvious. Rio de Janeiro, for example, was really two cities, whose population was half Afro-Brazilian and where immigrants flooded in by the thousands: the poor, on whom the authorities cast suspicious eyes, and "decent" upper- and middle-class folk, who made up less than 20 percent of the population. The upper classes imposed their will on the lower classes through cleaning up downtown spaces by instituting new health and housing codes, regulating recreation, and strictly enforcing laws against public nuisances such as prostitution.

Massive urban renewal took place in Rio de Janeiro from 1902 to 1910. Working-class neighborhoods were cleared and their inhabitants moved to the city's outskirts. As migrants continued to flow into the city, urban services remained woefully inadequate. Terrible epidemics tormented the city. By 1920, the downtown streets were ravaged by disease and littered with abandoned girls, beggars, and prostitutes.

The most startling example of superurbanization during this era may be Mexico City. Country people have thronged into the city in increasing numbers from 1940 to the present. Much of the nation's new industry was established in Mexico City—one-fourth of the country's factories were located there by 1970. Thus, between 1940 and 1970, millions of people left the countryside to seek their fortunes in the metropolis, increasing the capital's population from 1.5 million to 8.5 million. The number of automobiles jamming city streets also grew exponentially during that time, choking the city with carbon monoxide fumes. The government erected architectural splendors such as the National Autonomous University and the Museum of Anthropology. Skyscrapers sprouted in the core of the city and along the beautiful, tree-lined, statue-ornamented Paseo de la Reforma, while migrants overflowed burgeoning barrios, such as Netzahualcóyotl.

Generally, life was better in the city than in rural areas and offered more opportunity to improve one's conditions. In 1960, *capitalino* (resident of Mexico City) family income was 185 percent more than a rural family's income.

Life on the Edge: The Middle Class

The middle class expanded because government bureaucracies grew larger, the presence of foreign businesses multiplied opportunities trickled down in growing economies, and education became available to more than just the wealthy. What mattered to the members of the middle class, as it had to the gente decente in the nineteenth century, was maintaining their respectability and their distance from the lower classes. Because their economic situation was chronically precarious, middle-class people—who were only marginally more financially well off than the working class—concerned themselves primarily with keeping up the appearance of their status (see Table 13.1).

White-collar workers lived perpetually on the edge; their paychecks barely covered basic living expenses (see Table 13.1). Pawnshops were the only source of ready credit. White-collar workers found it nearly impossible to buy a home. It was difficult to save money, whether to build a down payment or create a financial cushion in case of emergency, and there were no banks to keep savings, even if they had existed, or to provide mortgages.

Their health was barely better than the working class. Lima's white-collar workers were less likely than poorer Peruvians to die of epidemic diseases such as typhoid, cholera, bubonic plague, or yellow fever, but they did succumb to tuberculosis. This disease accounted for one-third of all white-collar mortality in Lima and resulted from working in badly ventilated spaces or residing in damp, overcrowded apartments. It is likely that they were malnourished as well.

Despite these obstacles to financial security, white-collar workers tried to emulate the rich and were mostly concerned with appearance. Middle-class women followed European fashions, while men who worked in commerce in Lima during the 1920s

---

TABLE 13.1
_____

A Typical Middle-Class Budget in Mid-Twentieth-Century Peruvian Soles

	Soles
Rent	100
Food	240
Soap, toothpaste	20
Transportation	36
Water, electricity, garbage	14
One servant	50
Kerosene	12
Movies, once a week	20
School fees for oldest child	80
Total	572 on income of 600 (a meager sum at the time)

Source: *Ya!* No. 16 (July, 1949), pp. 18–19, cited in D. S. Parker, *The Idea of the Middle Class: White Collar Workers and Peruvian Society, 1900–1950* (University Park, PA: Penn State University Press, 1998), p. 212.

How Historians Understand   THE VOICE OF THE LOWER CLASSES

The most difficult task historians confront is the construction of the past of the rural and urban lower classes. Mostly illiterate, they did not often record their own histories. The upper classes, whose fear of the masses we have discussed extensively in these pages, were in charge of governments, universities, and media and excluded the stories of those who were not of their own status in national histories. The less well-born, among them the poor, country people, urban workers, and nonelite women, appeared in official history books only as no-account, lazy subjects of justifiable oppression, exotic objects of sympathy, criminals, or irrational protestors. As in the cases of the well-known Mexican historian Lucas Alamán and the liberal historians of nineteenth-century Argentina and Chile, upper-class fear and disdain of the lower classes was clearly evident.

Foreign visitors, the most famous of whom was Fanny Calderón de la Barca, the wife of the Minister of Spain to Mexico, who recorded her observations of nineteenth-century Mexico, were perhaps the best sources for glimpses into the lives of everyday people. They tended, however, to see Latin Americans through the narrow focus of wealthy, white Europeans or North Americans, with their racism and condescension undisguised. Their best-selling books provided pictures of half-naked gauchos and tropical villagers, noble at their best, savage at their worst.

Pressured by the events of periodic, violent upheavals during revolutions in Mexico (1910), Bolivia (1952), Cuba (1959), and Nicaragua (1979) and the challenges of Marxism, populism, and feminism, twentieth-century historians of Latin America

Women workers on strike in Mexico in the 1920s.

delved into the histories of lower-class people. The first efforts used traditional methods, exploring national institutions, such as labor unions, which had records to consult.

Traditional sources seemed to provide neither description nor insight. Newspapers of the day, unless in opposition to the government—and these were rare—hardly paid attention to the poor. Few treated the lower classes with any degree of fairness. Strikes, for example, were seen as the result of the manipulations of outside agitators. Not many reporters explored the lives of the people driven to these radical actions.

In the 1960s, dismayed by the massacre of 300 civilian protestors in Mexico City by government secret police forces, and in the 1970s, horrified by the emergence of vicious, repressive military regimes in Argentina, Chile, and Brazil, historians pushed harder to write the stories of everyday people. Local records provided the sources for this history.

The best sources for the history of common people lie in judicial, police, notary, and municipal archives, located in villages, towns, and cities. In addition, most recently, historians have discovered illuminating materials in the records of large companies. There are also some records from modern large estates. Foreign mining companies in Brazil and Chile, in particular, have proven rich depositories. Most of the archives contain "official" documents, of course, which reflect views of events that are hardly impartial.

Historians, despite the difficult conditions in local archives, such as poor lighting and ventilation, the threat of dangerous parasites from dust, and uncooperative bureaucrats, have discovered invaluable materials. Judicial archives, for example, contain the records of suits concerning marriage, criminal trials, tax protests, litigation between heirs, and land disputes. Notarial records reveal family economic holdings, wills, business transactions, and contracts. Police documents tell us what crimes were committed and by whom. Municipal records detail taxes, rules, and regulations, the activities and tactics of local officials, and the reactions of the citizenry to official actions.

Although police and court records are not always representative samples of the general population, by using them historians can uncover the extent of such activities as drunkenness, wife beating, prostitution, and banditry. They can also estimate the extent of government interference in everyday life in its efforts to discipline the lower classes.

The picture produced by these records is, of course, never complete, but they have created history where none had existed previously.

Questions for Discussion

Why do you think that historians in recent decades have focused on the lower classes? Why do you think that historians ignored the masses for so long?

joined shooting clubs or played billiards or wore English cashmere. Because living spaces were so small and unpleasant, many people frequented cafés and streets. Walking the streets of Lima was a way to show off their respectability—of seeing and being seen. Crucial to the middle-class psyche was the notion that they were demonstrably different from the working class. Thus, middle-class workers were willing to commute for hours so they could reside in respectable areas of the city. The middle class sought forms of entertainment beyond films, radio, and sports—all favored by the working classes—and began to travel.

Women made up only 1 percent of the white-collar workforce in 1908 in Peru and did not enter this sector in numbers until the 1910s, when they began to fill positions in post offices, telegraph offices, and telephone companies. In the 1920s, they moved into retail, then banking, insurance, and commerce. Five percent of all working women were white collar by 1931. The typical images of white-collar workers, however, remained those of a young bachelor or of a family man whose wife did not work. Respectability demanded wives stay at home, even if the result of living on one salary meant that the family lived more modestly than it otherwise might have. Despite this tacit cultural injunction, however, it is probable that married middle-class women worked outside the home.

In Peru and elsewhere in Latin America, the number of white-collar workers expanded from 1930 to 1950 as businesses grew larger and more complex and public bureaucracies swelled. As in Chile's mines, traditional paternalism gave way to hierarchies and impersonal relations. As mentioned previously, many more women entered the white-collar ranks during this period, although usually at the lowest-paid levels. After the 1930s in Lima, mestizos comprised the largest number of white collars. And white-collar workers' children eventually gained access to university educations.

La Chica Moderna

Urbanization and industrial work, with its accompanying financial freedom, instilled a new attitude in women, many of whom became what the era called "the modern woman." (They were known in Mexico and elsewhere as *las chicas modernas,* or modern girls.) Although at the beginning of the twentieth century women office and factory workers—that is, women holding nontraditional jobs—were only a small minority of the female workforce, they caused much public discussion. At that time, most working women still toiled as domestics, as they had in the previous century. The 1920s, however, brought with them the notorious flapper—self-confident women who were racy, flirtatious, and assertive. This unprecedented image of the independent, sensuous female shook male culture, because female "virtue" was the very center of patriarchy—and such virtue certainly did not include self-reliance, self-determination, or a sense of self-worth that was inherent rather than bestowed by a father or husband. In Latin America, as elsewhere in the Western world at that time, modernity indicated economic progress and healthy, rational sexual and family relations when applied to men, but it meant a dissolute lifestyle and loose morals when applied to women.

In Brazil, as in other Latin American countries, the upper classes, government officials, and conservative Catholics worried about the low rate of marriage among the poor, the high rate of infant mortality, and the increasing numbers of women and children in the industrial workforce.

The irony, of course, was that middle-class women in Brazil (and other nations) were entering the white-collar workforce because it had become harder and harder for families to make ends meet on one salary. Thus, given this reality and despite governmental policies designed to keep women in their place, more and more middle-class women took advantage of educational opportunities and went into the professions. By the 1920s, women's employment did not elicit the disapproval among the middle class that it had in the past.

Women's fashions of the 1920s disconcerted the upper-class males who dominated Brazil (and probably disconcerted a significant percentage of middle- and working-class males and some females). Compared to the clothing of the previous century and the turn of the century, during the early part of the decade, women wore lighter, shorter, and more comfortable dresses. Later in the decade, hems came up all the way to the knee and were worn with silk stockings and high heels. Less-cumbersome bras and panties replaced corsets. Short haircuts and the use of makeup were the style. Bare arms and legs were exposed on the beach. Women were revealing themselves physically as never before.

Fashion wasn't the only aspect of women's lives that was changing drastically. Women now smoked cigarettes in public. Films and magazines celebrated a glamorous, decadent life and encouraged women to aspire to it. Dances and music became scandalous: The tango, foxtrot, Charleston, and shimmy were all the rage.

To upper-class males, women's virtue was under attack, and the Brazilian state, like the Chilean state, sought to defend patriarchy from these challenges. The regime of Getúlio Vargas (1930–1945) adopted policies that were intended to adjust the traditional role of women to meet the new economic and cultural conditions of the twentieth century while maintaining the patriarchal structure of society. Its targets, of course, were women and the poor, the groups believed to pose the greatest threat to upper-class men's—and thus the state's—status. The goal was to strengthen traditional marriage. Women were, after all, crucial to society not only because they reproduced but also because they educated their children. Therefore, it was necessary to "re-educate" women and reemphasize traditional values, so that women would inculcate their offspring with the "proper" values and attitudes. To accomplish this, the government adopted protective legislation limiting women's access to the workplace. It was hoped that this would, in turn, limit women's ability to support themselves, thus essentially forcing them to find husbands simply to survive. The government also instituted social service agencies to monitor the urban poor. In addition to these governmental policies, industrialists even set up model villages to control the domestic lives of their workers.

The Brazilian ruling class and government were, however, willing to make minimal concessions to women. Early in the century, Brazilian legislation altered the wife's status to "companion, partner, and assistant in familial responsibilities." (Nonetheless, this legislation firmly maintained the husband as head of household, and women still did not have the power to control their own property.) In 1940, the government's penal code eliminated the distinctions between male and female adultery. There was also an attempt to end the legal tolerance of crimes of passion. (Law permitted a husband to kill his wife, if he caught her in adultery.) Thus, women, like the middle class, had struggled enormously to better their conditions, and succeeded somewhat, but their situation remained precarious. As the middle class had not achieved equal status with the wealthy and powerful, neither had women obtained legal, economic, or cultural equality with men.

POPULAR AND HIGH CULTURE

The vast movement of people from the countryside to the cities and from the rest of the world to Latin America during the first half of the twentieth century deeply affected the region's popular culture (folk songs, dance, and crafts) and its so-called high culture (orchestral music, theatrical dance, painting, sculpture, literature, etc.). Improved communications and transportation not only brought more people together domestically but facilitated travel among countries and, thus, the introduction of foreign influences. The arts were closely tied to the constructions of national identities, and Latin Americans struggled to find their way in the space between their own artistic traditions and those of Europe and North America, which were much admired by upper classes. The changes wrought by industrialization, migration, and urbanization on Latin American dance, music, and painting, in particular, are discussed below.

The tango, which was born in the slums of Buenos Aires, Argentina, during the late nineteenth century, was a fitting symbol for the profound transitions mentioned above. Before World War I, the tango was performed primarily in the outskirts of Buenos Aires, where rural tradition was still stronger than in the heart of the city. It was connected with rural music and songs that protested the miserable conditions in the teeming tenements and the industrialization of urban work. Rural people, newly transplanted, despised city ways as exemplified by the *cajetilla,* or dandy.

The tango melded various aspects of Argentine society, combining the music of the rural milonga, the Spanish *contradanza,* and influences of African Buenos Aires. Its very form was a protest against conventional mores: Danced by couples whose bodies were closely entwined, the tango was modern, urban, and explicitly sensual, eschewing more innocent traditional (folk) dances performed in groups. Radio and film made the tango part of popular culture, and the upper and middle classes, who disdained the dance for the first several decades of its life as being symbolic of the poor, later embraced it as a symbol of Argentina.

The Brazilian samba, too, was an object of upper-class scorn during the nineteenth century. In fact, the Brazilian government outlawed it for a time. Nonetheless, the samba became the symbol of Brazil's mixed heritage of African and European culture. Arising from the poor Afro-Brazilian neighborhoods of Rio, during the 1920s samba clubs took over Carnival (the festival before Lent). The clubs' leaders were able to shed the bad reputations of their predecessor organizations and convince parents in the poor neighborhoods to allow their daughters to participate. Thus, not only did samba—the dance of the poorest Brazilians—become the symbol of the nation, but it also illustrated how women, who were now active and public participants in Carnival, were no longer restricted to private spaces.

In painting and literature, the conflicts inherent in the processes of urbanization, modernization, and finding national identities emerged at the turn of the twentieth century in movements such as *modernismo* and *indigenismo* (nativism). Nicaraguan poet Rubén Darío founded modernismo, a literary movement that sought to express the Latin American experience. The visual arts followed, also seeking a uniquely Latin American presentation of the region's culture. Latin American artists, most of whom trained in Europe, set aside the perspective of the continent and began to look at their homeland up close. Mexican artist Saturnino Herrán (1887–1918), for example, depicted Indians and mestizos living and working in their local environs in such paintings as *El Trabajo* (*Work*) (1908) and *La Ofrenda* (*The Offering*) (1913). Herrán, who never studied in Europe, was one of the first twentieth-century Mexican artists to look to the country's pre-Columbian past for subject matter. Similarly, Ecuadorian painter Camilo Egas (1899–1962) depicted the life of Indians over the centuries since the conquest in huge horizontal panels, such as the *Fiesta Indígena* (*Indian Festival*) (1922).

At the heart of the Mexican search for national identity and art's place within it was Geraldo Murillo, widely known as Dr. Atl (1875–1964). He was a crucial link among European movements (such as impressionism), Mexican popular culture, the famous Mexican muralists, and the revolutionary government. Dr. Atl was an important sponsor of the muralist movement in the 1920s, and he brought *arte popular* into the forefront in 1921 when he organized an exhibition of popular art and wrote its accompanying text, *Las artes populares en Mexico.* A talented painter in his own right, Dr. Atl's works, such as *El Volcán Paricutín en erupción* (1943), for instance, showed his eclectic approach to art. Uruguayan Pedro Figari (1861–1938), son of an Italian immigrant, depicted life on the vast plains of the Pampas, as well as creole and black dance. He, like Herrán and Egas, painted the lower classes in the countryside, as one critic observed, "never before represented with such boldness and candor. . . ."

Perhaps the most well-known and the most important artistic movement that grappled with the intertwined dilemmas of modernization and national identity—most crucially the place of indigenous peoples within the revolution—were the Mexican muralists. The most famous of these were Diego Rivera (1887–1957), David Alfaro Siqueiros (1896–1974), and José Clemente Orozco (1883–1949), but the group also included Alva de la Canal, Charlot, Fernando Leal, Xavier Guerrero, Roberto Montenegro, and Dr. Atl. According to one art historian, Jacqueline Barnitz, "The artists faced two major challenges: that of introducing a new public monumental art requiring special technical skills, and that of creating an effective visual language for propaganda purposes." José Vasconcelos, the minister of education during the administration of

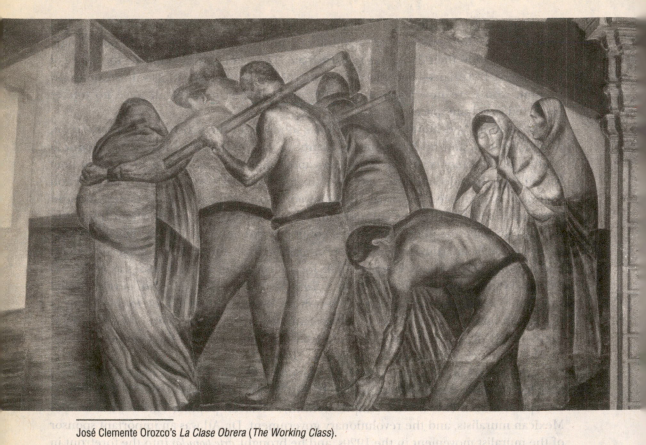

José Clemente Orozco's *La Clase Obrera* (*The Working Class*).

President Álvaro Obregón (1920–1924), set out quite pointedly to incorporate and indoctrinate the masses through public art. Vasconcelos sought to educate the mostly illiterate Mexican population about their country's culture and identity—in short, to make them Mexicans.

Siqueiros's manifesto of 1923 set out the muralists' goals: "the creators of beauty . . ." must ensure that "their work presents a clear aspect of ideological propaganda." The muralists introduced workers and country people into their art on a grand scale and rewrote Mexican history in their enormous paintings on walls. The stairwell murals in the National Palace in the Zócalo (central plaza) of Mexico City depict Mexico's history from the conquest through the Cárdenas (1934–1940) era. Art, to the muralists, was inherently political. In a nation in flux during the 1920s, art seemed a way to help construct a sense of nationhood in a country blown apart during the previous decade's revolution.

During the 1930s, artists' concern for the lower classes intensified. In Mexico and Peru, indigenismo art took center stage as these nations struggled, as they had for centuries, over the place of the Indian population in their societies. The Mexican muralists were the primary purveyors of the new indigenous image, which romanticized pre-Columbian

The Exploiters by Diego Rivera.

LATIN AMERICAN LIVES

FRIDA KAHLO

FRIDA KAHLO (1907–1954) was a tortured artist famous for her striking self-portraits and her stormy marriage to muralist Diego Rivera. Long after her death at 47, she became celebrated for her incorporation of distinctively female concerns, such as reproduction, children, and family, into her paintings. Critics consider her avowedly feminist in her treatment of her own body. She, like Elvia Carrillo Puerto (see Chapter 12), was a prominent example of Mexico's "new" woman who defied convention. Kahlo has reached cult status among feminists for her merging of personal emotions and politics.

Her life was determined by four factors: a terrible automobile accident that left her with a fractured spine and pelvis and constant pain throughout most of her life, her tumultuous marriage to Rivera, her inability to bear children, and her prodigious talent (though unrecognized, for the most part, while she was alive).

When she was 15, a bus she was riding collided with a trolley. The crash inflicted terrible injuries, which resulted in 35 hospitalizations and operations. The remainder of her life was spent in constant physical torment. Kahlo and Rivera married in 1929. They divorced in 1939 and remarried in 1940. They were international stars, consorting with world-famous artists and leftist politicians and thinkers. Rivera's notorious philandering marred their dreamlike lives, though Frida, herself, had affairs as well.

Personally and professionally, Kahlo was in the forefront of the movement to incorporate popular culture into art. She was flamboyant in her dress, wearing the traditional garb of the women of Tehuantepec, the isthmus in southern Mexico, and styling her hair in indigenous coiffures with bows, combs, and flowers. She bedecked herself in jewelry. She was an avid collector of popular, folk, and pre-Columbian art. Her artistic work was rooted in pre-Columbian and colonial sources. Some commentators regard her as the Mexican artist who best combined popular art with the "modernist avant-garde." The merger of her concerns as a woman and her feeling for country people manifest themselves in her painting *My Nurse* (1937), in which she suckles on the breasts of a dark-skinned Indian woman.

In her most famous paintings, we can observe her obsessions with her pain, her love, and her barrenness. In her work *Raices* (*Roots*, 1943), she portrays herself with vines growing out of her chest as she lies in barren land. Despite her inability to bear children, she insists on herself as part of and a contributor to the "natural environment." In *El abrazo de amor del universo, la tierra* [Mexico], *Diego, yo y el señor Xolotl* (*The Love Embrace of the Universe, the Earth [Mexico], Diego, Me and Señor Xolotl*) (1949), she holds a baby with Diego's face in her arms, combining both her obsession with motherhood and her love of her husband. *Las Dos Fridas* (*The Two Fridas*, 1939; see Plate 17) resulted from her divorce from Rivera. The two women depict her traditional and urbane sides, only the former loved by Diego.

In the male-dominated art world, Frida Kahlo was unappreciated until the 1980s, when her striking depictions of motherhood and her body fit into the new feminist art history. Some historians, however, have criticized the treatment of her as a victim, obsessed with her physical and emotional pain. Overlooked, they maintain, is "her active role in the formulation of the language of art, which questioned neo-colonial values." Interpreted as "'the other,' the feminine and the unconscious," she is marginalized in a similar way in which Latin America finds itself made exotic. Kahlo, however, does not interpret Mexican women (or herself) as victims, but rather as "an assertive presence with the power of life and death."

Questions for Discussion
Discuss how you think that art reflects its time. Why is art such an effective instrument of social protest?

civilizations and denigrated Spanish colonial culture. Indigenismo, both in art and literature and as a political problem, was a complex phenomenon. On one hand, intellectuals sought to extol the great heritages of the Indian civilizations. On the other hand, modernizing upper classes saw the Indians as backward rustics. At best, the more thoughtful members of the upper class sought to place the Indians in industrializing society. Pride in the accomplishments of native peoples dovetailed nicely with intensifying nationalism, which was a crucial aspect of populism, the political answer to the Social Question during the 1930s and 1940s. Nonetheless, to the upper and middle classes, modern Indians were impediments to progress.

Brazil had to confront its national and cultural identity not only in terms of Indians, but of African peoples, as well. Traveling the path of the Mexican muralists, Tarsila do Amaral (1886–1973) returned from her European training in the early 1920s to paint the everyday existence of poor Brazilians, who comprised the nation's largest population. Another Brazilian painter, Candido Portinari (1903–1962), according to Barnitz, also depicted the "poor and the dispossessed, haggard and weak, with the staring eyes and distended stomachs of the malnourished."

During the 1920s, with a movement centered in São Paulo, modernist Brazilian artists ended the nation's denial of its past and set about incorporating it into a national culture. They rejected regionalism and sought to make Brazil Brazilian. Novelist Mario de Andrade became a leader of the search for what constituted "Brazilianness."

Similarly, sociologist Gilberto Freyre sought Brazilianness in the country's various traditions and regions. Brazil could be whole, he argued, only by allowing regional differences to flourish within the nation. Both men rejected foreign models, none of which had stood up to Brazilian requirements.

CONCLUSION

At the core of Latin American struggles during the first half of the twentieth century were economic and physical survival. Most people were poor and struggling day by day to survive. Although great gains were made in education and health care—more people were literate and they lived longer—Latin Americans' standards of living lagged far behind those of people living in Western Europe and the United States.

Latin Americans also grappled with the widespread effects of industrialization and urbanization. Everyday people, particularly in the countryside, fought to retain their cherished traditions and control over their daily lives. The onslaught of the factories, railroads, highways, telephone, radio, electricity, and centralized government, however, was too strong. Nonetheless, the urban and rural working classes and small landowners were remarkably independent and resilient. They selectively adopted new ways and adapted to new conditions. Their resistance to the dictates of the upper classes and military, however, caused the latter to seek drastic solutions to the decades-old Social Question. Two decades of violence and trauma ensued.

LEARNING MORE ABOUT LATIN AMERICANS

Baily, Samuel L., and Franco Ramella, eds. *One Family, Two Worlds: An Italian Family's Correspondence across the Atlantic, 1901–1922* (New Brunswick, NJ: Rutgers University Press, 1988). The story of Italian immigrants in Buenos Aires.

Barnitz, Jacqueline. *Twentieth-Century Art of Latin America* (Austin, TX: University of Texas Press, 2001). An interpretive history of the region's brilliant art.

De Jesus, Carolina Maria. *I'm Going to Have a Little House: The Second Diary of Carolina, Maria de Jesus*. Trans. Melvin Arrington, Jr., and Robert M. Levine (Lincoln, NE: University of Nebraska Press, 1997). The sad story of a favela dweller.

De Jesus, Carolina Maria. *The Unedited Diaries of Carolina Maria de Jesus*. Ed. Robert M. Levine and Jose Carlos Sebe Bom Meihy. Trans. Nancy P. S. Naro and Cristina Mehrtens (New Brunswick, NJ: Rutgers University Press, 1999). The story of a favela dweller.

Farnsworth-Alvear, Ann. *Dulcinea in the Factory: Myths, Morals, Men, and Women in Colombia's Industrial Experiment, 1905–1960* (Durham, NC: Duke University Press, 2000). Women factory workers.

Fowler-Salamini, Heather, and Mary Kay Vaughn, eds. *Women of the Mexican Countryside, 1850–1990* (Tucson, AZ: University of Arizona Press, 1994).

French, John D., and Daniel James, eds. *The Gendered Worlds of Latin American Women Workers* (Durham, NC: Duke University Press, 1997). Essays on working-class women.

Herrera, Hayden. *Frida: A Biography of Frida Kahlo* (New York: Perennial, 1984).

James, Daniel. *Doña María's Story* (Durham, NC: Duke University Press, 2000). A woman in the meatpacking plants of Argentina.

Klubock, Thomas. *Contested Communities: Class, Gender, and Politics in Chile's El Teniente Copper Mine, 1904–1951* (Durham, NC: Duke University Press, 1998). Life in the mining camps.

Moya, José C. *Cousins and Strangers: Spanish Immigrants in Buenos Aires, 1850–1930* (Berkeley, CA: University of California Press, 1998). Traces the immigrant experience from Europe to Buenos Aires.

Parker, D. S. *The Idea of the Middle Class: White Collar Workers and Peruvian Society, 1900–1950* (University Park, PA: Penn State University Press, 1998). A rare view into middle-class work and society.

Parodi, Jorge. *To Be a Worker in Peru: Identity and Politics*. Trans. James Alstrum and Catherine Conaghan (Chapel Hill, NC: University of North Carolina Press, 2000). The hard life of the Peruvian working class.

14

REVOLUTION, REACTION, DEMOCRACY, AND THE NEW GLOBAL ECONOMY:
1959 TO THE PRESENT

THE POSTWAR WORLD'S promise of equitable politics and societies and prosperous economies went unfulfilled in Latin America. The region's leaders still grappled with the Social Question, seeking to satisfy the demands of the expanding middle and urban industrial working classes. In the early 1950s, as we saw in Chapter 12, Latin Americans turned to old dictators, such as Carlos Ibáñez in Chile and Getúlio Vargas in Brazil, or looked to new strongmen, as in Colombia and Venezuela. There seemed to be no answers, only failed formulas, tired politicians, and angry, impatient military officers. The major innovation of the era was the vast expansion of the electorate. Women at last won full suffrage, although the vote by no means ensured them an equal voice in political affairs. Governments eliminated literacy qualifications for political participation. The Cold War rivalry between communists in the Soviet Union and China on one side and capitalists in the United States and Western Europe on the other provided international context for the internal struggles.

The victory of the 26th of July Movement in Cuba in 1959 and the subsequent adoption of communism by the Revolution struck fear into the upper class–military alliance in Latin America. During the next 20 years, the Latin American Left surged and experienced an unprecedented degree of success. Chileans elected Socialist Dr. Salvador Allende (1970–1973) as president, and the *Sandinista* Revolution in Nicaragua (1979–1990) held power for a full decade. Major leftist insurgencies took place in Colombia, El Salvador, Guatemala, and Peru. Salvadoran and Peruvian rebels came within a hairbreadth of winning their wars. But at the same time, politics polarized into brutal violence. Leftist guerrillas staged robberies and kidnappings, attacked police, and bombed buildings, and, in response, Latin American militaries embarked

TIMELINE

1959
Cuban Revolution

1961
United States establishes the Alliance for Progress

1964
Brazilian military overthrows João Goulart

1968
Peruvian Revolution; Juan Velasco Alvarado

1970
Dr. Salvador Allende elected in Chile

1973
Allende ousted by Chilean military

1974
Juan Perón returns to Argentina

1979
Sandinista Revolution in Nicaragua

1982
Malvinas/Falklands War (Argentina vs. United Kingdom)

1983
Military rule ends in Argentina

1988
Pinochet voted out by plebiscite

1989
Sandinistas voted out of power

1990
Alberto Fujimori elected president of Peru

1999
Hugo Chávez elected president of Venezuela, marking the beginning of the so-called Pink Tide in Latin America

2000
Partido Acción Nacional (PAN) ends seven decades of one-party rule in Mexico

on a vicious reign of terror from the mid-1960s through the mid-1980s. Neither Left nor Right governments delivered sustained economic growth or social peace. Militaries ruled the major nations of the region through the 1970s and 1980s, seeking, at least in the beginning, to formulate new societies without popular organizations and political parties.

Eventually, if reluctantly, the armed forces, at times humiliated by defeat or scandal, withdrew from direct control over governments in the 1980s, pushed out to a large extent by the citizens of the nations they ruled. Democracy returned to every country in the region (except Cuba) by the 1990s. As the new century began and the new democracies struggled with widespread poverty and severely inequitable income distribution, a number of Latin American nations elected left-of-center leaders in a phenomenon known as the "Pink Tide." ("Pink" indicated that the leaders were not so far left as to be communist.)

At the outset of the post-1959 era, Latin American regimes continued to adhere to the import substitution industrialization (ISI) model of economic development. As we saw in Chapter 12, as the Right triumphed, it had presided over increasing government involvement in the economy. By the 1980s, however, ISI had failed resoundingly. Starting with Chile's military rule after 1973, Latin America gradually embraced free market economics. With the fall of communism in the Soviet Union and Eastern Europe in the late 1980s, there was no longer a Left alternative to capitalism. By the 1990s, it was clear that both the most extreme Left and Right regimes had ended in unmitigated disaster for most middle- and lower-class Latin Americans. The new left-of-center governments in several nations, such as Argentina, Brazil, Chile, and Peru, continued neoliberal economic policies, but modified their application by paying more attention to issues of social welfare. New programs have achieved some success in alleviating the worst poverty.

THE REVOLUTIONS: CUBA, NICARAGUA, EL SALVADOR, GUATEMALA, PERU, AND COLOMBIA

The Cuban Revolution shattered the fragile political equilibrium of the late 1950s in Latin America. The victory of Fidel Castro and his 26th of July Movement in Cuba introduced a whole new set of factors into Latin American domestic political equations. The "fall" of Cuba to communism mobilized the United States to intense involvement in the region. Fidel Castro's call for revolution throughout Latin America intensified the fears of the upper class–military alliance. Revolutionary insurgencies rose all over the region in the 1960s and 1970s, some obviously inspired by Cuba and others the result of entirely domestic factors. Often encouraged by the United States, Latin American militaries increased their political and economic activity in response.

Cuba

Cuba seemed an unlikely location for communist revolution in the late 1950s. After all, it was only 90 miles from the United States, filled with U.S. investment and tourists, dependent on the United States as a market for its sugar, and ruled by the Caribbean's strongest dictator, Fulgencio Batista. It also boasted one of the wealthiest, healthiest, and best-educated populations in Latin America. Nonetheless, on January 1, 1959, the revolutionary 26th of July Movement, led by Fidel Castro and other opposition groups, overthrew Batista (1940–1944, 1952–1959).

Batista had dominated the island's politics since 1934. He spent 7 years of comfortable, voluntary exile in Florida after the completion of his first term as president in 1944, and then returned as dictator in 1952. He and his followers hoped to regenerate Cuba, but, as his fellow former strongmen Ibáñez and Vargas discovered, ruling was harder the second time around, even if one was now a dictator. Fidel Castro was one of Batista's early opponents. Castro had grown up in the rough-and-tumble of Cuban student politics during the late 1940s and early 1950s, an era of blatant corruption, open violence, and deep disillusionment. On July 26, 1953, Castro led a small band in a disastrous attack on the army barracks at Moncada on the southern part of the island, barely escaping with his life. He was captured a few days later, however, and avoided execution only by luck. Amnestied after 2 years in prison in 1955, he left for Mexico, where he plotted and raised money to mount a new invasion of Cuba. He returned in late 1956, making his way with a small group of rebels to the mountains in the southeastern part of the island. There he established a small guerrilla movement, supported by local rural people. During the next 2 years, Batista's regime crumbled as the 26th of July movement and others, mostly urban rebels, grew stronger.

On the day the rebel army rolled into Havana, Castro declared that "This time the Revolution will truly come to power. It will not be . . . [as in the past] . . . when the masses were exuberant in the belief that they had at last come to power but thieves came to power instead. No thieves, no traitors, no interventionists! This time the revolution is for real."

Glorious victory soon gave way to grim reality, and Castro faced a number of daunting obstacles. First, the relatively small 26th of July Movement had to consolidate its power, because the group had never numbered more than a few hundred. Other rebel groups looked to share the victory. Second, at 32, Castro was the oldest of the revolutionaries. The revolutionaries' relative youth, which had stood them well during the rigors of guerrilla warfare, was a glaring disadvantage when the rebels became rulers: Neither Castro nor his followers had administrative experience, nor did they have a plan for governing. Castro thus needed reliable allies with expertise in governance. Third, Castro had to neutralize the United States, which had cut short Cuba's previous revolutions in 1898 and 1933.

Castro resolved these problems in the early 1960s by proclaiming his revolution socialist, breaking relations with the United States, allying with the Soviet Union, and taking on the Cuban communist party as a partner in governance.

His actions led to two confrontations with the United States that ultimately solidified his regime. In April 1961, his army defeated an informal force of U.S.-trained and U.S.-supported Cuban exiles who invaded the island at the Bay of Pigs, making him an even greater hero than previously. Then, in October 1962, the United States and the Soviet Union nearly went to war over the installation in Cuba of Soviet offensive intercontinental ballistic missiles. The U.S. Navy blockaded the island to prevent the arrival of additional weaponry. After a tense 13 days, the superpowers reached agreement: The United States promised not to invade Cuba if the Soviets removed the missiles from the island. The United States, however, has maintained an embargo on trade with Cuba from that time to the present day.

The Cuban Revolution has met with mixed success. Its economic program during its first two decades was marked by a series of unsuccessful attempts at diversification from its dependence on sugar exports and quixotic efforts to create a "New Socialist" Cuban who would work for the general good rather than individual gain. Castro then created a Soviet-style inflexible bureaucracy, the failures of which led him to occasional experiments with free markets and private enterprise. Cuba relied heavily on billions of dollars provided by the Soviet Union and the Communist bloc in Eastern Europe, which purchased most of the island's sugar. The collapse of the Soviet Union and its satellites in 1989 and the subsequent loss of their financial support caused an enormous crisis from which the nation recovered only slowly. There have been periodic shortages of staples and rationing. Nickel exports and tourism (mostly Europeans) have augmented the economy since 2000. Sugar has been in decline, with the 2009 harvest the smallest in a century. Despite the ups and downs of the economy, Cubans have been the best-educated and healthiest Latin Americans. The distribution of wealth is the most equitable in the region.

Politically, Fidel Castro, ailing at age 82, resigned as president of the Council of State in 2008, stepping aside for his younger brother (by 5 years) Raul. Fidel remains the First Secretary of the Communist Party.

Nicaragua

Central America suffered major upheavals after World War II, when long-term dictators, pressured by U.S. diplomacy, retired or were overthrown by more progressive forces.

The prolonged guerrilla wars and counterinsurgency in the region began in the aftermath of the Cuban insurrection and resulted in the deaths of hundreds of thousands of people and the displacement of millions more during the 1970s, 1980s, and early 1990s. By 2000, the nations of the region, their civil wars fought to stalemates, were at peace, and democracies governed all.

The road to this eventual outcome was long and agonizing, however. In 1979, the Sandinista National Liberation Front (FSLN) in Nicaragua overthrew Anastasio Somoza Debayle, making Nicaragua's leftist revolution the only one other than Cuba's to win power through force of arms. Later, however, it became the only leftist revolution in Latin America to lose control of the government through fair elections. The Somoza family, Anastasio Somoza García (1935–1956) and his sons Luis Somoza Debayle (1956–1967) and Anastasio Somoza Debayle (1967–1979), ruled Nicaragua for 46 years through control of the National Guard, which devolved into a lucrative criminal enterprise. Like many other Latin American insurgencies, the Sandinista National Liberation Front began in the early 1960s. It took its name from Augusto Sandino, who had led guerrillas against the U.S. occupation of Nicaragua during the late 1920s and whom Somoza's henchmen had assassinated in 1934. It attracted rural people, students, and the disillusioned children of upper- and middle-class families, perhaps numbering only about 3000 in 1978.

The Somoza regime began to disintegrate when it misappropriated relief funds after a catastrophic earthquake in 1972. Anastasio Somoza Debayle lost the support of the upper classes 6 years later when he ordered the assassination of longtime rival Pedro Joaquín Chamorro. The FSLN then took control of the National Palace in a daring raid, an action that clearly indicated the regime had lost its iron grip. Somoza fled on July 19, 1979. An estimated 50,000 Nicaraguans died in the brief but bloody civil war.

The Sandinistas ruled for the next decade. They governed without national elections until 1984, when FSLN leader Daniel Ortega won the presidency. Unfortunately for the Sandinistas, they encountered implacable opposition to their regime from the United States during Ronald Reagan's administration, which clandestinely and illegally backed the rival *Contras*, a conservative coalition, in a vicious civil war from 1981 to 1989 that cost another 40,000 Nicaraguans their lives. With the help of the other Central American presidents, the FSLN and the Contras finally reached a peace agreement in 1989.

The Sandinistas, again, like the 26th of July group, committed serious economic and administrative blunders mostly due to their inexperience. The civil war took an enormous toll not only in lives but also in billions of dollars in damages. The military draft, instituted to supply soldiers to combat the Contras, was very unpopular. But the single most important mistake of the Sandinista leadership was its failure to fully incorporate women. Much of the Sandinista guerrilla leadership was female, and many women heroes were wounded, raped, and tortured during the war for control of the country. The FSLN could not have won without the efforts of its women leaders and soldiers, but many of the movement's women felt dismissed and disdained after 1979, when the work of battle shifted to the work of governing. The Sandinistas also angered women in traditional roles, who did not want their children drafted into the army. This massive loss of women's support during the 1980s played a large part in the Sandinistas loss of the 1990 election.

Almost everyone in Nicaragua and abroad was surprised when Violeta Barrios de Chamorro, the widow of the martyred Pedro Joaquín Chamorro, won election as president that year. Nicaraguans were exhausted from years of civil war and sought an alternative to the ineffective Sandinistas. The FSLN remained a powerful influence in the National Assembly, where it was the largest single party, and in the army. Nonetheless, Nicaraguans were so disillusioned with the Sandinistas that they elected two more Conservative presidents to succeed Chamorro in 1996 and 2002, the first instances in Nicaraguan history when one democratically elected president succeeded another. However, in 2006, amidst the regionwide Pink Tide, Daniel Ortega staged a stunning political comeback, when he won election as president.

El Salvador

In El Salvador, a leftist insurgency nearly won control of the country in the 1980s. The nation's troubles dated back to the early 1930s, when the brutal dictatorship of General Maximiliano Hernández Martínez ordered the slaughter of 30,000 rural Salvadorans. The upper classes, fearing another uprising, backed Hernández Martínez (1930–1944) until his overthrow in 1944. Thereafter, an alliance between wealthy coffee planters and the military governed through electoral fraud and violent repression. El Salvador held its first open election in 1972, but the government nullified the results when it became clear that José Napoleón Duarte, the opposition candidate, had received the most votes. Twelve years passed before the next legitimate election, and this time Duarte (1984–1989) won (again) and took office in 1984.

Despite the democratic outcome of the election, a vicious civil war tore the country apart for the next 5 years. Guerrilla groups appeared in El Salvador in the late 1960s, drawing their support from El Salvador's vast, exploited, migratory rural working class., Between 1979 and 1989 the Augustín Farabundo Martí Front for National Liberation (FMLN) mounted a strong challenge to the military–upper class alliance, nearly winning the civil war, but for the massive assistance to the Salvadoran army provided by the United States. At their peak, the FMLN had an estimated 8000 combatants.

Exhausted by years of civil war, Salvadorans went to the polls in 1989 and elected Alfredo Cristiani, the candidate of the National Republican Alliance (ARENA), a coalition of right-wing groups. Much as in Nicaragua, people turned to the Right to bring peace. Cristiani reached agreement with the guerrillas in 1991, and three ARENA presidents succeeded each other in 1994, 1999, and 2004. In 2009 Salvadorans elected Maurisio Funas, a member of the FMLN, as president. As in Nicaragua, the guerrillas of the 1980s had in the new millennium taken power.

Guatemala

In 1944, Guatemala's longtime dictator, Jorge Ubico (1930–1944), was overthrown by a reformist group, led by young military officers, that redistributed land and fostered labor. This process ended in 1954, however, when the U.S. Central Intelligence Agency sponsored a successful revolt by Colonel Carlos Castillo Armas, who brutally overturned a decade's worth of improvements in the lives of the working classes. His successor, Miguel Ydígoras Fuentes (1958–1963), likewise served the interests of the upper classes, but without the repression practiced by Castillo.

In 1960, a guerrilla movement calling itself the Rebel Armed Forces, heartened by the Cuban example, took up arms. The military, in an effort to combat the guerrillas, ousted Ydígoras in 1963 and then ruled behind the scenes for the next decade, waging a campaign of terror and murder. Two successive generals ruled for the next 8 years. They intensified repression and presided over a measure of economic gains and an orgy of corruption. Death squads, determined to crush the rural insurgency, stalked the countryside, killing Indians, who supposedly supported the guerrillas. The scale of murder reached genocidal proportions. The war continued through coups and a string of presidents until 1996, when the government reached an accord with the rebels, ending nearly four decades of warfare that had caused 200,000 deaths. A semblance of democracy followed with democratically elected presidents in 2000, 2004, and 2008. As in the cases of Nicaragua and El Salvador, Guatemala lies in ruins, only slowly recovering from decades of violence and destruction.

Peru

From the late 1960s through the 1990s, Peru experienced three distinct revolutionary movements. The first in 1968 consisted of reformist military officers who implemented far-reaching reforms. During the 1980s and 1990s, a violent guerrilla organization terrorized the country and nearly toppled the government. Lastly, a third upheaval occurred when the president who had defeated the guerrillas ruled as an elected dictator in order to rebuild the economy.

Each of the revolutions resulted from the long-term, frustrating impasse in Peruvian politics that pitted the military–upper-class alliance against APRA (see Chapter 12) and its leader Victor Raúl Haya de la Torre. The precipitating event for this series of upheavals was the election of 1962, which first resulted in a military coup to prevent Haya from becoming president. Fernando Belaunde Terry (1963–1968) won the new election, but governed ineffectively, paving the way for another coup, led by General Juan Velasco Alvarado, who set out to establish a "third way," neither communism nor capitalism. Velasco redistributed more land from 1968 to 1975 than either the Mexican or Bolivian revolutions, giving over half the nation's land to 375,000 families, one quarter of all rural dwellers. He also vastly expanded the government's role in the economy, financing his program through massive borrowing abroad. But Velasco became ill in 1975 and stepped down. His successor Francisco Morales Bermúdez rolled back some of the reforms and adopted austerity policies to repay the debt. New elections took place in 1980 with

Belaunde winning the presidency, again with little to show for his term (1980–1985). These years, however, marked the emergence of the Sendero Luminoso (Shining Path), in the Andes mountains.

Abimael Guzmán, the self-proclaimed "Fourth Sword of Marxism" (Marx, Lenin, and Mao were the first three), was the mastermind of the movement, which began in 1970 as a splinter of the fragmented Peruvian Communist Party. The name derived from a quote from José Carlos Mariátegui, Peru's leading communist thinker, which proclaimed that "Marxism-Leninism will open a shining path to revolution." Guzmán dismissed other leftists in Latin America as traitors. He called the Cuban Revolution, for example, "a petty bourgeois militaristic deviation." He also believed in violence. The Sendero brutally murdered thousands of political officials, especially small landowners and those regarded as do-gooders. The awful violence not only intimidated many Peruvians but also earned the group many enemies.

The Sendero organization was extremely disciplined and cohesive, in part because it offered its members opportunities they did not have otherwise. Sendero drew its strength from young people with poverty-stricken backgrounds in the countryside and the shantytowns of Lima. Many of these youths had achieved a university education only to find that neither government nor the private sector could provide them with satisfactory employment. This made the Sendero, which paid its soldiers well by Peruvian standards (by using large amounts of money from taxes on narcotics traffickers), extremely appealing. In addition, the Sendero was fairly egalitarian in terms of gender: Half of its leadership was female. At its height, the Sendero had perhaps 10,000 guerrillas under arms and as many as 100,000 sympathizers.

By 1992, Sendero Luminoso had brought Peru to the verge of demoralization and collapse, and the war had cost 30,000 lives. Guerrilla victory appeared inevitable as the military seemed to fall apart and panic gripped the nation. Then on September 12, 1992, the tide turned, when the army unexpectedly captured Abimael Guzmán and much of the Sendero leadership. Without its highest echelons, the movement disintegrated. The Shining Path had brought Peru to its knees. Like the FMLN in El Salvador, the guerrillas came very close to victory, and the war cost the country dearly in terms of human life and economic destruction.

The third Peruvian "revolution" occurred in 1990, when Peruvians, desperate for a savior as Sendero violence devastated the country, elected little-known Alberto Fujimori president (1990–2000). Having used the military and rural community organizations to defeat the Sendero, Fujimori won reelection in 1995. Fujimori governed autocratically, but with the nation finally at peace, the Peruvian economy grew rapidly. This third "revolution" ended when Fujimori had to flee the country in 2000 in order to avoid arrest amid major scandals. In 2001, Alejandro Toledo became the first Indian to be elected president. In 2006 Peruvians elected Alan García to be president once again.

Colombia

In Colombia during the middle of the twentieth century, as in Peru, dysfunctional politics led to prolonged guerrilla warfare, which, predictably, exacted a heavy toll on its people and economy. Colombian history had long been marred by bloody civil wars between its two major political parties, the Liberals and Conservatives. Following the overthrow of the dictator Gustavo Rojas Pinilla (1953–1957) in 1957, the two political parties formed the National Front. They agreed to alternate the presidency every 4 years and to distribute elected and appointed political offices equally. This arrangement endured for 16 years, finally ending the long-running violence between the two parties.

But Colombia was hardly democratic during these years, given that the National Front permitted little dissent. Lacking outlets for peaceful protest, some citizens banded together into a number of guerrilla groups sprung up during the early 1960s. By the 1980s, the M-19 (founded in 1972) and the Revolutionary Armed Forces of Colombia (FARC) had become the largest and most effective of these groups. The guerrillas often controlled various regions of the country, but they were fragmented and unwilling to unite to obtain victory. In the mid-1980s, there was a brief peace, but from 1986 to 2001, an estimated 300,000 Colombians perished in the violence and an additional 2 million were displaced. By the end of the century, the FARC, its army numbering 15,000, controlled nearly half the country. The Colombian government often seemed on the brink of collapse. The election and reelection of Alvaro Uribe as president in 2002 and 2006 reinvigorated the government's struggle against the rebels, but the FARC remained the largest Marxist insurgency in the world.

THE TYRANNIES: BRAZIL, ARGENTINA, AND CHILE

Beginning in the mid-1960s and lasting through the late 1980s, several Latin American nations endured prolonged rule by rightist, military governments that seized power illegally and maintained control by using terror. Unlike past military regimes, these governments determined to remain indefinitely and to remake their societies, seeking to return to traditional patriarchal values with women subordinate to men and dedicated exclusively to caring for the home and their children. The military regimes sought and achieved the elimination of leftist organizations, including political parties, labor unions, and university students and faculty. Tens of thousands of people perished in the onslaught, many of them tortured. They spared no one, as rich, poor, men, women, children, bureaucrats, priests, and nuns were victims. Most citizens of these countries looked the other way in the face of the horror, fearing leftist takeovers more than their loss of freedoms.

The support for the rightist governments came from the armed forces, which despite their internal divisions united in common fear of the Left, the middle classes, whose members were terrified by the threatened disorder brought on by protesters, and the U.S. government, which regarded the Latin American military as the last bastion against communism in the resurgent Cold War against the Soviet Union. The military relied on well-educated technocrats to operate the government bureaucracy and state-owned enterprises, creating a political structure that became known as "bureaucratic authoritarianism."

The military regimes also looked to further economic development through a strategy that included attracting foreign investment by keeping wages low and enabling the accumulation of vast wealth by the domestic upper classes. State-run businesses proved enormously inefficient and corrupt. Moreover, their economic policies were often detrimental to their core constituencies, the middle classes.

Brazil

The Brazilian military took over in 1964 after a tumultuous 3 years during which President Janio Quadros (1961), an eccentric independent with no political party backing, abruptly resigned after only months in office and was succeeded by João Goulart, the vice president, a former close ally of Getulio Vargas, whom the military despised. Goulart lasted less than 3 years.

The first military governments were led by General Humberto de Alancar Castello Branco (1964–1967) and General Artur de Costa e Silva (1967–1969), who severely limited civil rights and established the wage suppression–foreign investment economic development policy. The war on the Left intensified under Emílio Garrastazú Médici (1969–1974), who also presided over the so-called Brazilian "economic miracle." By the late 1970s, however, the military had proven as inept and corrupt as its civilian predecessors, and it began a slow transition to democratic government. The first elected president in two decades, Tancredo Neves (1985), died after 2 weeks in office, but his successor José Sarney (1985–1990) managed his way through difficult economic times. Since 1985 Brazil has maintained its democracy.

Argentina

After the coup that overthrew Juan Perón in1955, Argentina experienced a decade of alternating military and civilian governments with neither the armed forces nor the various factions of the Radical Party able to find a way to accommodate the Peronists.

In 1966, General Juan Carlos Onganía overthrew Arturo Illia (1963–1966) and set about to renovate society. He outlawed political parties and expelled leftist students and faculty from the universities. These actions resulted in widespread protests, led by automobile workers and students in the interior city of Córdoba in May 1969. Within a year, these protests were followed by series of spectacular kidnappings by guerrillas known as the *Montoneros*. Although it proved ineffective, the group provoked an unprecedented, vicious response from rightwing military and upper-class-sponsored gangs. Argentina descended into murder and chaos. With the nation disintegrating, it turned once again to Juan Perón, then long exiled in Spain. Even though in failing health, 78-year-old Perón won election as president in 1974. He died in July after only a few futile months in office. His third wife María Estela Martínez de Perón ("Isabelita") succeeded him with no better results until she was overthrown in early 1976.

From 1976 to 1983 was the darkest chapter in Argentine history. Under the brutal rule of General Jorge Videla (1976–1981) due process of law vanished and was replaced by torture and murder. By 1978 the military had eradicated the guerrillas and killed most labor union leaders, even shop stewards. The cost was dear, for the armed forces, police, and right wing gangs killed an estimated 30,000 people. Known as the "disappeared" ones (*desaparecidos*), they were executed without trials or public records.

As in Brazil, however, the military's popularity waned over time as they proved inept economic managers. In a desperate measure to regain support, the regime went to war against Great Britain in April 1982. Argentine forces occupied the Malvinas in the South Pacific, a territory that the British had seized 150 years earlier and which had remained in dispute ever since. President Leopoldo Galtieri (1981–1982) badly miscalculated both the British response and the reaction of the United States, expecting the former not to fight for the islands and the latter to back Argentina. The war was disastrous, resulting in 2000 casualties and $2 billion in expenditures. The humiliating defeat discredited the Argentine armed services and forced them to relinquish power.

Raúl Alfonsín (1983–1989), who had long opposed the military dictatorship, won election as president in 1983. His term was difficult, because the Peronists were uncooperative and the armed forces staged a number of rebellions. He had begun the healing, however, and paved the way for the peaceful succession of Peronist Carlos Menem (1989–1999) in 1989. It was the first time since 1928 that one elected Argentine president followed another. Menem served two terms. Four presidents fulfilled the next term, as an economic downturn buffeted the nation. Left-leaning populist Néstor Kirchner (2003–2007) and his wife Cristina Fernández de Kirchner (2007–2011) were Argentine versions of the "Pink Tide" that swept South America after the turn of the millennium.

Slice of Life   ON THE STREETS OF NUEVO LAREDO

MORE THAN ONE-FOURTH of all working Latin Americans are employed in the informal sector of the economy, which includes petty entrepreneurs selling a broad range of items and providing services, as well as small-time criminals, prostitutes, and street children. In Peru, more than half of the working people toil in the informal sector. High unemployment rates, especially among unskilled, inadequately educated people, many of whom are recent migrants from the countryside, have left millions of Latin Americans on the economic margins, struggling daily to make a living.

Perhaps the most well-known of these petty business people are the street vendors seen almost everywhere in the large cities, where they fill the public spaces outside of the underground (subway) and bus stations and the sidewalks of busy neighborhoods. But there are several hundred thousand more who scratch out their subsistence as trash pickers, known as *pepenadores* in Mexico, *cartoneros* in Argentina, *catadores* in Brazil, and *moscas* in Peru. They constitute an extensive recycling enterprise throughout the region, scavenging bottles, cans, and cardboard. One study in 2002 estimated that 150,000 Brazilians earned their living collecting aluminum cans, some 9 billion of them a year. In some cases, trash picking has moved beyond the informal economy. In Mexico City, the pickers have their own union which controls the municipal dumps.

The cardboard pickers, known as *cartoneros,* of Nuevo Laredo, Mexico, while not entirely typical of the informal economy, nonetheless, provide us with a graphic insight into its operations. Nuevo Laredo is a city of 400,000, in the State of Tamaulipas, in northeastern Mexico directly across the Rio Grande River from its twin city Laredo, Texas. For a century and a half Mexicans have recovered wastes from both cities. According to Martín Medina, who has meticulously studied the cartoneros in Nuevo Laredo, Mexican scavengers have collected cardboard in Laredo since before World War II. Medina's informants describe a large number of cartoneros collecting in Laredo and bringing the cardboard across the border during the 1940s. Because U.S. sanitary regulations did not permit them to bring their horses into the United States, the collectors had to use pushcarts. They use horse carts in Nuevo Laredo to the present day.

As a result of the considerable expansion of Laredo as a retail center and the establishment of border manufacturing plants, known as *maquiladoras,* in northern Mexico, the amount of cardboard boxes has grown enormously over the past few decades. During the 1950s, a Catholic priest in Laredo helped found a cartonero cooperative, the Sociedad Cooperativa de Recuperadores de Materiales de Nuevo Laredo, and to negotiate a legal working arrangement with local government in Laredo. The scavengers suffered a setback in the 1960s, when the Mexican government outlawed importation of waste cardboard. The cartoneros innovatively smuggled the material by throwing the cardboard into the river and having accomplices pull it out on the other side. During the 1980s, the Mexican government instituted a quota system, requiring an expensive permit to transport cardboard within Mexico. The cartoneros, however, circumvented and outlasted all these impediments.

Recycling of paper products in Mexico has become an important business. The paper industry has been chronically short of raw materials, as the consequence of the high cost of logging in Mexico (paper is made from wood). By the 1990s, only a quarter of the fiber used in Mexican paper came from wood pulp. The rest was from recycling. Therefore, what began as an illustrative case of the informal economy has become attached (and vital) to the formal economy, the paper industry. Middlemen connect the two sectors, with the cartoneros selling to the middlemen and the middlemen selling to the industry.

Medina cites a survey conducted in 1994, which presents a picture of the average cartonero: He is a 40-year-old married male and is literate in Spanish, despite having had only 4 years of education. Most cartoneros are male, because the usual method of transporting the cardboard is a three-wheeled cart, known as a *tricicleta,* which requires strength enough to move more than 800 pounds of cardboard at a time. The cartoneros work 8 or 9 hours a day, 6 days a week. Many augment their income by collecting aluminum cans and other salvageable materials, and occasionally helping smugglers move their goods, mostly electronics, across the border. According to the 1994 survey, three-quarters of the cartoneros owned homes and had a higher median income than the average resident of Nuevo Laredo.

Although some observers sometimes dismiss the informal economy as having marginal economic value, it is clear, at least in the instance of the cartoneros of the

Another occupation in the internal economy is begging. In the words of one mother: "Shame is for those who steal, not for those who beg for their children."

two Laredos that the operators of the informal economy not only perform a valuable economic function but also allow a better-than-average standard of living for themselves and their families.

Questions for Discussion

What are the obstacles to entering the informal economy? What are the obstacles to making a decent living? Do you think that the cartoneros are part and parcel of an inherently corrupt political and economic system?

Chile

The tyranny that emerged in Chile during the 1970s was as shocking as that in Argentina and lasted a decade longer. Chile's long-held reputation for democratic, nonviolent politics was forever shattered.

In the 1950s, Chileans had turned to familiar names for their leaders, Carlos Ibáñez (1952–1958), a former president, and Jorge Alessandri (1958–1964), a son of a former president, with little results. Fearing that Socialist Salvador Allende, who had narrowly lost the 1958 election, would win in 1964, the moderate and conservative parties coalesced to support Christian Democrat Eduardo Frei (1964–1970). Despite considerable assistance from the U.S. Alliance for Progress, he could not sustain economic development, paving the way for Allende's election in 1970.

The first elected socialist head of state in the Americas, Allende, had a promising start, but his regime ended in tragedy. He ultimately failed, because he was unable to rein in the most radical factions of his coalition; he lost the support of the middle classes, which were wary of his radical program; and, lastly, the military abandoned its commitment to civilian constitutional rule. High prices for copper, Chile's leading export, boosted the economy during his first year, but the fierce opposition of the upper classes, the opposition of the U.S. government and foreign corporations, the loss of middle-class backing, and deteriorating economic conditions led to a military rebellion on September 11, 1973. Allende died in the fighting.

The commander of the army, General Augusto Pinochet, led the coup. He set out to not only depose the socialist president but, like the Argentine military, also to renovate Chilean society by eliminating the Left. The armed forces and their right-wing allies imprisoned, tortured, and murdered thousands. Pinochet closed congress and outlawed political parties and labor unions. He also privatized government-run enterprises and deregulated the economy. During his 16 years of dictatorship, however, Pinochet never suppressed Chileans' democratic tradition. A national plebiscite in 1988 ended military rule. Moderate Christian Democrats succeeded each other in the 1990s, accompanied by a measure of economic prosperity.

THE EXCEPTION: MEXICO

Only in Mexico, among the largest nations of Latin America, did the military play a subordinate role, though it too experienced a hidden "dirty" war against the Left during the 1970s and 1980s. As we learned in Chapter 11, after the revolutionary decade 1910 to 1920, a single-party political system evolved that began relatively responsive to the middle and lower classes, but which over time cared less and less about its constituents and became more and more corrupt. The regime used selective violence and patronage to maintain its power. From the 1940s through the 1960s, Mexico underwent a prolonged era of economic growth that redistributed wealth downward from the upper-income strata and upward from the lowest strata. The middle classes and skilled working class enjoyed a measure of prosperity. The Institutionalized Revolutionary Party (PRI) ruled unchallenged.

By the 1960s, however, the PRI had lost touch with the common folk. Growing protests from students and workers in 1968 caused PRI leaders to panic, leading to the slaughter of an estimated 500 people in the Plaza of the Three Cultures in Mexico City on October 2. Mexico was to host the Summer Olympic games, and the government feared embarrassment. The massacre at Tlateloco, as it became known, discredited the regime at home and abroad.

The discovery of vast oil reserves in the 1970s seemed at first as the way to continue economic growth and maintain the PRI in power. But mismanagement and corruption squandered the oil revenues. In order to continue the orgy of spending and theft the government borrowed heavily abroad, which left the nation with a mountain of debt, which, when oil prices fell from the boom time heights, was beyond Mexico's ability to repay.

The PRI continued to elect presidents through 2000, when the conservative *Partido de Acción Nacional* ended 70 years of one-party rule with Vicente Fox (2000–2006), a former executive with Coca Cola, winning the presidency. He was succeeded by another Panista Felipe de Jesús Calderón Hinojosa (2006–2012). Faced with a national legislature split between the PRI, PAN, and PRD (Party of the Democratic Revolution), neither Fox nor Calderón have accomplished very much reform. Calderón also confronted the drastic economic downturn in the United States, Mexico's largest trading partner, and the debacle of the war on drugs. The latter led to a widespread outbreak of violence, especially along the northern border.

LATIN AMERICAN LIVES

AN ARGENTINE MILITARY OFFICER

THE YEARS FROM 1976 to 1983 were Argentina's nightmare. The military, police, and vigilantes kidnapped, tortured, and killed thousands of its citizens. Military officers threw naked, drugged civilians from airplanes over the South Atlantic Ocean. Squads of white Ford Falcons arrived at homes in the middle of the night and took away their occupants, whom no one ever saw again. Soldiers raped female prisoners. Terrorist gangs kidnapped pregnant women, taking the babies and killing the mothers. Even today, few military officers are repentant for the deeds of this era. Who were the soldiers who could have committed such acts? What was it about the institution of the military that led it to turn viciously on its own people?

In 1995, retired Naval Captain Adolfo Scilingo and a half dozen other ex-officers publicly confessed to murder. While stationed at the Navy Mechanics School as a junior officer in 1977, Scilingo had flown on two flights during which he personally threw more than 30 living people into the ocean. He reported that his superiors had told him that these were extraordinary times requiring unusual actions.

The Argentine military was at almost every point before 1976 divided into two main groups: those who would maintain the constitutional order, even if they opposed the policies of the civilian government, and those who would overthrow any civilian government. There were also splits between the generals and the lesser-ranking officers. They argued over personalities and management styles. Finally, there were disagreements between the Army, Navy, and Air Force. The military previously had taken over the government in 1930, 1943, 1955, 1962, and 1966. Although their divisions never entirely disappeared, the armed forces unified from 1976 to 1983 in what they believed was a holy mission to save their fatherland. This time they vowed to remain in control.

Prior to 1976, Latin American officers trained at their individual nation's military academy. They chose their branch (cavalry, infantry, or artillery) during the first year of their 4-year course. Supply officers attended the academies, but they did not develop the same bonds as the line officers. The rigorous training emphasized character and tradition. The academies turned out men who had "a very subjective and very romantic . . ." worldview.

New officers experienced rigid discipline. They fell under the complete authority of their commanding officer, who often took an interest in the junior officer's social life and whose approval was necessary to marry. They earned promotions periodically: sub-lieutenant to lieutenant in 4 years, to captain in 8. Officers attended new schools at regular intervals. Selection to the status of general staff officers through examinations assured higher ranks. Those who reached the rank of colonel after about 20 years had received a year of higher military studies, which educated them in important national concerns. They also traveled abroad, often to the United States. The Argentine military was heavily influenced by German practices prior to World War II and by U.S. doctrine thereafter.

An officer's experience throughout the twentieth century would also include eroding salaries, outmoded equipment, and an intensifying sense of loyalty to the military. The officer corps believed itself above civilian petty politics in the abstract, but was mired in them in reality. Officers saw their duty was to defend their nation, but they disdained the civilians they swore to protect.

The generation of officers that came of age during the 1970s was either from small towns in the interior or sons or grandsons of immigrants. The previous cohort of officers had included many second-generation Argentines (half of the generals in 1950). As ethnic Argentines, they were often superpatriotic. Many sons of officers followed their fathers into the military. They lived to great extent in an insular world with military friends and family, which created a mentality of the military against the world. These officers did not trust civilians. The burst of leftist terrorism in the 1970s struck hard at their psyches, traditions, and beliefs. They saw themselves under siege by international communism.

By 1976, the Argentine military was desperate. It had intervened repeatedly in politics since 1930 to no effect. The nation seemed to regard the military with respect. Peronism was a sore that would not heal, but after his death in 1974, bringing back the dictator clearly was not an option. The international situation frightened the military, for insurgencies were everywhere: Vietnam, Africa, and other parts of Latin America. Fidel Castro had sponsored guerrillas (unsuccessfully) in neighboring Bolivia. Reflective of their middle-class backgrounds and decades of indoctrination, the office corps struck hard against its real and imagined enemies. The results scarred Argentina forever.

Captain Adolfo Scilingo, one of the Argentine military officers who admitted murdering civilians during the "Dirty War" (1976–1983).

> **Questions for Discussion**
>
> How did the Argentine military become so integral to the years of terror during the 1970s and 1980s? What factors caused the struggle between Left and Right to degenerate into brutality? How would you compare the years of the terror with some of the internecine strife during the nineteenth century, such as the civil wars between Liberals and Conservatives?

RESURGENT DEMOCRACY AND THE "PINK TIDE"

Latin Americans freed themselves from right-wing tyrannies beginning with the fall of the Argentine military in the wake of the humiliation of the Malvinas War in 1983, the Brazilian *Abertura* (democratic opening) during the mid-1980s, and the Chilean plebiscite (1988) and end to Pinochet's dictatorship in 1990. With the exception of Colombia, the terrible civil wars and insurgencies that had raged in the region ended by the mid-1990s. The new democracies that replaced the dictatorships, however, confronted overwhelming problems, such as the increased number of poor and the extreme maldistribution of wealth, which were the results of the inability of Latin American economies and societies to create sufficient employment or to provide crucial elements of social welfare, including basic education and health care. The exuberant return to free elections, unfortunately, did not bring about immediate amelioration of the harsh conditions many Latin Americans endured. Consequently, in some nations, though notably not Colombia, Mexico, or those in Central America, by the turn of the twenty-first century voters turned leftward for solutions.

The first of the new, elected leftist leaders was Venezuela's Hugo Chávez, a former military officer who had attempted to forcefully overthrow the government in 1992. He took office in 1999. Over the course of the next 7 years, left-of-center Ricardo Lagos and Michelle Bachelet in Chile, Luiz Inácio "Lula" da Silva in Brazil, Néstor Kirchner in Argentina, Alejandro Toledo in Peru, Evo Morales in Bolivia, and Tabares Vázquez in Uruguay ascended to the presidencies of their countries, comprising what became known as the "Pink Tide." Daniel Ortega's election in Nicaragua in 2006 and the FMLN's Mauricio Funes winning the presidency in 2009 continued the leftward trend.

Hugo Chávez quickly became notorious for his bellicose oratory, loudly berating both his domestic enemies—all political parties—and the United States, and for his friendship with Fidel Castro. The rapid increase in world oil prices after the terrorist attack on New York City in September 2001 heralded a bonanza for Venezuela, which had the largest petroleum reserves in the world outside of Saudi Arabia, providing Chávez with billions to implement his programs. Despite a slow start, his regime lowered the poverty rate to 39 percent from 50 percent, and the rate of extreme poverty by half. Inequality also fell substantially. There was a one-third decline in infant mortality and a doubling of the number of students in higher education. Inflation, however, remained a critical problem, remaining at over 30 percent. The country continued to be at the mercy of erratic oil prices. Chávez pushed through a number of political reforms that concentrated power in his hands and limited the rights of his opposition.

Latin American political leaders who came from the socialist and communist Left were somewhat more successful in alleviating the extreme inequities in income and the widespread poverty that plagued the continent. They were also less likely to challenge the neoliberal economic programs of their predecessors. In Chile, a left-of-center coalition of Christian Democrats and Socialists governed after the end of the Pinochet regime in 1989. Ricardo Lagos (2001–2006) and Michelle Bachelet (2006–2011) came from the old Socialist Party of Allende. The Left alliance brought a considerable measure of prosperity to Chile, reducing poverty, growing the economy, and investing in human capital (education, for example). Christian Democrats and Socialists alike continued the neoliberal policies of their predecessor Pinochet. Chile, however, suffered a major setback in 2010 when an enormous earthquake struck in the vicinity of the port city of Valparaíso. In Uruguay, Tabares Vázquez (2005–2010) won the presidency with the support of the old Left, including many former guerillas, but nonetheless did not tamper with the neoliberal economic program that had resulted in his nation having the lowest rate of poverty in the region. Uruguayans elected a former Tupamarú guerrilla José Mujica as president in 2010. Alejandro Toledo (2001–2006) in Peru, another socialist, restored stability to the nation's ruined politics in the aftermath of Fujimori's resignation in 2000. But he, too, did not alter the neoliberal economic policies of his predecessor. Peruvians then rejected further movement leftward by electing Alan García, the former president who had allowed the Shining Path insurgency to expand, as president in 2006. Both Uruguay and Peru experienced steady economic growth from 2003 through 2008.

"Lula" da Silva (2003–2011) in Brazil, perhaps, more than any other Latin American leader, epitomized the new wave of Left politics. He had founded the Brazilian Workers' Party in 1980 at the height of the military dictatorship. But he, too, did not adopt a radical program as president. His economic record has been cautious. Lula chose to continue the policies of his predecessor Fernando Henrique Cardoso (1995–2003), emphasizing fiscal conservatism and maintaining low inflation. The centerpiece of his social program was the Bolsa Família, which involves direct payments to poor families in return for their sending their children to school and taking advantage of preventive medicine programs. There has been as a result a halving of the number of Brazilians living in extreme poverty. Nonetheless, income distribution remains the most unequal in Latin America with the top 10 percent controlling 50.6 percent of the wealth and the bottom 10 percent 0.8 percent. In the new millennium, Brazil has emerged as one of the most important economic powers in the world, particularly as a leader in the production of food.

The most obvious old-line populist to emerge in the Pink Tide was Néstor Kirchner (2003–2007), a Perónist like Saul Menem, in Argentina. Kirchner rescued his nation from the depths of economic crisis and employed many of the familiar redistributive policies that made Perón popular among the working class. This resulted in a considerable reduction in the rate of poverty and extreme poverty and an improvement in the unequal distribution of wealth, though Argentina remains one of the most inequitable societies in the region. His wife Cristina Fernández de Kirchner, a prominent politician in her own right, succeeded him as president in 2007.

Perhaps the most radical of the emerging left leaders was Evo Morales (2006–2014) in Bolivia, the first elected indigenous president. Morales, contradicting a generation of political economic policies in the region, nationalized Bolivian natural gas resources in his first months in office. He also severed Bolivia's long-standing relationships with the International Monetary Fund and the World Bank. Taking over the revenues from hydrocarbon production provided the government with windfall revenues to finance its programs. Bolivia remains the poorest country in South America.

Democratization has proven inefficient in Latin America (as it has everywhere else), with presidents often at odds with their legislative bodies. In Venezuela, impatience with indecisive and often corrupt politics resulted in a popular president enhancing executive powers. A tendency toward authoritarian politics has also marked Nestor Kirchner's career. But for the most part, the Left has maintained a strong commitment to democracy.

The Left has not surged to power everywhere in Latin America, however. In Colombia, dissatisfaction with the displacements of decades of guerilla warfare led voters to elect conservative hard-liner Álvaro Uribe (2002–2010) as president twice. In Central America, the people of El Salvador, Guatemala, and Nicaragua elected conservatives as presidents for a decade after their prolonged civil wars. Mexico turned to the rightist Partido de Acción Nacional (PAN) and Vicente Fox, rather than to the Left to break the hold of the long rule of the PRI, and then elected another PAN president, Felipe Calderón, in 2006 (by a razor-thin margin in a bitterly disputed vote).

THE STRUGGLE FOR CONTROL OF EVERYDAY LIFE

Have Latin Americans given up the struggle to control their everyday lives? For two decades, terror overwhelmed this struggle, and currently, globalization threatens to eliminate differences between nations and peoples. Nonetheless, many Latin Americans retain their sense of locality, and they certainly continue to seek control of their lives. Local loyalties may have helped to save the nation-state from disintegration. The strong sense of local governance and tradition in the Peruvian highlands, for example, was the bulwark of opposition to the Shining Path guerrillas during the 1990s. The Shining Path thoroughly alienated much of the countryside by killing village leaders and priests and by brutally intruding on local prerogatives. The local organizations brought together to protect villages against the guerrillas were crucial participants in the eventual defeat of the insurgency. In Mexico, the deterioration of the official revolutionary political party (PRI), which led to its loss of power in 2000, was caused in large part by its unresponsiveness to local needs and sensibilities. Power had grown overcentralized in a nation where local traditions were so strong. The victorious opposition party, the National Action Party (PAN), was to considerable extent a product of Mexico's peripheral states, particularly in the north.

Unquestionably, contemporary factors have altered this unending struggle for control of everyday life. It was transformed by the vast migration from the countryside to the cities (see Chapters 13 and 15), which shattered the old ways. The migration resulted in far more people residing in urban slums, barrios, or squatter settlements than in villages. Thus, village life and identity were no longer the basis for people's politics, and the struggle for local (village) autonomy became largely irrelevant for urban dwellers. Instead, people formed neighborhood organizations to obtain services, such as water, electricity, schools, and roads. Also, new arrivals in the cities found it difficult to maintain the traditions of their country homes in the face of mass media that perpetually touted the benefits of a consumer culture.

In the workplace, the new migrants discovered that most workers had to negotiate their own way; only the fortunate might join a labor union. Those who were self-employed, as street vendors, for example, faced similar conditions, though a very few joined associations that represented them.

For those who remained in the countryside, much of the isolation that once defined rural life disappeared. Few could earn a living solely in agriculture, and, as a result, even those who stayed in the villages often had to supplement their income by working elsewhere. Mexicans regularly crossed the border to the United States to work on farms during planting and harvest seasons and then returned home. Rural dwellers' lives were also made difficult by bureaucratic-authoritarian and dictatorial regimes that determinedly undermined local prerogatives the 1970s and 1980s, perceiving local political efforts as impediments to the government's mission. The end of tyranny and the resurgence of democracy, however, have given new life to local autonomy.

INDIGENOUS POLITICAL MOVEMENTS

One of the most extraordinary developments arising from the democratization of Latin America since 1990 was the emergence of indigenous political movements. They have taken up the struggle to enhance local autonomy and to preserve their traditions. Indigenous peoples comprise approximately 11 percent of Latin America's population or 60 million. They are the majority in Bolivia and Guatemala and significant minorities in Belize, Ecuador, Honduras, Mexico, and Peru. Most live in rural communities, barely subsisting by farming their own plots and augmenting their incomes by working elsewhere or by crafts production.

Some historians have surmised that the movements originated with the guerrilla insurgencies of the 1960s and 1970s. Dormant during the years of the terror, they reorganized in thae space afforded them by more open democratic governments. By the 1990s the organizations had adopted up-to-date strategies that included sustained protests and use of mass media. The most famous of the efforts took place in Mexico in 1994, when the Zapatista Army of National Liberation (EZLN) rebelled in Chiapas, a state in southern Mexico, ostensibly against the implementation of the North American Free Trade agreement. Indigenous protests pushed out governments in Ecuador in 1997, 2001, and 2005 and in Bolivia in 2003 and 2005.

A striking aspect of the new movements was their creating new political parties that won considerable success in Colombia, Ecuador, and Bolivia. Peasant and indigenous groups (most notably coca growers) became part of the Movement to Socialism (MAS) that won the presidency in Bolivia in 2005; Evo Morales became the first indigenous elected leader of a South American nation in 2006.

In some ways the indigenous movements are a throwback to the struggles of the nineteenth and early twentieth century, when country people fought to retain their control over their everyday lives. The issues remain much the same: local control, national government interference, taxes, and land alienations. It was no accident that the EZLN took the name of Zapatistas.

THE NEW GLOBAL ECONOMY

As the new millennium began, democratic elections and relatively smooth transitions of power prevailed throughout Latin America. But these new regimes still faced the daunting economic challenges and mounting social tensions that had proven the downfall of the military dictatorships that preceded them. During the half century after World War II, the countries of the region pursued three general strategies to achieve economic development. The first was to promote and diversify exports, either by finding new primary products (oranges in Brazil or petroleum in Mexico, for example) or by using the advantage of inexpensive labor costs to manufacture goods for European or the U.S. markets. The second was import substitution industrialization. There were two versions of ISI: one set forth by democratic governments and the other by military dictatorships. Both export enhancement and ISI required extensive government involvement, costly importation of capital goods, heavy foreign borrowing, and massive foreign investment. Widespread poverty sharply limited domestic markets, placing a brake on economic development based on ISI. The third strategy, neoliberalism, adopted after policymakers declared ISI a failure, threw open Latin American markets, and removed governments from direct participation in the economy.

Despite so-called economic miracles in Mexico from the 1950s through 1970, in Brazil during the late 1960s and early 1970s, and in Chile during the 1990s, major problems hampered sustained economic growth in Latin America in the post-1959 era. The region experienced increasingly volatile cycles of booms and busts because all of the strategies for development depended on external markets, capital, and technology. Periodic downturns cost many people their jobs. Prolonged periods of steep inflation eroded the standard of living of the working and middle classes. Staggering foreign debt

How Historians Understand   THEORIES OF ECONOMIC DEVELOPMENT AND HISTORY

Since World War II, successive theories of economic development not only have greatly influenced the policies of Latin American governments, the behavior of businesspeople, and the plight of hundreds of millions of people but also the interpretation of historical events and trends.

During the nineteenth century, ideas advocating free trade and comparative advantage dominated. Accordingly, Latin American nations were to produce agricultural and mineral commodities for export and open their markets for imports of manufactured goods. The Great Depression of the 1930s challenged these perspectives. Economists no longer universally believed that the export of primary products was sustainable as a means to develop. In the late 1940s, the United Nations Economic Commission for Latin America (UNECLA or CEPAL), led by Raúl Prebisch, an Argentine, put forward the center-periphery paradigm, also known as structuralism. This view dominated Latin American economic thinking through the 1970s. It argued export economies tended in the long run to suffer from a decline in the terms of trade. In other words, the prices received for primary goods decreased because the demand for primary products would not rise as fast as income, while at the same time the prices of industrial products rose over time. The only way structuralists believed that Latin

Women sorting coffee beans on a fazenda in Brazil. Coffee was Brazil's leading export for more than a century.

America could develop was to substitute domestic for imported manufactures. This encouraged import substitution industrialization (see Chapters 12 and 14) as the development policy widely adopted in Latin America after World War II.

By the 1960s, however, ISI had clearly failed. Dependency analysis arose to explain Latin America's lack of development. There were two schools of *dependencia*—the neo-Marxist and the reformist. Dependency advocates believed that peripheral (underdeveloped) countries, like those in Latin America, and center nations (the United States, Western Europe, and more recently Japan) were involved in an unequal exchange that would always exploit the former and benefit the latter. Consequently, the only way to change the system was to either overthrow it, which the Marxist school advocated, or reform it. The most important translation of dependency into policy resulted in further government involvement in the economies of Latin American nations to mitigate the influence of the developed center. Ironically, in order to finance their economic interventions, governments borrowed huge sums from the industrialized nations.

In opposition to the dependency school, the diffusionist model maintained that technology, capital, trade, political institutions, and culture spread out from the advanced nations to the backward countries. Within the underdeveloped nations, there also were dual societies in which a more advanced urban sector and a backward rural sector coexisted. The diffusionists maintained that ideas and capital spread from urban to rural. Accordingly, they believed that policy should be directed so that the more advanced nations cooperate with the middle classes in less advanced nations to modernize the latter. Contrary to the diffusionists, the *dependentistas* believed that the diffusion of ideas and capital made the less developed nations dependent on the giving country and therefore widened the gaps between developed and less developed nations. This situation was duplicated in the dual domestic society.

Because no Left regime (with the exception of Cuba) endured for more than a decade in Latin America after 1945, due to the opposition of upper class–military alliances throughout the region, the intervention of the United States, and communist regimes everywhere falling into economic crises by the 1980s, Latin Americans became disillusioned with governments' strong involvement in the economy. Pressured heavily by the United States and international lending agencies such as the International Monetary Fund and the World Bank, Latin American policy makers turned to the century-old liberal paradigm, now known as neoliberalism. The idea that market forces will eventually bring equity dominated once again.

How did these differing views affect historians? These theories overwhelmingly emphasized outside factors as causes of Latin American underdevelopment. This tended to lessen the importance of domestic circumstances. In a sense, these theories removed culpability from the upper class–military alliance, from individual leaders, political parties, traditions, and culture. They reduced the lower classes to

(*continued on next page*)

THEORIES OF ECONOMIC DEVELOPMENT AND HISTORY (*continued from previous page*)

meaningless nonparticipants. The emphasis on international factors tended to push aside the consideration of the regional and local, which had predominated in Latin America since pre-Columbian times, leaving out the most meaningful aspects of culture and society, and overemphasizing economics. Finally, dependency, especially, did not incorporate change over time, perhaps the most crucial aspect of an historian's purview.

In recent times, historians have reduced their concerns with economics and turned to the occurrences of everyday life and culture. This has placed the lower classes in a more central place in their studies. There has been a shift from international to local and from great forces to people.

Questions for Discussion

Why have the various models of economic development failed in Latin America? How has the struggle for control over daily life fit into the various models of development?

---

interest payments absorbed the preponderance of government revenues, leaving little or nothing for social welfare. The already sharp inequalities in the distribution of wealth and income widened, as the rich grew ever richer and the poor even poorer. Corruption ran rampant.

The world petroleum crises of the 1970s constituted a twofold curse for Latin America. Not only did the rise in oil prices cause general inflation and economic downturn, but it also exacerbated the debt crisis in many countries. The members of the Organization of Petroleum Exporting Countries (OPEC) earned enormous sums from the increases in oil revenues, which they deposited in Western financial institutions. The banks faced the dilemma of where to invest this money. Latin American nations (mostly Argentina, Brazil, Mexico, and Venezuela) required vast funds to develop. Latin American nations were able to pay the interest on the debt as long as their economies grew. Badly damaged by the second oil crisis, however, Latin American countries could not pay by the early 1980s. Mexico nearly defaulted in August of 1982. Rescheduling the debt and a short-lived upturn avoided the collapse of the international banking system, but the enormous burden for Latin America was not lessened in the long term. From 1978 to 2000, Argentina increased its foreign debt tenfold. Brazil quadrupled it. Mexico increased it by 500 percent. Argentina, Brazil, and Mexico in 2000 owed more than a half billion dollars abroad.

There are some indications the new millennium has brought some interesting changes. First, the vast movement of peoples, particularly to the United States, has had some surprising consequences. Funds sent by Latin American workers to their families back home, known as remittances, have had an enormous economic impact. In Mexico, remittances (*migradollars*) constitute the third-largest source of income after oil exports and tourism. In a number of the poorest Latin American nations, remittances account for more than 10 percent of the Gross Domestic Product. Until the economic crisis that began in 2008, remittances had grown at a rate of 15 percent per year for a decade, reaching an estimated $70 billion, 80 percent of which came from the United States. These funds have mitigated the harsh conditions in much of the region, lessening the precariousness of survival in many instances. It is not clear to what extent the remittances have alleviated poverty, however.

Second, there are several examples of nations that have diversified sufficiently to no longer suffer as badly from the swings of the world economy. Brazil with its array of agricultural commodity exports would be a prime case. Third, Brazil among others has also succeeded in diversifying its export customer base. As of 2010, China was its leading trade partner. Lastly, with Brazil again the major case, Latin America has begun to expand its domestic markets, lessening its dependence on markets abroad.

CONCLUSION

Momentous changes marked the half century after the Cuban Revolution in Latin America. Guerrilla wars and military reigns of terror caused the deaths of countless thousands and dislocated hundreds of thousands more. At times, it seemed as if the region had descended into madness. An era of democracy followed those dark days. The end of insurgencies in Guatemala and Peru in the 1990s left only one major rebellion—that in Colombia.

Though democracy rules almost every nation of Latin America, there are threatening clouds overhead. Who can guess what will happen when Fidel Castro finally passes from the stage in Cuba? Mexico at times seems near to descending into chaos as a result of the economic crisis in the United States from 2008 to 2010 and the U.S.-sponsored war on drugs. In 2010, violence on the northern border had reached epic proportions. Colombia with its still-strong insurgencies remains precarious. The Pink Tide's social programs offer at least the threat of inflation. Latin America continues to be deeply in debt. Most important, however, is the problem of how Latin America can assure the continuation of democracy when, as we will see in Chapter 15, poverty and misery pervade the region.

LEARNING MORE ABOUT LATIN AMERICANS

Diamond, Larry, Plattner, Marc F., and Abente Brun, Diego, eds. *Latin America's Struggle for Democracy* (Baltimore, MD: The Johns Hopkins University Press, 2008). Reasoned analysis of the Pink Tide.

Domínguez, Jorge I., and Shifter, Michael, eds. *Constructing Democratic Governance in Latin America* (Baltimore, MD: The Johns Hopkins University Press, 2008). An analysis of the recent wave of democracy in the region.

Gwynne, Robert N., and Cristobal Kay, eds. *Latin America Transformed: Globalization and Modernity*, 2nd ed. (New York: Arnold, 2004). Filled with statistical data and interesting analyses.

Masterson, Daniel. *Militarism and Politics in Latin America: Peru from Sánchez Cerro to Sendero Luminoso* (New York: Greenwood, 1991). Clarifies the role of the military in Peru.

Menchú, Rigoberta. *I, Rigoberta Menchú: An Indian Woman in Guatemala*. Trans. Ann Wright (New York: Verso, 1984). Heart-breaking story of rural women in Guatemala in the midst of civil war.

Miller, Francesca. *Latin American Women and Social Justice* (Hanover, NH: University Press of New England, 1991). Relates the participation of women in organized social movements.

Pérez-Stable, Marifeli. *The Cuban Revolution: Origins, Course, and Legacy*, 2nd ed. (New York: Oxford University Press, 2003). Fair-minded assessment of the revolution.

Smith, Lois, and Alfred Padula. *Sex and Revolution: Women in Socialist Cuba* (New York: Oxford University Press, 1996). Explores the disappointing treatment of women in Cuba.

Stern, Steve, ed. *Shining and Other Paths: War and Society in Peru, 1980–1995* (Durham, NC: Duke University Press, 1998). Essays on the Sendero Luminoso and its relations with people in the countryside.

15

EVERYDAY LIFE:
1959 TO THE PRESENT

THE UNPRECEDENTED REIGN of terror perpetrated by rightist military dictatorships in Argentina, Brazil, Chile, and Uruguay, and the vicious civil wars between rightist militaries and rightist and leftist guerrillas in Central America, Colombia, and Peru, described in Chapter 14, created an era of deep political tensions and economic hardships across Latin America. Not only were hundreds of thousands of people killed, wounded, and displaced, but nearly everyone else suffered uncertainty. Latin Americans risked imprisonment, torture, or death for speaking their minds in public. In countries such as Argentina and Guatemala, few people were not related to or familiar with someone who had been "disappeared": taken away in the middle of the night, never to be seen again, or killed by leftist guerrillas or rightist death squads. To make matters worse, military regimes often installed nonpolitical technocrats as the managers of their governments. Because neither the military nor the technocrats saw themselves as accountable to voters, they disregarded the potential repercussions their new economic programs might have on the middle and lower classes. They instituted policies that dismembered direct government involvement in business enterprises and opened national borders to free trade and foreign investment. As a result, many Latin Americans suffered extensive job losses and a large-scale erosion of their standard of living.

The end of the terror and the ensuing democratization of the region over the course of the 1980 and 1990s did not immediately improve economic conditions. Almost every nation in the region experienced periods of sustained economic growth, which after the new millennium lessened the dire inequalities between the wealthiest and the rest of the population and decreased the numbers of desperately poor. The Pink Tide governments that won elections after 1998 adopted a number of programs aimed at alleviating the worst poverty. In Venezuela, Chávez used the increased revenues derived from the government takeover of the national oil company in 2003 to lower the poverty rate from 54 to 26 percent of the population. Extreme poverty fell by 72 percent to under 10 percent. Inequality lessened as well. However, with the exception of Venezuela and Bolivia, the new left governments were extremely cautious financially, maintaining surpluses, which limited to a considerable extent their ability to alleviate the plight of the poor. Nonetheless, they benefitted almost uniformly from the boom in export commodities after 2003 that raised their revenues. Thus, from 2003 to 2008 Latin America enjoyed a period of economic growth and low inflation. Despite the significant improvement in the lives of Latin Americans, in 2008, 33 percent of the region's population or 180 million people lived in poverty and 12.9 percent or 71 million lived in extreme poverty.

In the new millennium, globalization transformed not only the economies but also the material culture and communications of Latin America. The impact of U.S. consumerism and popular culture, carried by the mass media all over the region, was widespread. (Even in the most remote villages, for instance, one could find Coca-Cola.) Indigenous Latin Americans, much like their ancestors in the sixteenth century, had to choose which aspects of their tradition and which aspects of the modern culture generated, in part, by globalization they would use to construct new and unique cultures. In art, as well as in politics and everyday life, Latin Americans sought to make sense of their shifting reality. When brutal regimes suppressed their creativity, artists found new means of expression, while at the same time melding their views and techniques with those from abroad to construct distinctly Latin American art.

The last quarter of the twentieth and first decade of the twenty-first century brought on extraordinary challenges for the people of Latin America. Their efforts to pull themselves upward economically produced unanticipated adverse consequences for the environment. And natural disasters, such as hurricanes, floods, and earthquakes added to their struggles.

THE REIGN OF TERROR

Dictatorships and guerrilla insurgencies tormented Latin America from the mid-1960s through the mid- or late 1980s. Citizens in all of the nations discussed in Chapter 14 lived in fear of the police, military, guerrillas, and informal paramilitary death squads. The human and physical damage that resulted from this long era of terror was breathtaking. There were tens of thousands of casualties. Hundreds of thousands of people were dislocated from their homes. If this were not enough, civil and human rights were nonexistent. Regimes, such as in Chile, ruled under a state of siege, eliminating due process of law.

The human toll exacted during this period surpassed that of the incessant conflicts of the nineteenth century. Between 1975 and 1995, 33,000 Colombians were casualties of the civil war. In 1997 alone, 200,000 people had to abandon their homes because of intensified fighting. El Salvador suffered 70,000 civilian deaths in its terrible civil war during the 1980s. The guerrilla war and counterinsurgency in Guatemala destroyed

---

LATIN AMERICAN LIVES

WOMEN REBELS

IN THE CUBAN REVOLUTION and subsequent movements, women have mobilized in response to widespread political oppression. They have led the resistance to dictatorships in Argentina, Brazil, and Chile. They have joined the revolutionary organizations in Guatemala, El Salvador, and Nicaragua. In Bolivia, Mexico, and Peru, women have actively participated in rural and urban protest movements. They have fought time and again to protect themselves and their families from economic crises and political mistreatment and to end long-standing gender-based oppression.

Two of these women, Vilma Espín and Doris María Tijerino, are examples of the endurance, sacrifice, and extraordinary courage and leadership women have provided to the movements for social justice.

Vilma Espín Guillois (1930–2007) was a chemical engineer with degrees from the University of Oriente (in Cuba) and the Massachusetts Institute of Technology, whose father was a high-ranking executive in the Bacardi Rum Company. In 1955, she joined the 26th of July Movement in Cuba, led by Fidel Castro. As a student, she had participated in protests against Batista, written and distributed antigovernment pamphlets, and joined the National Revolutionary movement. She was in Mexico briefly when Castro was in exile there, and when the 26th of July struggled in the Sierra Madre Mountains during 1956 and 1957, she was a member of its national directorate, along with two other women, Haydée Santamaría and Celia Sánchez (later Fidel Castro's longtime companion). Working in the cities, she went underground, narrowly escaping arrest in May 1957. Espín coordinated the group's work in Oriente province and then took over much of the overall leadership in the province when police killed Frank País, her boss. Espín was one of the leaders of a national strike in April 1958, which failed. She married Fidel Castro's brother Raúl, one of the rebel commanders, after the triumph of the revolution in 1959 (the couple reportedly separated in the 1980s). In 1960, she became director of the Federation of Cuban Women (FMC), a post she held through the 1990s. The FMC eventually included 3 million women, 80 percent of the women in Cuba. She also served as a member of the Central Committee, the Council of State, and the Politburo, the highest leadership group of the Communist Party. Espín was outspoken against the sexual double standard and other gender inequities that were still prevalent in Cuban society. She was one of only a small number of women to hold the top leadership posts in the government and Communist Party, which is clear indication of the mixed success achieved by the Cuban Revolution in granting equal rights to women.

Doris María Tijerino Haslam (b. 1943) was one the earliest Sandinistas. Her father worked as an engineer for the Nicaraguan National Guard, which was notorious for its corruption and oppressive tactics. A veteran of the guerrilla insurgency from the late 1960s, Tijerino was arrested, jailed, and tortured in 1969 by the Somoza regime. She was imprisoned until 1974, when the infamous Sandinista raid on a high-society Christmas party obtained the release of political prisoners. The government captured her again in 1978. Another daring raid, which took over the National Palace, secured her release. Tijerino received the rank of full commander in the Sandinista army, the only woman to do so. She paid a terrible personal price for her achievements, however—the Somoza government murdered two of her husbands. In postrevolutionary Nicaragua, she headed the National Women's Association, was head of the national police, and was a member of the national legislature. She kept her seat as a Senator even after the Sandinista defeat in 1989. Tijerino, like Espín, suffered from discrimination by the very revolutionary government she helped place in power and then helped lead, because its men would not allow women to attain the highest ranks within the government, despite their obvious ability to lead and the wrenching sacrifices they had made.

Questions for Discussion

Given the traditional role of women in Latin America, why do you think women were such important contributors to the revolutions in Cuba and Nicaragua from the 1950s through the 1990s?

440 hamlets. Hundreds of thousands fled into exile in Mexico and the United States. Forty thousand died in the civil war in Nicaragua during the 1980s. Between 1980 and 1995 in Peru, the Shining Path guerrilla movement and the government counterinsurgency led to the deaths of more than 20,000 people and produced perhaps 200,000 internal refugees.

The economic cost of all this destruction was staggering. The Shining Path, for example, caused an estimated $15 billion in damages. The real income of Peruvians dropped by one-third just in the period from 1990 to 1992: One million people lost their jobs in Lima alone. In the late 1990s, because of the long civil war, three-quarters of the people of Guatemala lived in poverty, more than one-half of these in extreme poverty.

THE QUALITY OF LIFE

The terror visited upon Latin America by the right-wing regimes and leftist insurgencies brought unspeakable misery to the region. Latin Americans, after two decades of economic growth and equalization of income after World War II, plunged once again into overwhelming poverty. Latin America and the Caribbean suffer the most unequal distribution of income in the world.

The deterioration of Latin Americans' well-being was all the more tragic in light of the fact that after World War II several decades of relative growth and prosperity had offered hope to millions by reducing poverty in terms of percentage of the population and redistributing wealth to the middle and lower classes. From 1950 to 1980, per capita income rose by an average of 3 percent a year. This pushed down the percentage of the population living in poverty from an estimated 65 percent in 1950 to 25 percent in 1980.

Between 1970 and 1982, the share of the income of the wealthiest 20 percent fell, and the share of the poorest rose 10 percent.

By 1980, however, after a decade of dictatorships, sustained growth ended and during the next 10 to 15 years the widespread adoption of free market, neoliberal strategies badly exacerbated conditions. From 1982 to 1993, the number of people living in poverty in Latin America increased from 78 million to 150 million. Relatively speaking, the wealthiest nations in the region, Argentina, Uruguay, and Venezuela, experienced the sharpest increase in poverty. Economic stagnation or decline, rampant unemployment, widespread underemployment, and inflation characterized the years of the terror and incipient democracy. During the 1980s, the per capita gross domestic product fell more than 20 percent in Argentina, Bolivia, Nicaragua, Peru, and Venezuela. The only countries that did not suffer net decline in gross national income from 1980 to 1992 were Chile, Colombia, and Uruguay. In Latin America, 1990 per capita income was 15 percent below the 1980 level. As a result, the number of poor rose to 210 million by the mid-1990s. There was a clear correlation between the establishment of right-wing regimes or the presence of a prolonged insurgency and the impoverishment of the population. The percentage of people below the poverty line in Chile, for example, went from 17 in 1970, the first year of the government of Salvador Allende, to 45 in 1985 after a dozen years of Agustin Pinochet's dictatorship. Thirty years of war in Guatemala immersed 60 percent of the total population of 10 million in poverty.

The onset of democratization has improved the lot of the poor. Current poverty and indigence rates are far below those of 1990, the approximate date by which the terror had ended. Peru's rate of poverty went from 48 to 36 percent since 2006. In Uruguay, under Pink Tide president Tabare Vázquez (2005–2010), the unemployment rate fell to 6.4 percent, the lowest ever recorded.

What Does It Mean to Be Poor?

The poor in Latin America are overwhelmingly rural, female, and Indian or black and most likely live in Brazil, Mexico, or Peru. Poverty levels in the countryside are twice those in the cities. Women are more likely to be poor than men. The percentage of the indigenous population living in poverty in Bolivia in 2002 was 72, in, Mexico 90, and Peru 65 (see Table 15.1).

Malnourishment, disease, and high infant mortality are an inescapable fact of life for the poor. In 1980, more than 50 million people in the region had a daily calorie intake below the standards set by the World Health Organization (WHO). Twenty million of those were seriously malnourished. In Mexico, the diets of an incredible 52 percent of the population did not meet WHO standards. Urbanization and globalization increased malnourishment. In 1960, for example, Mexicans mostly ate tortillas, beans, bread, and small quantities of vegetables, eggs, and meat. Two decades later, poor city dwellers consumed more processed food (such as white bread) and soda. Consumption of milk in Mexico declined about 10 percent during the 1980s, while consumption of beans dropped even more. Mexicans ate only minimal amounts of eggs, fruits, and vegetables, and 60 percent

TABLE 15.1

Latin Americans Living in Poverty and Extreme Poverty, 1980–2002

Country	Percentage of Population in Poverty			Percentage of Population in Extreme Poverty		
	1980	2002	2006	1980	2002	2006/7
Argentina	10.5	45.4 (Urban)	–	2.8	20.9	–
Bolivia	–	62.4	–	–	37.1	31.2
Brazil	45.3	37.5	33.3	22.6	13.2	8.5
Chile	45.1	18.8	13.7	17.4	4.7	–
Colombia	42.3	51.1	19.2	17.4	24.6	–
Costa Rica	23.6	20.3	–	6.9	8.2	5.3
Ecuador	–	–	43.0	–	–	16.0
El Salvador	–	48.9	–	–	22.1	–
Guatemala	71.1	60.2	54.8	39.6	30.9	–
Honduras	–	77.3	71.5	–	54.4	45.6
Mexico	42.5	39.4	31.7	15.4	12.6	8.7
Nicaragua	–	69.4	–	–	42.4	–
Panamá	41.0	–	29.9	19.7	–	12.0
Paraguay	–	61.0	–	–	33.2	31.6
Peru	34.0	54.8	44.5	17.4	24.4	–
República Dominicana	–	44.9	–	–	20.3	–
Uruguay	14.6	–	–	4.0	–	–
Venezuela	25.0	48.6	30.2	8.6	22.2	8.5
Latin America	40.5	44.4	–	18.6	19.4	–

Source: Economic Commission for Latin America and the Caribbean (ECLAC), Statistical Yearbook for Latin America and the Caribbean, 2004 (LC/G.2264-P/B), Santiago 2005, figure 50.0, pp. 118–119. United Nations Publications, Sales N° E/S.05.II.G.1.

ate no meat at all, leaving them easy prey for dysentery, malnutrition, and anemia. Their diets were marked by consumption of less protein and more sugar. The complex combination of corn (tortillas), beans, and chili (hot sauce), which had provided their sustenance since the beginning of civilization, gradually gave way to widely advertised Pan Bimbo (the equivalent of Wonder Bread) and Coca-Cola. Maternal malnutrition has been the primary cause of high child mortality rates, which in 1996 stood at 102 per 1000 births in Bolivia. In Nicaragua, the infant mortality rate in the 1990s was a stunning 138 per 1000 births among the poorest sector of the population. Ironically, at the same time, overall life expectancy improved: It was 47 years in 1950 and 68 in 1990.

To be poor not only means that you would not have enough to eat and that your children would likely die before they were a year old but that you would have limited or no access to health care, sanitation, and housing. Routine health services are not available to one out of three Latin Americans. An estimated 1.5 million people under the age of 65 die each year from causes that are avoidable. Unfortunately, neoliberal policies have cut expenditures for health care, and, as a result, the incidence of diseases associated with poverty, such as dengue, cholera, hepatitis, typhoid, and tuberculosis, has risen. Access to safe drinking water and adequate sanitation is badly limited, leading to the proliferation of disease. Less than 2 percent of Latin American sewage is treated, resulting in the proliferation of typhoid and cholera. The lack of health and sanitation facilities in indigenous communities allows outbreaks of influenza, measles, dengue, and respiratory infections to quickly become epidemics. Between 20 and 30 percent of all Latin American children grow up in overcrowded lodgings (three or more in a bedroom). In Brazil, perhaps 200,000 children live on the streets.

The biggest hope for Latin Americans to struggle out of poverty is education, but it is seemingly unattainable beyond the first few grades. While overall educational enrollment expanded from the 1960s through the 1970s and the percentage of children ages 6 to 11 in school reached 71 in 1970 and 82 in 1980, the percentage of children ages 12 to 17 in school only went from 15 to 24. Today in Guatemala, a poor child will complete on average just 1 year of schooling. In Bolivia, only one-third of those who enter primary school finish. Even in Chile, a poor child will complete only 6 years of school. The situation worsened with the neoliberal reduction in government expenditures as Latin American per capita public expenditures on education fell 12.5 percent during the hard times of the 1980s. Latin Americans are imprisoned in their poverty.

Some observers saw the rapid population growth after World War II as a major cause of the increase in poverty. During the post–World War II boom, reproductive rates rose so that by 1960 the region's population was increasing at the rate of over 3 percent per year, more than doubling between 1950 and 1980. It became clear, however, that Latin American economies could neither sustain sufficient economic growth to provide employment for the increased number of workers nor could governments provide services, such as health care, housing, and education, for them. Consequently, Latin American governments have implemented policies to lower the birth rate, expecting that this would alleviate poverty. Since 1980, in fact, the population growth rate in the region has declined as a result of the expanded use of contraception. The Mexican government program to encourage the use of contraceptives resulted in more than a twofold increase in their use from 1976 to 1995 (30.2 percent in 1976 to 66.5 percent in 1995). However, the poorest Latin Americans have resisted contraception use and maintained high levels of fertility. Geographer Sylvia Chant provides the example of Melia, a 27-year-old woman who lived in a one-room hut in a barrio in Puerto Vallarta, Mexico, with her husband, a construction worker, and six children ranging from ages 3 to 9 years. Melia is a devout Catholic who had not used nor planned to use contraception, calling her offspring "gifts from god."

Although the sharp increase in population contributed to unemployment and poverty, no other phenomenon of the post-1959 era has damaged the status and well-being of the lower and middle classes more than inflation. Inflation reached staggering rates during the 1970s and 1980s (see Table 15.2). Bolivia's consumer price index, for example, rose an average of 610 percent between 1980 and 1985, with the largest

TABLE 15.2

Inflation (Average Annual Rate)

	1970–80	1980–85	1985	1992	1995	2000	2003
Argentina	118.5	322.6	672.2	17.6	1.6	−0.7	13.4
Bolivia	18.8	610.9	11,749.2	10.5	12.6	3.8	3.3
Brazil	34.2	135.1	301.8	1,149.1	22.0	5.5	14.7
Chile	130.2	21.3	30.7	12.7	8.2	4.7	14.7
Colombia		22.3	24.1	25.1	19.5	8.8	7.1
Mexico	16.5	60.7	57.8	11.9	52.1	8.9	4.5
Peru	30.3	102.1	163.4	56.7	10.2	4.0	2.3
Latin America				414.4	25.8	8.7	

Source: ECLA, *Statistical Yearbook for Latin America and the Caribbean*, 1990, pp. 98–99; ECLA, *Statistical Yearbook for Latin America and the Caribbean*, 2000, p. 751, and *2005*, p. 136.

increase in 1985 at over 11,000 percent. Brazil's inflation topped 1500 percent in 1989, Nicaragua's 9700 percent in 1988, and Peru's 3398 percent in 1989. Only Colombia, Guatemala, Honduras, Panama, and Paraguay escaped inflation rates of more than 30 percent per year during this era. Inflation badly eroded real wages. No one could live without difficulty during these periods of hyperinflation. Fortunately, in the first decade of the new century the Pink Tide governments have, for the most part, reined in inflation with only Venezuela's rate above 10 percent in 2010.

It is perhaps not surprising that in an environment where the currency might decline 2 percent in value each day, conditions created desperation. Thus, to be poor also meant that one lives amid crime, which has risen sharply, further exacerbating the decline in the quality of everyday life. Crime in Mexico City, for example, rose by 40 percent from 1963 to 1980, by more than 40 percent more in the 1980s, and by more than 40 percent again in the first half of the 1990s. Many other cities in Mexico, such as Guadalajara and Tijuana, also suffered from surging lawlessness. Conditions deteriorated to the extent that police subjected passengers to weapons searches before the passengers were allowed to board first-class buses traveling between Mexican cities.

Latin Americans have proven extraordinarily resourceful in adapting to these difficult conditions. They have survived economically in great part because they have constructed an informal economy and because they have left their homelands to go elsewhere, sometimes to the cities, but often to other countries, in search of security and economic opportunities.

Informal Economy

The informal economy, which includes activities that take place outside of regulation and law, consists of small-scale, low-technology, family-run farms, mines, artisan shops, services, and vendors, nearly all of which are run by Indians, blacks, mulattos, and mestizos.

Neoliberal policies resulted in a substantial increase in the informal sector because 81 percent of the new employment they generated was in the informal or small enterprise sector. From 1980 to 1992, in Latin America as a whole, employment in small enterprises increased from 15 to 22 percent of the workforce. The informal sector's share of employment went from 19 to 27 percent. With domestic service (6.4 percent), these two accounted for over half the workforce. At the same time, employment in large- or medium-size businesses fell from 44 to 31 percent and public employment from 15.7 to 13.6 percent. La Paz, Bolivia, where the number of vendors in the markets jumped from 15,000 in 1967 to nearly double that number in 1992, provides a good example of the consequences of neoliberalism for the informal sector. The informal sector continued to grow through the era of democratization In Bolivia, Colombia, Ecuador, Paraguay, and Peru it accounted for more than 40 percent of the Gross Domestic Product. In Paraguay it amounted to nearly 70 percent.

The streets of Latin America's cities are filled with individual petty entrepreneurs, who will sell items ranging from gum and candy bars to hot food to appliances. These small businesses are usually the product of a continuum, in which migrants move to the cities, take jobs—if they can find them—as domestics and menial laborers, and then, when they are more established, begin their own enterprises, using the skills learned from parents and other family. They rely first on the unpaid labor of nuclear family, but also extended kinship networks. When necessary, they obtain additional labor from workers seasonally unemployed by the export sector, and illiterate, unskilled residents of urban slums. Some proprietors of informal-sector businesses manage to rise above the poverty level. Many others are not so fortunate, however, because the informal economy also includes street children, small-time criminals, and prostitutes.

The informal economy not only provides a living for increasing numbers of Latin Americans but also supplies the daily needs of much of the population. In the bustling central market of Cuzco, Peru, for example, vendors sell anything a consumer might want, such as watches, hats, medicinal herbs, clothes, and endless quantities of food, some prepared and hot. In Lima, the informal sector built most of the public markets and delivers 95 percent of Lima's public transportation. In Bolivia, half the economically active population works in small businesses. In Latin American cities, vendors set up shop anywhere that space is available. The sound of bargaining is relentless, as the market women and their customers dicker back and forth over prices. The noisy market, teeming with people and overflowing with smells of food, is still the very lifeblood of the city.

Women play exceptionally important roles in the informal economy. They dominate the markets today, much as they have since before the Europeans arrived in the sixteenth century. In Cuzco, women run the stalls, caring for children, gossiping, and helping their neighbors at the same time. Often, the women begin work as domestic servants, then move on to itinerant peddling, and lastly to the market. Necessary skills, including relentless haggling with customers to get the best prices for their merchandise, are passed on from mother to daughter or aunt to niece. Work in the market provides

MEDICAMENTOS
SUEROS
VACUNAS
ANTIBIOTICOS
ALIMENTOS
GRANILLO
SEMA
SALVADILLO

Women vendors in market.

women with income, flexibility to care for children, and autonomy from men. Some women work only part-time in the market so that they can hold additional jobs. Some vendors journey in from the countryside periodically to sell agricultural products, while others invest in a license for a permanent stall.

Life is by no means easy for market women, though. Most of them are single mothers or widows. Competition with other sellers is relentless. They must be shrewd in their dealings with local authorities. They depend heavily on family members to help them. They must be willing to work long hours. The pressure on them is enormous. As one market woman put it: "From the time I wake up until I go to bed, it's the preoccupation a mother has to feed her children, to find food for her children, whether we sell or not, because if we don't sell, there's no food to eat."

A few examples illustrate the complex adaptations required by men and women who earn their livelihoods in the informal economy. Doña Avenina Copana de Garnica is an artisan in La Paz, Bolivia. Born in the city, she nonetheless speaks Aymara, an indigenous language, as well as Spanish. She and her husband and their six children live in small, rented quarters above their small workshop in an artisan district of the city. The upstairs has one bedroom with bunk beds. They sleep and work there. The shop has a small stove for soldering and shares space with a cooking area demarcated by a piece of cloth.

The Garnica family uses metal, cardboard, and cloth to make numerous items used in rituals and celebrations, including masks, noisemakers, whips, and costumes for miniature figures. Avelina's parents live across the street, and the whole family works in the business. They learned their trades from relatives. Avelina comes from a family of costume makers. She embroiders the costumes for the miniatures. She also cuts and pastes the decorations for the costumes. Her husband, a tinsmith, apprenticed with her aunt and makes objects out of sheet metal. The family employs seasonal workers. Avelina keeps the books and supervises the workers, often making 40-minute bus rides to their homes. The Garnicas actively promote their products through sponsorship of local fiestas, selling to tourist stores in the city, and even traveling to Peru to expand their market further.

Slice of Life   THE BARRIO/FAVELA

THE VAST INCREASE in the population of Latin America's great cities is the most important development in the region since the 1940s. As we saw in Chapters 13 and 14, the enormous influx of migrants created gigantic, unmanageable urban areas, and shantytowns now dominate these megacities. Known as barrios in Mexico, barriadas in Peru, and favelas (also *mucambos*) in Brazil, they incorporate hundreds of thousands, sometimes millions, of poor people, most of whom have fled desperate conditions in the countryside. These huge, filthy shantytowns are noisy monuments to the resourcefulness and resilience of impoverished human beings who, seemingly against all odds, survive, and occasionally prosper, with dignity and humor. It is one of the mysteries of twentieth-century history that they have not erupted into bitterness, resentment, and widespread violence.

The shantytowns appeared in empty spaces owned by absentee landlords or by the local governments, arising overnight as people heard by word of mouth of any empty space and assembled to occupy it. After moving in from other parts of the city or from the countryside, residents constructed their abodes with materials salvaged from others' trash, such as scrap wood, corrugated metal, cement blocks, and, sometimes, cardboard and cloth. Unrecognized by city authorities, the settlements initially had no water, electrical, or sewage services, nor did they have schools or medical clinics. If lucky, inhabitants would line up for hours to fill cans and bottles with water from a public spigot or a visiting water truck. Inhabitants obtained electricity by stealing it—and paid exorbitant prices.

As cities expanded, the shantytowns always stayed on the outskirts, often on the steep sides of hills or in low regions susceptible to flooding. No one wanted these lands, for they were scarcely habitable. In some areas, shantytown residents organized and won self-government as municipalities. One such case is Netzahualcóyotl, now a city in its own right in the state of Mexico with 1.2 million residents, which began as a squatter settlement on the dried-out bed of Lake Texcoco, where strong winds swirl volcanic soil about and flooding is chronic. The government sold the land during the 1920s to developers whose project never materialized. Later, real estate promoters illegally sold 160,000 plots of land to low-income people. Ciudad Netzahualcóyotl incorporated 40 irregular settlements northeast of Mexico City in 1964. In the 1970s, still without services, residents protested by withholding mortgage payments. Eventually, the government furnished the services and granted legal titles to the residents. Similarly, in many other cities, squatters banded together to organize protests to acquire their properties legally and to obtain services. The fight was often hard, because governments and landlords frequently used violence against the protestors.

In Rio de Janeiro, the seemingly chaotic nature of the settlements hides innovation and resourcefulness. Dwellers employ clever techniques to maximize the use of difficult space. They build their homes literally brick by brick as they accumulate enough money to acquire more building materials and add to their structures, making them more permanent. The favelas are not obsolete, retrograde remnants of rural culture. Rather, they were and are places of transition and persistence.

The shantytowns in many ways are twenty-first-century urban versions of rural villages. Just as country folk fought to maintain their local autonomy and traditions in the nineteenth and much of the twentieth centuries, the residents of shantytowns have struggled to assert their control over everyday lives.

Questions for Discussion

How do the circumstances of twentieth- and twenty-first-century struggles for control over everyday life in urban shantytowns differ from those of villages in the countryside in the nineteenth and early twentieth centuries? How are they similar?

Like Avelina Copana de Garnicas, Sofía Velázquez grew up in La Paz, Bolivia, and earns her livelihood in the city's informal economy. She began her working life helping her mother sell candles in the markets and then sold vegetables in the market on days when there was no school. Later, she sold eggs, beer, onions, mutton, and pork. Separated from her husband, she earned enough to send her one daughter, Rocío, a teenager in the early 1990s, to private school. She continues to buy and sell pork, but she and her daughter now supplement their income by working as food vendors: Rocío cooks and Sofía sells the food in front of their home. Sofía also plays an active role in community affairs. She heads the organization that controls the local market, a position that carries with it the considerable expense of sponsoring local fiestas.

Narcotics

The most notorious aspect of the informal economy is the production and commerce in illegal drugs, primarily cocaine, marijuana, and methamphetamines. At various times over the past three decades, the United States has pushed for campaigns against the production and distribution of drugs in Bolivia, Peru, Colombia, and Mexico. The so-called "War against Drugs" has not appreciably diminished consumption. There have been, however, important ramifications to these efforts. By one estimate, illegal drugs just in Mexico generate $17 to $38 billion a year. The war has had mixed success. In Peru, cocaine production fell by 70 percent from 1995 to 2001, but experts attribute this drop to low prices for coca (the plant from which cocaine derives), and so when prices rose in 2002 acreage in production increased.

One of the unanticipated consequences of the antidrug campaign, U.S. antidrug intervention in Latin America has been an adverse impact on the environment. For example, erradication programs in Colombia have led to the clearing of over 1.75 million acres of Amazon rainforest. Aerial eradication efforts are responsible for the destruction of legal subsistence crops, and the pesticide glyphosate is suspected of causing a variety of health problems in Colombian children, including diarrhea, hair loss, and skin rashes.

The antidrug campaigns have affected primarily Bolivia, Peru, Colombia, and Mexico. But the most notable impact has been in Mexico, where in 2007 the newly elected president Felipe Calderón started a major campaign against the criminal cartels, called the Mérida Initiative, that caused an unprecedented outbreak of violence and by 2010 the deaths of 23,000 people, more than 7000 in 2009 alone. At one point Calderón sent an occupying army of 6500 to the state of Michoacán. By 2010 there were 45,000 Mexican troops involved in the national campaign. The militarization of the conflict resulted in widespread human rights abuses.

There has been a considerable economic and political cost, as well. Tourism, Mexico's third-largest enterprise (oil and remittances rank first and second, respectively), worth about $11 billion annually, has declined since 2007 because of the violence. The vast sums of money involved have led to widespread corruption at all levels of the police, military, and civilian government, which has eroded the respect for both the government and the law.

The Great Migrations

Since the 1960s, vast numbers of Latin Americans have left their homes to find security and work in other countries. This movement of people has to some extent alleviated the pressures on governments to provide employment for their citizens. It also has been an enormous source of funds for Latin American economies. Since 1960, more than 10 million people have immigrated from Latin America to the United States. Most came from Mexico, but hundreds of thousands arrived from the Dominican Republic, El Salvador, Cuba, Colombia, Guatemala, and Honduras. Cubans fled the communist regime. The Central Americans and Colombians sought to escape the region's civil wars.

The economic impact of this migration of people has been enormous, because the new immigrants have remitted billions of dollars to their home countries. In 2008, Latin Americans sent a total of $70 billion to the region, funds that benefited every country. Mexicans sent back more than $25 billion, and even Uruguayans remitted $116 million. The flow was set back somewhat by the worldwide economic downturn in 2009, which cut remittances. In some years, in countries such as the Dominican Republic, these remittances have kept the economy afloat during tough times.

A short summary of migration in Central America illustrates the importance of these movements of people. Before the 1960s, Central Americans moved within the region to find work. More than 350,000 Salvadorans, for example, made homes and found work in neighboring Honduras until the mid-1960s, when the Honduran authorities deported them. Guatemalan Mayan Indians crossed back and forth over the Mexican border for centuries to labor in the plantations in Chiapas. The civil wars of the 1980s, however, changed these patterns of migration, when endemic violence pushed hundreds of thousands to the United States and other nations.

One of the recent developments is the movement of people from Latin America to the nations of southern Europe (Spain, Portugal, and Italy) and the United Kingdom. A million people from Latin America and the Caribbean resided in Spain, for example, in 2010.

The impact of both the vast movement of people and the transfer of large sums of money from immigrants to their former homelands are much discussed. There is, for example, concern about the loss of workers in the prime of their lives economically, particularly the highly educated. In villages in Mexico it is not uncommon for the entire population of working age men and women to migrate at least for part of the year, leaving only the very old and very young. Remittances are a major source of income for many low-income families; in some places, as much as 40 percent of the households draw a substantial portion of their support from them. But the impact of the remittances is not certain. Beyond alleviating the worst conditions by allowing for the purchase of staples, there are few linkages that might lead to development.

THE CITIES

The massive movement of people to the cities that began in the nineteenth century has continued unabated. From 1950 to 1980, 27 million Latin Americans, almost all of them poor, left the countryside for the cities. The percentage of people living in urban areas rose from 40.9 percent to 63.3 percent. In the last third of the twentieth century, the people of Latin America moved to the cities in overwhelming numbers. By 1995, the proportion of urban dwellers reached 78 percent of Latin Americans. (In the United States, they comprise 76.2 percent.) Many Latin American nations' populations are predominantly urban: Argentina's is 87.5 percent urban, Brazil 78.7 percent, Chile 85.9 percent, Uruguay 90.3 percent, and Venezuela 92.9 percent. Furthermore, the population is concentrated in a very few enormous cities. Forty percent of Chileans live in Santiago. São Paulo and Mexico City each may have as many as 20 million inhabitants. With Buenos Aires and Rio de Janeiro, these cities make up four of the ten largest cities in the world.

The statistics for Mexico City are staggering. It is spread over 950 square miles, three times the size of New York City. Mexico City contains 25 percent of Mexico's population, 42 percent of all jobs, 53 percent of all wages and salaries, 38 percent of the value of all industrial plants, 49 percent of sales of durable goods, and 55 percent of all expenditures in social welfare. Its inhabitants consume 40 percent of all food production, buy 90 percent of all electrical appliances, use 66 percent of country's energy and telephones, and purchase 58 percent of the automobiles.

The great cities are virtually unmanageable. Less than half of Brazilian urban residents have garbage collection with almost all these waste materials dumped into streams or open spaces. The only factor that mitigates this enormous environmental problem is that poor people generate less waste than more affluent people. Many lack sanitation facilities. As of 1990, only 16 percent of the households of São Paulo were connected to municipal sewage treatment plants. Consequently, human wastes contaminate the water. In Brazil, it is estimated that 70 percent of all hospitalizations are the consequence of diseases that result from the lack of sanitation. Twenty-seven percent of Latin America's urban residents—80 million people—breathe air that does not meet World Health Organization guidelines. The only factor that keeps the cities from being overwhelmed by toxic emissions from automobiles is that Latin America has relatively few autos compared to the United States.

To Be Poor in the Cities

Latin American cities are really two cities—one for the rich and the other for the poor. Lima, for example, has a modern downtown with paved streets dotted with skyscrapers. Surrounding the center are millions of people living in *barriadas,* or squatter settlements. Many of the *barriadas,* also known as *barrios* or *colonias* elsewhere in Spanish America or as *favelas* in Brazil, were rural into the 1940s and even the 1950s. Gradually, as the city grew outward and as people searched for less expensive living quarters, farmland disappeared. The residents of these settlements have migrated from the Andean highlands. Dirt roads lead through the houses built from scrap lumber, woven mats, and other materials. The stink from open sewers is noticeable. The bustle is everywhere and noise abounds. The marketplaces are busy.

Beneath the apparent squalor, the odors, and the hustle are real communities. And it is here that the twenty-first century's version of the struggle for control over everyday life occurs. In Lima's barriadas and other squatter settlements throughout Latin America, people assist each other in much the same ways as they had when planting and harvesting on collectively operated farms in the highlands. Networks of relatives and friends from their home villages make life more bearable. When Jorge and Celsa settled in Lima's Chalaca barriada, for example, Jorge's sister and brother helped them build a house on the same plot where the sister and her husband lived. An aunt also provided support. Later, Celsa's sister, her husband, and four small children moved in.

Most barriada families started with next to nothing and have painstakingly built their homes. The typical house at first had one story and was built with reed matting or wooden boards. Later, residents reconstructed with wood or perhaps brick and cement. In the city of Callao, the port for Lima, dwellers salvaged bricks and wood from the buildings destroyed by an earthquake in 1967. There were a variety of furnishings depending on the economic status of the inhabitants. Barriada dwellers cooked over small fires or kerosene stoves. Only a few dwellings had electricity, initially pirated from main lines. Because there was no refrigeration, residents bought their food at the market every day, buying only what they needed. People shared space with goats, sheep,

How Historians Understand   FROM THE COUNTRYSIDE TO THE CITY

The vast movement of people from rural areas to the cities that has taken place since the 1940s in Latin America has left historians with many questions: Who were/are the migrants? From where did/do they come? Why did/do they leave the countryside? Three types of analysis have arisen to explain the phenomenon: The first interprets migration as a "rational" act by people seeking to better their economic situations; the second sees wider forces resulting primarily from capitalist market forces at work; and the third incorporates both individual motivations and structural causes. Generally, the latter, more eclectic approach has won the day. We realize now, thanks to a long series of case studies, that although the search for economic betterment is crucial to any decision to migrate, much more enters into it.

Migrants are difficult to characterize. At first glance, it appears that young, single males are the likeliest to move from rural villages. Some early observers concluded that these men migrated because they had fewer attachments and the best chance for employment. But, in fact, women have comprised the majority of migrants, especially in Mexico, Peru, Honduras, and Costa Rica. In general, however, there seems to be no pattern according to marital status or age. We cannot with certainty even maintain that the very poorest migrated. Some investigators believe that migration is selective and that only the "more dynamic members of the rural population" migrate to the cities. Nonetheless, women were less educated, were more discriminated against, and had fewer possibilities for employment, but were the majority of migrants.

There is considerable disagreement, too, over from where migrants originated. Some investigators have found that migrants overwhelmingly came directly to the cities from rural areas. Others claim a pattern of movement from village to a small town, such as a provincial capital, and then to the larger cities. Proponents of the first theory thought that migrants were totally unprepared for city life. Proponents of the second theory offer the opposite view, maintaining that the migrants were "pre-urbanized." Small cities, however, were not the same as large cities. Thus, while migration may be a step-by-step process, and this is debatable, acculturation was not so easy in any case. What seems the most likely conclusion is that migrants came from villages, small towns, small cities, and larger cities, depending on their particular circumstances. Geography and time period affected their plight and resulted in different migrants moving through different patterns.

Leaving one's home, abandoning what one knows for the unknown, was/is an act of enormous courage. But what were the reasons behind it? Were people "pushed" out of

and pigs and raised guinea pigs (a traditional South American delicacy) and rabbits in their kitchens.

The homes were functional with few possessions. A typical home might have a table and utensils hung from the walls. Sleeping areas had cots or beds with straw mattresses. Clothes were hung from poles or lines strung overhead. There were boxes or trunks for

Shantytown where newly arrived migrants make their homes.

their rural homes by shrinking access to and deteriorating quality of land? Or did they leave because of the unavailability of employment due to the adoption of large-scale agriculture and widespread use of technology? The first investigators thought the relentless poverty of the countryside provided the impetus for migration. Later studies, however, found that the process was not so simple. There were both "push" and "pull" aspects to migrants' decision making. One observer called what was involved no less than a "substitute for social revolution."

One survey found that the migrants themselves, when surveyed, mentioned economic concerns as a motivation factor less than half the time. Migration had more to do with family (to join a spouse, to find a partner, to escape civil war) or health. The same study was unable to get migrants to "describe the decision with any precision."

It seems there was/is no one reason why a person or family moves from the countryside to the cities: There is no typology for migrants. Nor was/is there a specific route of migration; it was too personal a process. The migrants themselves do not experience or depict their lives as linear. As historians, nor should we.

Questions for Discussion

If you lived in a rural area in Latin America, what would motivate you to migrate to the cities or immigrate to another country? Would you have the courage to leave your home?

storage. Larger animals, such as goats, sheep, and pigs, were kept in the courtyard and ate scraps. Nothing was thrown away, for everything had its uses. Nothing was fancy anywhere.

Little by little, these settlements and similar settlements throughout Latin America acquired community governance and services. Residents built cement basins with a number of spigots and a drain area at strategic points. There people waited in long lines in early morning and in the evening to draw water. Women washed laundry and bathed their children during less busy times.

An Urban Migrant's Story

The story of Percy Hinojosa (related by Jorge Parodi) of Lima, Peru, is typical of the hundreds of thousands of Latin Americans who left their rural homes and moved to the cities in search of better lives. Percy, like many others in Peru and elsewhere, left his village at 15 because the countryside offered nothing but endless poverty. Like most migrants who arrived in Lima from the countryside, he came with at best an elementary school education. In order to find work, it was important to have relatives or friends already in the city who could provide the migrant with contacts to obtain employment in factories, but Percy did not have any personal contacts. He toiled for 12 years in various jobs until he got a steady position in a factory. He began as a domestic servant and went to school at night. He then embarked on an odyssey very typical of migrants:

> I worked at Coca-Cola, at Cuadernos Atlas, and in the Italian bakery. Later on, I would work at Pepsi-Cola, in small shops, in furniture factories, and carpentry shops. I would work two months and a half or three and I'd be laid off. I think the companies didn't want you to have a steady job at that time.

Percy did everything from counting bottles to packing notebooks and sanding furniture. He earned enough to get by, though no more. In search of higher-paying, more secure employment, he entered the construction trade, but this meant enduring long periods without work. He then acquired a position as an apprentice auto mechanic. He had to quit that job, however, when he became too vocal about getting a raise. Percy returned to the countryside for a year. By the time he left for Lima again, jobs were even harder to come by. Eventually, he used a contact from his earlier employment as a domestic to obtain a factory job. Like so many Latin Americans, Percy did whatever was necessary.

THE ENVIRONMENT

The push for economic development in Latin America, as elsewhere, has come at a high cost to the environment. Air and water pollution, the deterioration of agricultural lands through overuse or misuse, and the destruction of tropical rainforest areas are among Latin America's chief environmental disasters. These conditions have exacerbated the health problems, especially among the poor that we discussed earlier.

Mexico City is one of the most disheartening examples of environmental degradation over the past half century. The air is dangerous to breathe and the smog is so thick that residents rarely see the beautiful mountains that surround the city. Three million cars clog the thoroughfares of Mexico City, often bringing traffic to a standstill—residents sometimes refer to their freeways as the "largest parking lot in the world." Motor vehicles are the primary contributors to air pollution, emitting enormous quantities of sulfur dioxide and other contaminants into the air every day. The government has tried to clean up the air by prohibiting cars from being driven into the city 1 day a week and by ordering emission tests and the use of cleaner fuels. These measures have helped a bit, but not enough. Motor vehicles, however, are only part of the problem. Erosion; exposed trash and feces; untreated water seeping into the subsoil; and emissions from electric plants, refineries, petrochemical plants, incinerators, and internal combustion engines spew tons of contaminants into the air each day.

Safe drinking water is hard to find. The sewage system filters only 70 percent of the city's water. Thirty percent of municipal solid waste is not collected, and people dump it into the streets, rivers, lakes, and open fields. Lake Guadalupe, the closest lake to the Federal District, is essentially a huge septic tank: Its 30 million cubic meters of residual waters are polluted with unspeakable wastes. Consequently, agricultural products produced in the region of the lake are dangerous because they are infested with harmful microorganisms from the lake water used to irrigate crops.

Outside the cities, conditions are no better. Tropical rainforests in Latin America are being depleted at an annual rate estimated between 113,000 and 205,000 square kilometers per year. This results mostly from the conversion of rainforests to open land suitable for agriculture, especially in the Amazon region of Brazil, as waves of immigrants have flowed into the area during the last third of the twentieth century. The population of the Amazon went from 3.6 million in 1970 to 7.6 million in 1980 and 18 million in 2000. The number of agricultural properties increased by 90 percent, and the number of cattle herds doubled. From 1973 to the mid-1980s, farmer colonists in the western Amazon region razed 60,000 square kilometers. Fewer than half of these settlers stayed more than a year. The cutting of wood for use in homes and industry has contributed considerably to the destruction of the rainforests. Oil wastes have devastated the tropical rainforests of Ecuador. Black slime formed in pools and slush filled with toxic wastes contaminated the countryside. Seventeen million barrels of oil spills ruined the rivers. The soil is so contaminated in some areas that it is crusty when poked with a stick.

Natural Disasters

From 1970 to 2000 there were, by one estimate by the Inter-American Development Bank, 972 natural disasters (hurricanes, floods, earthquakes, volcanic eruptions) in Latin America that caused 226,000 fatalities (an average of 32.4 disasters and 7,500 deaths per year), costing about $29 billion in direct damages and $21 billion in indirect damages. Just in the 1990s alone, these events made 2.5 million people homeless. The two most well-known disasters are the earthquake that struck Mexico City in 1985, which killed 10,000 people and damaged or destroyed thousands of buildings ($6 billion in damages), leaving countless people without shelter, and the 2010 earthquake in Haiti which caused the deaths of 200,000 people, erasing the entire infrastructure of Port-au-Prince. However, there have been other devastating tragedies, such as an earthquake in Peru in 1970 that killed 66,000, a 1976 earthquake in Guatemala with 23,000 dead, and floods/mud slides in

Venezuela that caused 30,000 deaths. There were also recurring events, such as the prolonged drought in Northeast Brazil (10 years of drought between 1970 and 1993) and *El Niño* on the Pacific Coast in Ecuador and Peru. El Niño is the variation in climate caused by change in the surface temperature of ocean water. The phenomenon occurs every 5 to 7 years and lasts several months to 2 years, causing droughts and/or flooding. The two climatic catastrophes have cost enormous sums in damages and lost production. In this suffering Latin America appears to follow a growing worldwide trend. In the same time period, the number of major natural disasters has risen by 300 percent globally.

THE GLOBALIZATION OF CULTURE

During the second half of the twentieth century, globalization shaped the lives of people in Latin America and everywhere else. Borders between rural and urban, local and national, and national and international culture have broken down. Massive migration from the countryside to the cities and across international boundaries has been one factor in this profound change. The advent of modern mass communications, especially television, has perhaps played an even more decisive role, touching the lives even of people who never ventured very far from their homes. Meanwhile, newspapers, comic books, magazines, popular theater, radio, movies, and television deeply influenced what were formerly entirely locally focused societies. The Internet has immeasurably widened the horizons of those fortunate enough to have the resources to use it. No culture exists in isolation anymore.

Brazil provides an excellent example of how mass media had transformed culture since the 1960s. Magazine circulation increased from 104 million to 500 million between 1960 and 1985. Between 1967 and 1980, the number of record players grew by more than 800 percent. The number of commercial records went from 25 million to 66 million just during the 1970s. The expansion of television was spectacular: In 1965, there were 2.2 million televisions in Brazil, but that number rose to 4.2 million in 1970 and to 16 million by the 1980s, when 73 percent of Brazilians had TV sets. By 1996, Brazil had become the seventh-largest advertising market in the world, with advertising expenditures at $10 billion, more than half of which was accounted for by television. The Brazilian television industry illustrates well how Latin Americans have used the mass media not only to increase their own cultural output but also to spread their culture across the world. From 1972 to 1983, the percentage of foreign programming decreased from 60 to 30 percent. Brazil exports its truly amazing soap operas all over the world (especially to Mexico and Portugal).

Without question, the globalization of popular culture brought a steady influx of movies, music, fast food, and fashions from the United States and Western Europe to Latin America. McDonald's golden arches are a familiar icon throughout the region, and Walmart operates 600 retail stores in Mexico, some under its own name and some under their original names, which were retained after Walmart acquired them. The mass media have heightened demand for consumer goods in the countryside, sometimes with negative consequences for the quality of life. According to the cultural commentator Néstor García Canclini, "The penetration of consumer goods into rural areas frequently generates a crisis. New needs for industrial goods are created, forcing the rural household to rationalize production and work harder, longer hours, thus making it difficult for the peasant family to continue participating in [traditional] magico-religious practices."

Latin Americans have found myriad and creative ways to blend old and new. On Sunday afternoon in the Praça de Se in São Paulo, Brazil, one can observe *capoeira* (a form of martial art used as self-defense, formerly practiced by slaves, now a dance), electric guitars playing rock music, and poetic duels by *cantadores*. In Peru during the 1980s, chicha music (*chicha* refers to an Andean maize beer often linked with traditional rituals) enjoyed widespread popularity. A combination of elements from Andean and tropical cultures, the music illustrated the mass immigration from the countryside into the cities. Although the mixture of electric guitars with tropical and Andean rhythms appears at first instance a degradation of tradition, it may in fact be a way of preserving the memory of the past within a practical acceptance of current reality. In Latin American homes, technology and tradition exist side by side. Television sets often rest on tables that stand right next to altars bearing religious images. In Brazilian favelas, residents paint their rooms pink to remind them of their rural homes.

Latin American popular culture has found worldwide markets and enthusiasts. Growing numbers of Latinos in the United States can watch soap operas on television, attend concerts of popular Latin American musicians, and celebrate traditional holidays. In June 2004, there were reenactments of *Inti Raymi*, the ancient Inca summer solstice festival, in cities as far away as Chicago, Seattle, New York, Brussels, Barcelona, and Budapest. The indigenous people of Otavalo in northern Ecuador have long been known as savvy marketers who sell their fine textiles to tourists visiting their picturesque community. Now a wide selection of their products is available on the Internet. Sometimes popular culture has changed its form to suit foreign tastes, while retaining cultural meaning at home. Andean music has shown a noticeable Western influence as it has become familiar to audiences around the world. In Peru and Bolivia, however, music has kept its place at the center of the annual cycle of ritual.

Transitions to the new hybrid folk art are ambiguous at times. In the late 1960s, the artisans of Ocumicho, Michoacán, in Mexico began to create ceramics depicting devil figures associated with elements of the modern world previously unknown in the village, such as police, motorbikes, and airplanes. Some observers have suggested that the devils provide a way of controlling the destructive effects of modernization, by placing them within a traditional repertory of symbols. Carlos Monsiváis, the Mexican essayist, reports an interesting twist on the intrusion of modernity into rural society that occurred when the Mexican government introduced video cameras to municipal meetings in the state of Hidalgo. The Otomí Indians, who comprised most of the population of the municipality, showed more enthusiasm about watching the videotapes of the meetings than attending gatherings in person.

International market forces and national political considerations have, without doubt, altered many local traditions. Mexican governments have encouraged handicraft production so as to provide sustenance for rural people and to thus keep them from migrating to the cities. Cultural commentator Néstor García Canclini maintains, for example, that the urban and tourist consumption of handicrafts "causes them to be increasingly decontextualized and resignified on their journey to the museum and the boutique. . . . Their uses on the land, in the household and in rituals are replaced by exclusively aesthetic appreciation," which in turn affects how they are made and the form they take.

Art

Latin American artists have continued to develop their innovative style and techniques in the age of globalization. The stark political art of the 1930s and 1940s gave way temporarily to geometric and abstract art by the 1950s, but neither proved satisfactory to artists concerned with contemporary conditions. In Mexico, there was a reaction against the muralists, led by José Luis Cuevas, who believed the world more complicated than that depicted by Rivera and Siqueiros. Instead of depicting a world of simple contrasts between heroes and villains, these artists portrayed humans as victims of greater forces. Perhaps the most famous artist to emerge from this era was Colombian Fernando Botero, who also dropped socialist realism. Like Cuevas, Botero was more comfortable using European painters' techniques, but he added exaggeration and parody to his portrayal of characteristic types in Colombian politics and society.

By the 1960s, Latin American artists again embraced social protest, but this new protest was more diversely applied than that of the earlier generation's socialist realists. According to art historian Jacqueline Barnitz, however, some artists working under the brutal regimes of the 1970s through the 1980s employed a "strategy of self-censorship" in which "they invented new symbols or invested previously used ones with new meaning." For example, Brazilian Antonio Henrique Amaral painted bananas in the 1970s as a parody of Brazil as a banana republic, a tinhorn dictatorship that deferred to the United States. Other artists challenged not the political state but the commercialization of art and official art institutions. This conceptual art, comprised of various media ranging from prints to performance, provided the means for ideological expression without actually confronting the terrifying regimes in power. Some artists, nevertheless, paid a high price for even veiled protests. After the Chilean coup in 1973, Guillermo Nuñez was arrested, imprisoned, tortured, let go, and then watched closely. After being jailed and tortured a second time 2 years later, he was forcibly exiled.

Latin American artists in the late twentieth century struggled and succeeded brilliantly in forging their own art out of the different strains of influence from their homelands and abroad. They fought to make sense out of a world of bitter poverty and profound disappointment. They explored their past and future with the same persistence, courage, and humor displayed by their ancestors for the preceding 600 years.

CONCLUSION

As they entered the new millennium, Latin Americans lived in a world very different from what their ancestors had known when they embarked on their journeys as independent nations nearly two centuries before. As we saw in Chapter 9, nineteenth-century governments struggled mightily to persuade their people to think of themselves as citizens of a nation rather than residents of a particular village, town, or region. Those who governed in Latin America after 1880 had a much easier time in getting people to see themselves as part of a national community. The coming of railroads, telegraphs, and telephones consolidated national territories as never before. Public education systems and mandatory military service provided ideal vehicles to inculcate patriotic values to students and raw recruits. Modernizing governments saw local governance and culture as impediments to their mission and took decisive steps to undermine both.

The development of modern mass communications in the twentieth century created national popular cultures as more and more people followed the same soap operas, read the same comic books, watched the same movies, and enjoyed the same music. Televised spectator sports also encouraged people to think of themselves as Peruvians or Mexicans or Costa Ricans as they cheered their national teams in international soccer competitions. Winning the World Cup in soccer has probably done as much as any government program to make Brazilians proud to be Brazilians and Argentines proud to be Argentines. In the age of globalization, even a nation's citizens who worked and lived abroad could partake of national patriotic observances and reaffirm their loyalties to their home countries. Each year on the night of September 15, for example, the medium of satellite TV permits Mexican citizens living in the United States to watch their president stand on the balcony of the National Palace in Mexico City and reenact Father Miguel Hidalgo's famous "Grito de Dolores," the spark that ignited the country's struggle for independence nearly 200 years ago. The Internet and cheap long-distance telephone service enable people living abroad to keep in touch with friends, family, and local happenings back home.

Meanwhile, globalization has also generated forces that weaken national loyalties. Traditional ways of life distinctive to a particular country are rapidly giving way to international consumer culture. At the same time, strong local and regional loyalties persist alongside wider national and international allegiances. In recent years, the end of tyrannies and the comeback of democracy have allowed more local autonomy. The rise of Mexico's most active opposition party, the Partido Acción Nacional, and its ultimate success in capturing the presidency in 2000 began in part as a resurgence of regional identity, particularly in the north. Ethnic and linguistic minorities continue to reassert their languages and traditions against homogenized national and international cultures.

Whether they work for multinational corporations or continue to work in the countryside, whether they never venture much beyond the localities where their ancestors have lived for centuries or travel great distances in search of work, education, or entertainment, whether or not they have access to the Internet, and regardless of their income levels, Latin Americans of the twenty-first century still see the struggle to retain control over their daily lives as their paramount objective, and one that is perhaps as unattainable today as it has ever been in their history. For a large majority of people in the region, poverty and its related ills—malnutrition, substandard housing, and disease—seriously interfere with that quest. Even those who live comfortably for the moment can remember all-too-recent times of political uncertainty, galloping inflation, and war and terror—and they fear a return to those conditions. The natural environment that nurtured the first civilizations in the Americas and provided a host of commodities used and valued all over the world faces the dire consequences of modernization. But ever since their first ancestors migrated across the Bering Strait thousands of years ago, Latin Americans have shown great ingenuity in meeting their needs for survival and for cultural autonomy. Their energy and cultural creativity will serve them well in the years to come.

LEARNING MORE ABOUT LATIN AMERICANS

Pacini Hernández, Deborah, Fernández L'Hoeste, Hector, and Zolov, Eric, eds. *Rockin' Las Américas* (Pittsburgh, PA: University of Pittsburgh Press, 2004).

Scheper-Hughes, Nancy. *Death without Weeping: The Violence of Everyday Life in Brazil* (Berkeley, CA: University of California Press, 1992). The author presents a gut-wrenching picture of favela life.

Tardanico, Richard, and Rafael Menjívar Larín, eds. *Global Restructuring, Employment, and Inequality in Urban Latin America* (Miami, FL: North-South Center Press at the University of Miami, 1997). The editors include all the dismaying statistics about the present state of Latin Americans.

Timerman, Jacobo. *Prisoner without a Name, Cell without a Number* (Madison, WI: University of Wisconsin Press, 2002). Argentine Jew who was jailed during the Dirty War tells his terrifying tale.

Ulloa Bornemann, Alberto. *Surviving Mexico's Dirty War: A Political Prisoner's Memoir.* Ed. and trans. Arthur Schmidt and Arora Camacho de Schmidt (Philadelphia, PA: Temple University Press, 2007).

Winn, Peter. *Weavers of the Revolution: The Yarur Workers and Chile's Road to Socialism* (New York: Oxford University Press, 1986). Winn gets inside the minds of workers to an unprecedented extent.

GLOSSARY

Aguardiente (ah-gwar-dee-EN-tay)   Sugar cane alcoholic beverage.

Arrendatarios (ah-rehn-dah-TAH-ree-ohs)   Permanent workers on Colombian coffee farms.

Atole (ah-TOH-lay)   Corn gruel eaten for breakfast in Mexico.

Barretón (bah-ray-TOHN)   A heavy wedge with an iron tip and long, straight wood handle used to poke soil in order to insert seed.

Cacique (kah-SEE-kay)   Originally, a traditional chief in Caribbean societies; later an indigenous local ruler in Spanish America; this term was also used to describe local political bosses in the nineteenth century, after Latin American independence.

Calaveras (kah-lah-VAY-rahs)   Skeletal figures used in celebration of the Days of the Dead in Mexico.

Candomblé (kahn-dohm-BLAY)   Afro-Brazilian religion.

Cantadores (kahn-tah-DOR-ays)   Singers.

Capataz (kah-pah-TAHS)   Foreman on a cattle ranch.

Capitalino (kah-pee-tah-LEE-noh)   Resident of Mexico City.

Capoeira (kai-poh-EH-rah)   Formerly a slave dance, evolved as form of self-defense in Brazil.

Caudillo (kow-DEE-yoh)   Strong leader with a local political base.

Centralist   Favors strong national government.

Chica moderna (CHEE-kah mo-DEHR-nah)   Modern woman.

Chicha (CHEE-chah)   Maize beer drunk in the Andean region.

Cofradía (koh-frah-DEE-ah)   In Spanish America, an organization of lay people devoted to a particular saint or religious observance; members maintained village churches and sponsored festivals.

Colono (coh-LOH-noh)   Temporary worker on a Colombian coffee farm; medium-scale Cuban sugar planter.

Compadrazgo (kohm-pah-DRAHS-goh)   Godparent relations; an individual who agrees to look after the child of another.

Concordancia (kohn-kor-DAHN-see-ah)   Argentine political coalition of the 1930s with Conservatives, Radicals, and Independent Socialists.

Conservative   Favors strong central government and the Roman Catholic Church.

Conventillos (kohn-vehn-TEE-yohs)   Buenos Aires tenements.

Corticos (kor-TEE-kohs)   Crowded slums in Rio de Janeiro.

Debt peonage   Debt incurred by rural laborers on large estates in order to pay for baptisms, weddings, funerals, and to purchase supplies that debtor cannot repay.

Descamisados (des-kah-mee-SAH-dohs)   Shirtless ones; working class supporters of Juan Perón in Argentina.

Enganchadores (ehn-gahn-chah-DOR-ays)   Dishonest labor recruiters.

Estado Novo (eh-shta-doo-noh-voo)   Dictatorship of Getúlio Vargas in Brazil (1937–1945).

Estancia (eh-STAHN-see-ah)   Large estate in Argentina and Uruguay that generally raises livestock.

Estanciero (eh-stahn-see-EH-roh)   Large landowner in Argentina and Uruguay; owner of an estancia.

Farinha (fah-REEN-yah)   Coarse flour made from cassava.

Fazenda (fah-ZEHN-dah)   Large estate in Brazil.

Fazendeiro (fah-zehn-DAY-roh)   Large landowner in Brazil; owner of a fazenda.

Federalist   Favors weak national government with political power vested in states or provinces.

Finca (FEEN-kah)   Colombian coffee farm.

Frijoles (free-HOH-lays)   Beans, a staple of Mexican diet; usually combined with corn tortillas.

Gaucho (GOW-choh)   Argentine cowboy known for fierce independence.

Guano (goo-AH-noh)   Bird excrement used for fertilizer, collected from islands off Peru.

Hacendado (ah-sen-DAH-doh)   Large landowner in Spanish America.

Hectare   2.47 acres.

Hombres de bien (OHM-brays day bee-EHN)   In colonial Spanish America, men who had honorable reputations in their communities; in the nineteenth century, decent people; professionals of some means who often managed government in nineteenth century Mexico.

Huaraches (wah-RAH-chays)   Sandals.

Indigenismo (een-dee-hehn-EES-moh)   Admiration for the advanced culture of pre-1500 societies in Latin America; efforts to bring native peoples into the modern economy.

Jefes políticos (heh-fays poh-LEE-tee-kohs)   District political bosses under Porfirio Díaz in Mexico.

Léperos (LEH-peh-rohs)   Beggars of Mexico City.

Ley fuga (Lay FOO-gah)   Shot while trying to escape; ruse used by Rurales.

Liberal   Favors weak central government, opposes the Roman Catholic Church, and encourages individualism rather than collective landownership.

Liberto (lee-BEHR-toh)   Slave born in Brazil after 1813 who was to remain a slave until age 21.

Matador (mah-tah-DOR)   Bullfighter.

Mayordomo (mai-yor-DOH-moh)   Manager of an estancia or hacienda.

Metate (may-TAH-tay)   Grinding stone for corn used in making tortillas.

Molino de nixtamal (moh-LEE-noh day neex-tah-MAHL)   Corn-grinding machine.

Panela (pah-NEH-lah)   Brown sugar cakes.

Patron–client relations   Unequal relationship between upper-class individual and lower-class individual (hacendado and peon, for example) in which the former obtains protection and patronage in return for loyalty.

Peinilla (pay-NEE-yah)   Machete.

Petate (pay-TAH-tay)   Sleeping pallet.

Pulque (POOL-kay)   In Mexico, a fermented beverage made from the agave cactus.

Quilombos (kee-LOHM-bohs)   Communities of runaway slaves in the interior of Brazil.

Rebozo (ray-BOH-soh)   Narrow, long shawl for women.

Rurales (roo-RAH-lays)   Rural police during era of Porfirio Díaz in Mexico.

Santería (sahn-tay-REE-ah)   Afro-Caribbean religion.

Siesta (see-EHS-tah)   Nap after the midday meal.

Tithe   Contribution to the church of 10 percent of one's income.

Vaqueros (vah-KAY-rohs)   Cowboys in Mexico.

Vecindades (vay-seen-DAH-days)   Mexico City tenements.

Voudoun (VOO-doon)   Afro-Caribbean or Afro-Brazilian religion.

Yerba mate (YER-bah MAH-tay)   Strong tea in Paraguay and Argentina.

CREDITS

Front Matter
Opener Stamps: Fotolia, LLC and Flavia Morlachetti/Fotolia, LLC
p. xxxii: Cheryl Martin
p. xxxii: James Wasserman Photography

Chapter 8
p. 220: CORBIS All Rights Reserved
p. 227: The Bridgeman Art Library International
p. 230: © (Pablo Corral)/CORBIS All Rights Reserved
p. 234: Gianni Dagli Orti/The Art Archive at Art Resource, NY

Chapter 9
p. 248: The Bridgeman Art Library International
p. 256: Public Domain
p. 264: The Granger Collection, New York

Chapter 10
p. 277: Edward E. Ayer Collection/The Newberry Library
p. 283: Art Resource, New York
p. 288: Art Resource, New York

Chapter 11
p. 309: Donald c. Trupen/Center for Southwest Research
p. 319: Art Resource, New York
p. 324: © (Bettmann)/CORBIS All Rights Reserved

Chapter 12
p. 335: Courtesy of Susan Besse and the Author
p. 338: Hubert Stadler/Corbis
p. 348: Biblioteca Nacional de Chile

Chapter 13
p. 364: © (Bill Gentile)/CORBIS All Rights Reserved
p. 370: Schalkwijk/ Art Resource, New York
p. 371: Art Resource, New York

Chapter 14
p. 387: © (Barry Lewis)/CORBIS All Rights Reserved/In Pictures
p. 390: © (Reuters)/CORBIS All Rights Reserved
p. 396: Hulton Archive/Getty Images

Chapter 15
p. 410: © (Nik Wheeler)/CORBIS All Rights Reserved
p. 417: © (Paul Almasy)/CORBIS All Rights Reserved

COLOR PLATES (13–23) *Front of book*
Plate 13: New York Historical Society/The Bridgeman Art Library International
Plate 14: Index/The Bridgeman Art Library International
Plate 15: The Bridgeman Art Library International
Plate 16: Erich Lessing/Art Resource, New York
Plate 17: Schalkwijk/Art Resource, New York
Plate 18: Keystone Pictures USA/Alamy
Plate 19: Schalkwijk/Art Resource, New York
Plate 20: Sean Sprague/Alamy
Plate 21: © (Howard Davies)/CORBIS All Rights Reserved
Plate 22: © (Susan Gonzalas)/CORBIS All Rights Reserved
Plate 23: Art Resource, New York

INDEX

Note: The letters 'b' and 't' following the locators refers to boxes and tables cited in the text.